INVISIBLE

The Essential Guide for Aliens Stranded on Earth

TONY MATTHEWS

First published 2023

All enquiries should be made to the publishers.
Big Sky Publishing Pty Ltd
PO Box 303, Newport, NSW 2106, Australia
Phone: 1300 364 611
Fax: (61 2) 9918 2396
Email: info@bigskypublishing.com.au
Web: www.bigskypublishing.com.au

Cover design: Big Sky Publishing
Cover photographs:
Front cover artist: lazyllama, Shutterstock
Back cover: Can Stock Photo/denbelitsky
Author Photo: Tony & Lensie Matthews Collection

Typesetting: Lensie Matthews
The names of several people in this book have been changed for reasons of privacy.

ISBN: 9781922896421 (Paperback, C Format)
Printed and bound in Australia by Griffin Press

A catalogue record for this book is available from the National Library of Australia

INVISIBLE

The Essential Guide for Aliens Stranded on Earth

TONY MATTHEWS

Dedication

This book is dedicated with love and admiration to my wife, Lensie, who also knows how to duck for cover at just the right moment.

Contents

The monotony and solitude of a quiet life
stimulate the creative mind.

— Albert Einstein

Introduction

This is a story about a young, spindly, grocer's lad, slightly addicted to illicitly bought cigarettes, and rather more addicted to his beautiful art teacher's astonishingly long legs. Tony Matthews, or Anthony, as he was then known, who is now a long established Australian writer and historian, spent much of his boyhood alone, wandering the chemically-saturated, coal-dust-tainted hills, swamps and abandoned copper-smelters of 1950s Swansea, South Wales, hiding in old air-raid shelters or bomb-ruins or the crumbling World War Two concrete gun emplacements at the base of a rocky island lighthouse situated on a headland, musically called Mumbles. It was a name which, for some unfathomable reason, immediately conjured up images of Hobbits or dwarfs or possibly little Welsh goblins. All this makes Tony sound as mad as a fruit-fly but in fact he was just a young, tousle-headed boy with a torch, a book, a wobbly bladed penknife and a slightly different mission in life.

Tony Matthews was something of a loner from the very beginning although he did not know it at the time. When he wasn't hiding in secretive silence in the ruins of a disused R.A.F. Spitfire airbase eating wild blackberries with one hand while shooting down imaginary *Focke Wulf Fw 90* bandits with the other, he was alone in an abandoned cottage somewhere in the wilderness of the Gower peninsula where his only companions were the ghosts of Neolithic cave-dwellers. They were probably a little miffed that Tony was camping on their burial mound but the young lad never went in fear of them. He even spent some of a summer holiday alone in the same cave where those ancient people had once lived. There, with just a rolled up newspaper as a flaming torch, he discovered the fossil of an amazing creature that had died sixty-five million years, seven months and three days before Tony had even come into existence. Ordinary boys don't normally do that, but then young Tony Matthews was anything but ordinary.

He was invisible!

Often choosing to be alone during his boyhood, Tony Matthews was seeking something he didn't even know existed — the inner self of solitude, a quiet place in a world that seemed full of noise, confusion and brightly colourful people. Noises, crowds and bright lights either hurt his eyes or made him want to find a dark place where he could sit alone like a Devil's Hole Pupfish and there are only fifty of those little guys left on the entire planet.

In this funny and, at times, brilliantly perspicacious book, Tony Matthews writes about how the world is viewed through the eyes of an intensely introverted and overly self-conscious recluse who, in addition to living a life largely secluded from the rest of society, also describes what it is like to be an ethical vegan on a planet where the killing and consumption of animals is considered perfectly normal and where millions of animals are killed daily for food or sport or fun.

This is a story that, at times, is emotionally touching, and at other times touchingly comic but it describes an unusual world that relatively few people have seen, despite the fact that we are an intrinsic part of that world and it is everywhere around us.

All his life Tony Matthews has sought ways that would render him virtually invisible to the rest of society, and despite the fact that he has written more than thirty books, mainly histories or historical novels, including several publisher's best sellers, he remains something of an enigma, a shadow in the literary world. As a writer who has travelled extensively in twenty-seven countries, including the odd war zone or two, he has experienced much during his life and has had a unique opportunity to study people of various races and religions and is able to see the abnormal in what we would consider normal. From boarding gold smugglers' dhows in the Persian Gulf to surviving one of the bloodiest military coups in modern history or being almost comically headhunted by the C.I.A. for one of their stultifyingly goofy covert missions in darkest Africa, Tony has lived through extraordinary times.

Yet personal participation in fascinating events such as these has never been Tony's ambition. Whenever possible he has always attempted to be the observer, standing back, watching carefully and analysing, usually from a vantage point where he is able to see but without being noticed. Looking at society from the outside gives him a unique and often prismatic perspective of life. Sometimes it is intensely moving, at other times it raises our awareness of how quirky we can be or how wonderfully full of compassion and love. He questions everything, asking why the world is what it has become today and where we might be heading in the future. As he does so he is acutely conscious that holding up a mirror to the rest of the world also requires him to do exactly the same to himself even though this examination can, at times, be both cutting and outrageously satirical.

Introspection and seclusion are powerful vantage points from which to study our fellow humans and this book demonstrates that it can be possible to do so with clarity, honesty and an abundance of raw humour that is sometimes as penetrating as an alien's rectal probe.

This is a book filled with a precise and edgy observation of life on planet Earth told in a style of wry self-deprecation and vividly expressed good humour. It is also an intensely moving description of a life lived as a reclusive writer, a super-self-conscious, socially awkward hermit, a vegan and introvert, and, as Tony describes himself: 'An honorary extraterrestrial with a forged hall-pass to Earth'.

As a boy, and right through his entire life, Tony Matthews has craved anonymity and invisibility — a state of being that is not only well beyond the laws of physics as we know them but also one largely at odds with his chosen profession of writer, historian, poet, radio broadcaster and documentary filmmaker.

In *Invisible — the Essential Guide for Aliens Stranded on Earth*, the author commences his journey through the strange, other-dimensional world of the born recluse, vegan, hermit and introvert. Reflecting his own young confusion, he questions why he appears to be a round doughnut irrevocably stranded in a square biscuit-tin. His quest for understanding takes him on a roller-coaster ride through boyhood into adolescence when finally he comes to understand that he is about as comfortable on this strange world called Earth as a crocodile in a handbag factory.

Author's Note

This is a book about really scary introverted vegans. Actually, it's worse than that. It's a book about really scary introverted vegans who live in a kind of grey(ish) underworld of seclusion. You might think from this description that it is a simple life and a simple story but nothing could be farther from the truth because vegan introverts are, by definition, a breed apart, and this book will be a character-filled insight into our strange personalities, foibles and fears, (well, mine at least!). This is the odd, stupidly funny, vaguely ridiculous and sometimes mischievously risqué story of a vegan recluse stuck inexorably to Planet Earth like an insect stuck to flypaper.

In fact this is going to be a rather topsy-turvy kind of book filled with all the vibrant observations, anecdotes and chilling horror stories of living the life of a vegan recluse in a world where everyone loves to party; where noise is king and silence is borderline psychotic. In short, it is a world where introverts and especially introverts who are also vegans and recluses are seen as cone-headed aliens. That's actually not a bad thing, but cone-headed aliens are somewhat disadvantaged because Earthlings have quite a lot of trouble understanding them. I hope this little publication will serve to deepen this confusion even more because when a mystery deepens people start to talk about it and talking itself is a road to understanding, even if it is only the weird kind of mind-battering reverse logic that I present here.

This is not a book designed to explain who reclusive vegans are or why they live as they do. This book has been written because it's about time we had a jolly good chuckle at ourselves and the world generally and where we all attempt to fit into it, or not fit into it, as the case may be. I don't fit into it particularly well and rather like that. It might also surprise you to learn that you also could be a closet recluse. It's called the 'friendship paradox' and demonstrates that most people have fewer friends than their friends have. Gregariousness is rapidly becoming a jar of vanishing cream. Welcome to the 21st Covid-apocalyptic century.

Since starting this book I've never really been sure if it is a serious story about a really silly subject or a really silly story about a serious subject. I can't decide. Perhaps it's both. Perhaps you should decide once you've read it — if you can see it through to the end, that is, which will be a challenge for anyone who suffers from nervous dyspepsia because at times a recluse's life can be hard to stomach without a spoonful of Mylanta.

I've been an introverted vegan for more years than Fred Astaire was dancing with Ginger Rogers. I've actually been an introvert since birth — or at least since a neighbour saw me bollock-naked in a pink plastic basin covered with insufficient soap-suds to hide my quite inadequate three-year old willy. Now *that* was the precise moment I also decided that I didn't particularly like being looked at, especially when attired in nothing but rapidly popping soap-suds smelling rather too strongly of coal-tar.

A whole lifetime is a long time to seek solitude especially when seclusion and quietude are almost impossible to achieve in a world designed for community expression, instant connectivity and stereophonic speakers that are now built into the bottoms of our mobile phones. I'm quite sure, the way things are going, with advances in digital implant technology, we will soon have stereophonic speakers built into our own bottoms. (It's called transhumanist technology, by the way, and it really is coming our way in the not too distant future). We are now so connected that somehow we seem to be falling apart at the same time, although with luck all our bottoms will remain firmly in place.

Social media, the Internet, texting, direct Twitter messaging, are all forming a new kind of human seclusion, and these are issues and skills we have learned to hone universally during the Covid 19 outbreak. Social skills are being lost as hyper-jittery (and sometimes rather pimply) little boys and girls sit tensely in their bedrooms staring zombie-like at computers or phone screens while shifting continuously in their chairs having twitchingly consumed three gallons of caffeine-impregnated carbonated water during the previous half hour. They exist almost alone but in a state of constant apprehension as they wait for some completely unknown and anonymous person to 'follow' or to 'like' them. It's a strange world where success is measured not by our achievements but by the number of little thumbs-up emojis we have on our Facebook pages. People call reclusive vegans really strange but how sad is that, and who invented emojis anyway? I'm not sure but I expect he's a multi-billionaire by now with a super yacht at Monaco crewed exclusively by Playboy Bunnies wearing nothing warmer than fluffy bum-tufts.

I'm a recluse because that's an indelible part of my psyche and has nothing whatever to do with caffeine drinks or fluffy bottoms, yet today many people are becoming reclusive because they no longer need community or human contact. Enforced seclusion during the Covid outbreak changed the way we think about these issues and we are all very definitely more protective of our own space — something that recluses have cherished all their lives. Everything is done remotely on touch-screens. What was once considered as the new revolution in bringing everyone together is actually helping to force us apart, and Covid has a lot to do with that too.

Time passes. In my experience it passes too quickly. When we are young the years stretch ahead as if life will never end. We long to grow up and grow larger willies (if one is adorned with a willy in the first place, of course), but as we grow we experience and learn.

I actually once believed that I would be the only person in the history of the world who would live forever. I was only seven at the time so it's understandable, but I also believed that I could fly. Yet as we grow older the years begin to speed up with astonishing rapidity. Time flashes past like a bullet-train. I'm sure the late and lamented Stephen Hawking, who predicted that we could travel through time at the speed of light, had something to do with that, and I'm not very pleased with him because personally at my age I'd like things to slow down quite a lot.

Yet there are advantages. When one gets up a bit in years it's perfectly possible to get away with just about anything. Old people are contagiously grumpy and they get away with that. Old people feign fragmentary memory discombobulation to forget conveniently that it's their round, even when they have no idea what discombobulation actually means. To be ageing gracefully is not the horrific spectre it's made out to be. In fact it can be quite fun, especially when one is a vegan reclusive introverted hermit and therefore by default an intergalactic alien with an uncanny ability to remain invisible — or at least, cunningly camouflaged when appropriate.

That will be me, I think!

It's okay to be a recluse but when one is both a recluse and a vegan, that's when the world really becomes interesting because suddenly one is not *of* this world. One is a binary distortion. Not only that, but being at an age which rather unkind young people sometimes call 'overripe' also means that one has now become unfathomably invisible and it's been achieved automatically. Now that's what all introverted recluses strive for. It's a major success. Complete invisibility at last. It's possible to go into any shop and be even more ignored by shop assistants than usual.

It's now possible to tote up the positives of being an aged, invisible, introverted, reclusive, vegan alien. Firstly, you are going to live forever because of your cruelty-free, cholesterol-emancipated diet. Secondly, nobody is going to ask you for a donation to save endangered dodgem cars or similarly ridiculous causes because you are invisible and they simply can't see you. Thirdly, being aged, even if people do magically manage to penetrate the invisibility shield you have placed around yourself, then it will be perfectly acceptable to tell them to get stuffed because you are old and that's what grumpy old people do.

God it's so bloody liberating!

Everything changes as you age. When you are young you go into a museum and think it's about as boring as watching old rail-lines rust (which I've actually done) and when you're in your middle-ish years you think that museums are, well, sort of interesting, and finally, when you become something of an old fart, you look in a museum glass-cabinet where there are relics of fossil scraps and sepia-faded press-stories from fifty years ago and you find yourself there. Really! It happened to me!

Everything has to change. That's both the beauty of life and its principal challenge. I look around me now, seated on a wooden bench, cleverly camouflaged amid a spread of shopping-centre potted palms and see a pale, pinkish, blueish tidal surge of people, mainly young women, sporting literally an indelible display of neck, arm, ankle, thigh and upper posterior tattoos, and I'm buggered if I know what this tsunami of blue-inked rind is all about. Tattoos were once the preserve of randy sailors and young bar-girls who served them pints of scrumpy in the shady taverns of Portsmouth. It was completely mad in those pubs and, in a way, you could understand why the bar-girls tattooed their boobs. But some people now have tattoos on their faces and some have even tattooed their eyeballs. One man I saw online had cleverly turned himself into an alien and had gone to the extent of cutting off his nose so that just two rather snotty holes were left in a completely tattoo-blackened face. These ingenious folk have the ability to remind me of the photographs I've seen of people in side-shows: the bearded lady; the man with three eyes; the strongest man in the world; the man whose penis sounds like Scottish bagpipes when he wees, or, my favourite: Stork-leg Man who stands on stage with two cotton-skinny legs and pretends very convincingly to eat live worms. That kind of thing. The world, I'm sure, is becoming successively crazier.

I am getting on in years and remain an inveterate introvert, vegan and recluse which is probably why I'm now hiding among all the shopping-centre potted plants dressed in a pair of really cheap Big W camouflage military pants — the type that a former U.S. president's militia supporters would wear when on brain-dead operations in the banjo-plucking bayous. I really am scribbling this down on a few scraps of paper and a napkin as I sit here, by the way. This is live action you're reading. I am also dressed in a secondhand brownish/greenish shirt which cost me four dollars at the Lifeline op-shop, and a mud-coloured *Raiders of the Lost Ark* type of hat that happily melts into the background rendering my head almost completely invisible — at least to the untrained eye. The hat cost me a completely mad fifty dollars at the organics shop and is not made of rabbit fur largely because I wouldn't wear a hat made from the residue of caged and once furry angora bunnies who have been repeatedly fur-ripped by some rather unpleasant gentleman in a very large Far Eastern country.

But I digress. Here in the shopping-centre I'm so invisible that people bump into me and don't bother apologising because they think I'm part of the potted plant arrangement. Standing perfectly still also helps with my quest for invisibility. I stand like stone. I studied Clint Eastwood to do that — *A Fistful of Dollars*. He could stand like a Boot Hill gravestone (after he'd thrown his poncho over his shoulder to reveal his shooting-iron, of course) and plug about a million people with his six-gun all in the same nanosecond. It was quite remarkable and I've always envied him that talent because there are, I reluctantly admit as a pacifist, one or two people whom I've known in the past who might benefit from a really good plugging. I'm talking of course about men in the TV industry who wear neck-danglers shaped like naked ladies, or those sporting gold bangles on really hairy wrists, and also those quite astonishing geniuses who like to hang fake testicles from the tow-bars of their 4WD vehicles — but that almost goes without saying.

In my constant quest for invisibility I sometimes stand so still that in the past I have actually been mistaken for a shop dummy. Really! It's a terrifying experience because you never quite know if shop assistants are about to interfere with your underpants (quite innocently of course). Honestly, I constantly have to be on my guard. Being invisible can sometimes get you into awful difficulties.

Okay, enough of this. Let's go back a bit. In fact let's go back to the moment I discovered that I was miraculously transforming into a little (untattooed) alien.

You'll love that.

Chapter One

From Earthling to Alien

When I was a child with the legs of a stork and teeth like splinters I believed it possible that I might at least be part alien. Not the horrid type of alien that drips gallons of smelly saliva and callously impregnates Sigourney Weaver without any thought of child support, but a rather curious kind of little-boy-alien with a slightly dozy, completely harmless look — a bit like Garfield, I guess, but without the embarrassing habit of coughing up furballs.

I was only a kid, of course, and had no real knowledge of the world or what the word 'beget' meant in real terms, although the Bible, which I was forced to read at my stunningly Catholic school where there were more nails and crosses on the walls than children at desks, appeared to be stuffed full of people begetting each other, so evidently it was important in an esoteric and possibly even a slightly erotic kind of way. I knew that it had something to do with procreation because so many people in the Bible had begat so many other people I guessed there must be some kind of link to the mysteries of human reproduction.

I was aware that although I was largely human I wondered if somehow during my own begetting some really weird element of space-dust containing microscopic particles of alien life from Mars had fallen onto my head, or perhaps into the holy water used at my christening, and somehow added another other-worldly component to my begetting and therefore I may have been partly from Mars or even another solar system entirely. It was a real conundrum for a boy of five years because by that time I was beginning to realise that I wasn't exactly the same as everyone else — something was wrong. Perhaps my brain had been installed back-to-front or upside-down because I was thinking about things that normal young chaps appeared not to be thinking about such as would it be possible to live forever on hot chips and if I flicked a rubber-eraser hard enough would it bounce off my headmaster's desk and lodge irretrievably in his nose?

My favourite place in our home was a small cupboard beneath the stairs. It was full of rubbish and old tin toys, cardboard boxes and spiders' webs. It smelled strongly of furniture polish and linseed oil because that was where my mother stored her cleaning materials and where my father kept his box of putty for fixing cracks in the window sills. It was dark in there with little chinks of light coming through the bottom and top of the ill-fitting door which was just large enough for a Hobbit. There was a part missing at the top through which I'd put my hands to open it. Not even the spiders could see me in there. I was alone, invisible, listening to everything that was going on in the house but no one knew I was there and I found that I really rather liked that.

I didn't then know what an introvert or a recluse or a hermit might have been but I did know that I liked to be alone and that was rather peculiar because everyone else, apparently, liked to cluster like paperclips to a magnet.

I'd sit in the darkness deep in thought. I was a retrospective little Hobbit. My favourite subject at school was history and I was always looking back into the past, trying to see what it had been like in those distant days. In that cupboard beneath the stairs, in addition to all the cleaning potions, smelly polishing rags, bags of stinking putty and an assortment of gardening tools (rarely used) I discovered to my delight a pair of ancient British Army-issue binoculars that apparently had been brought back from the Western Front by one of my uncles who had served during the First World War. The binoculars had seen better days; they were battered by rough usage, mute testimony to the terrible conditions on the shell-torn battlefields. I loved to take them to the top of the hill behind our house and look through them at the distant horizon, imagining what others had seen while also looking through those same lenses. One of the lenses was badly cracked so it was like looking through a strange kind of prism, but that only heightened the effect of being able to look back through time, to see events that had taken place years ago. Yet I was only able to do this when I was alone. If other boys were with me my window in time would never work. The magic of it was to be by myself. I never understood why, but was beginning to understand that being alone was often better and more exciting and interesting than being with other boys. It gave me a chance to be myself and to find elements in life that were elusive when in the company of others.

Now I know all this sounds about as crazy as Lord Such's Monster Raving Loony Party (although he wasn't actually crazy at all, as the British polls subsequently proved), but what I'm saying is real. It's quite possible for boys with lots of imagination and a need to be alone to see into the past. In fact my entire life has been based on that premise and I've written loads of history books to prove it. Not only that, but I've also been able on many occasions to see into the future. Now you're probably thinking I've been smoking far too many funny fags, but I assure you that later in this book you'll see that it all makes sense. Well, sort of.

I was a loner and eventually came to understand that. I just loved being by myself when everyone else apparently liked to party. Parties are all the same whether you are four years of age or sixty-four. Somewhere in the centre of those two ages an additional element is introduced into all such events and it's called raging hormones which are at the centre and heart of all parties from the ages of fifteen until about forty at which time parties appear to regress to become the same as all the parties you had attended when you were four, right down to the pink jelly which is about all you can eat when you're in your dotage anyway because there usually aren't too many teeth left in a functioning capacity.

I'm a recluse. That's just who I am. Parties make me feel like I'm trapped in a titchy little cell with far too many brightly coloured balloons and lots of noisy people. When I go to a party, which is about once every forty-five years, the first thing I want to do is prick all the balloons with the little pin that holds my PETA badge onto my cruelty-free tee-shirt and then run away to some place where it's super quiet. I do that a lot, even when I'm not at parties.

I remember the first party I attended. It was a street party being held right across the U.K. On almost every street and in every household people from all walks of life were coming out of their houses carrying tables and chairs, bottles of beer, cakes and slices of bread and butter. You could tell that something *really* important was going on because the bread had been buttered right to the edges, not just in the middle and then folded over to disguise the discrepancy. Oh no! No folded bread today. If it was going to be buttered to the edges then *everyone* should be able to see it.

This was, of course, the party to end all parties. It was the Queen's coronation, 1953. I was four and a half years of age and about as tall as a Meerkat in a sombrero. The street was a haze of people. The pavement had been lined with old trestle tables, much splashed with paint-drippings and wallpaper paste but cleverly covered with crisp white tablecloths and small vases of wildflowers. The food was impressive for those poverty-wracked years including pink blancmange and apple pie although the feast didn't last long as dockers, miners and smelter hands were a hungry lot and everything was scoffed in rapid time followed by bottles of frothing beer. After all the feasting came the speeches followed by lots of toasts in beer dregs to the Queen, God Bless Her, and then the singing, largely *God Save* etc with loud and quite beautiful Welsh baritones — voices fuelled by kegs of beer and throats greased by all the butter that had gone right to the edges.

I can't say that I really enjoyed it. I didn't even know what a queen was at that time other than the fact that ours must have been related to Cinderella because she went everywhere in gilt carriages drawn by a team of fairy-tale horses and every time she got out of the carriage a bunch of men dressed in funny long socks with pointy shoes played trumpets very loudly. It was as if Walt Disney had taken a week' sabbatical from drawing Micky Mouse by hand and had suddenly come to town.

As I grew a little older I realised that parties were not my thing. Everyone was expected to be happy and full of fun and life but all I ever wanted to do at a party was to find the cupboard under the stairs, ubiquitous in all working class terraced houses, and hide there until the bedlam had died down so that I could creep out like an undertaker's apprentice and disappear darkly into the night. Now I know that makes me sound a little freaky but it was just the reality of being a young introvert and a recluse-in-training with wing-nut ears that made me look like a startled possum.

Not that parties were particularly common at that time. The queen might have been in the process of building one of the most expensive royal yachts in the history of humankind and having frocks made at a cost that would have kept a hundred ordinary families for an entire year, but for mere mortals like us the austerity measures forced upon us by the costs of the fairly recent war were still quite real. These were the early 1950s. Life was tough, cold, grim and, at times, particularly bleak. There were bomb ruins everywhere. No one really wanted to party, and few could afford it.

The second party I attended, some years later, was held at the house of my school's headmaster, Mr Moran. I never quite managed to bounce a rubber up his nose, by the way. I was also never sure if he was really alive because he was tall and thin and had the pale, haunted face of a ghost. The big day came and off I went to the party. It was the birthday of one of the Moran children and Mrs Moran, despite nationally imposed government austerity, had spared no expense. The table was full of cupcakes with sprinkles on top and the bread had almost been buttered to the edges but not quite because even a headmaster had to show some economic constraint.

Actually, I believe that the entire party had been arranged for the sole purpose of showing off Mr Moran's brand new television set which only he in the entire neighbourhood had been able to afford.

No one had ever seen a TV before. I wasn't even sure what a television was or what it might be used for. It came in the form of a square wooden box, the wood panelling quite handsome and polished, in front of which was a grey glass screen that looked decidedly boring. Beneath that were a few Bakelite knobs. 'After we've had tea we'll all sit down and watch the television set,' Mr Moran enthused. 'Charlie Drake is on today.'

I liked Charlie Drake because he looked like a short duck with exploding hair but I was a bit wary of Mr Moran, I had to admit, mainly due to his ghostly element but also because he was about nine hundred feet tall.

After all the food had magically disappeared into the crumb-rimmed mouths of a dozen or two little boys and girls (we were all dressed in our Sunday best, by the way) Mr Moran ceremoniously switched on the television and sat in his favourite chair, well contented, politely belching boiled-egg-scented breath into one hand. While we waited for the wooden box to 'warm up', Mr Moran regaled us with a brief history of the invention and development of television from its earliest days of conception. It was like listening to Einstein expounding his Theory of Relativity and almost as incomprehensible. We learned that the 'TV' as it was known in the good old U.S.A. was going to be the new wireless of the future. We gawped wide-eyed at that because we couldn't possibly imagine anything taking the place of wireless sets and especially Tony Hancock's *Ha-Ha-Half Hour,* for those of you who remember that poor old chap who flew half way around the world to Sydney, of all places, to wash down a box of exceedingly nasty tablets with a pint of vodka — which was a peculiar kind of ending for someone who had laughed rather a lot — especially on our wireless sets.

Mr Moran went on and on talking about the wondrous invention of television. It was going to change the world, he said. He talked so much he neglected to notice that the television box was failing to warm up at all and when I put my hand on the glass, leaving a sticky mess of cup-cake jam, the screen was as cold as charity.

That was almost it, as far as our first demonstration of this earth-shattering device was concerned, although Mr Moran did manage finally to get power to the thing and after about five minutes it 'warmed up' to reveal a screen filled with nothing but some kind of electronic snow. We had entirely missed Charlie Drake, and all the station staff had gone out to enjoy a jolly good lunch because that's what TV staff did in those days — four hours on air and the rest of the day in the pub. We were all enthralled though. I mean, we'd never seen snow on a screen before. It was amazing at first but became boring after about fifteen seconds and we all went home to tell our parents that Mr Moran had a new box he called a tele-something and that it was really good if you wanted to see a lot of flickering snow. It was astonishing. It was going to change the world. We knew that was true with a strange childlike certainty because Mr Moran had told us so and as he was our headmaster we believed absolutely everything he said.

Anthony 'Tony' Matthews
The young 'grocer's lad', who, as a boy, loved to roam alone.
— Tony & Lensie Matthews collection.

Years passed. I began to shoot up like a daffodil but without the yellow head. In fact I think I did go through some peculiar illness when my head turned slightly yellowish for a while. Yet I was the perfect little boy. Not too bright, mind you. Really stupid at geometry, algebra and trigonometry but excellent at dropping my pencil at just the right moment to take a surreptitious look at Miss Edward's legs. In fact Miss Edwards, my art and English teacher, was the first female I ever noticed with legs. Up until then the gentle gender might well have been whizzing around on roller skates or snow-shoes for all I cared, or noticed, but Miss Edwards was different. She had legs and I thought they were rather spiffing. I would have done anything for Miss Edwards because not only did she have legs but she also had a number of other attributes including the capacity to give me a wry but good-natured smile even when I was being cheeky.

I sometimes wonder if Miss Edwards liked my legs as much as I liked hers. Probably not, although she might well have noticed my wobble which I thought was so pronounced at times I felt like one of those little tin clowns with spherical bottoms that sway in every direction as soon as you touch them. I was a spherical-bottomed daffodil-coloured clown and apparently everyone knew it. No wonder I was wobbling like buggery!

My first alien 'wobble' came when I was about nine. Not long after I'd peed my pants during my very first night as a Cub. I was a Cub-virgin, you see, and just as nervous. I didn't even have a uniform yet. All the tiny little Cubs had been looking at me and I found that it was rather disconcerting to be the centre of everyone's gaze, especially when standing in a warm puddle of well-used lemonade.

Perhaps that's what started it all. Not long after the deliciously mind-numbing saga of pissing all over the Cub-house planks, I was walking with my Auntie Eth along a street when I noticed a group of people on the other side of the street turn slightly to watch us. I had an unaccountable feeling of being examined and for some unfathomable reason this made my legs wobble a little and I felt as if I were staggering slightly. I know now that it was simply self-consciousness but at the time I thought I was either having a mini-stroke or Auntie Eth's lilac water was a smidgen too heady that day.

That was actually the day when I'd just got through telling my teacher at Wellsprings School in Taunton that she had misspelled the word 'inflammable'. For a boy of nine from working class Swansea that wasn't a bad effort. Perhaps I wasn't so stupid after all. Nine-year-old Wendy Turnbull looked at me adoringly which was really spiffing because she wore the cutest little white ankle socks, but then I suddenly noticed that everyone else in the class was also looking at me as if my bum had suddenly dropped off. In the playground the word went around quickly. I could see the elbow-nudging and the long looks. Some of them no doubt would have loved to be able to spell inflammable, even if they had no idea what it meant, but others were just teetering on the edge of astonishment that weedy little Anthony Matthews who'd just been transferred from some Swansea poo-hole of a school had actually had the temerity to *correct* a teacher! They had no idea, of course, that although I was just a lemonade-leaking sprout, I was also a bookworm with glow-in-the-dark eyes from reading beneath my blankets at night and I could spell the socks off most boys my age. All that would have been okay too but everyone was now *looking* at me and when I tried to walk nonchalantly my legs were beginning to go wobbly — a bit like the dockers in Swansea on Friday nights. I couldn't understand what was happening. Why did my legs feel like apple blancmange?

Since then the malady has grown. As a boy it wasn't too noticeable but when I got into my teenage years, tall, dorky, a bit like Stork-leg Man but without the whole worm-eating thing, that's when the wobble started to become really wobbly.

Anyway, because I shall be mentioning this 'affliction' later in this book, I just wanted to point out the fact that I often feel like I'm wobbling. It can be a little disconcerting at times, even if the wobbling is just in my own tiny, wasp-sized brain and no one has actually ever noticed the slightest waver in my walk.

I did not realise for years that my wobble was a direct result of my intense self-consciousness. I could feel people's eyes burning into me like Superman's fabulous see-through vision. Everywhere I walked, it seems, people were watching me. If I got on the bus everyone would turn to watch, or at least some of them would. When I stood to get off the bus they did it again. Sometimes I'd stay on the bus just so that I wouldn't have to get up and be watched by all the other passengers while I wobbled off. When that happened I usually had a long walk back to school but that was better than being looked at by a bunch of scruffy bus-people with greasy hair and neck-pimples. What was it about me that turned their attention? I wasn't James Dean. I wasn't even good looking. Yet I always felt that I was being noticed and it made me feel like an alien with his trouser-buttons open and that can be a little disconcerting for a young grocer's lad who had not yet noticed that most girls actually had legs and they went all the way up to their bottoms. Wendy Turnbull didn't count, by the way, I was only transfixed by her white ankle socks and possibly her dimple. No doubt she would have been equally enthralled with my little ankles which could clearly be seen because I wore sandals without socks even though I'd had a terrible row with my Aunty Eth because I wanted to wear socks with my sandals but she said they would make me look like a right twit and she was probably right. Even today, Spaniards on the *Costa del Sol* are still splitting themselves laughing at British tourists wearing socks with their sandals. It's a source of constant hilarity, especially when the tourists finally take the socks off revealing their bone-white ankles and feet in contrast to their *Costa del Sol* suntanned legs. It looks as if they are wearing white skin-socks — which is bloody hilarious!

I was a boy of the fifties. It was a different world. War rationing had ended only a few years earlier. You could tell. Everyone was skinny and had boils. There wasn't much money around and that made people even skinnier. Britain was attempting to recover from the mind-boggling cost of the war. The whole country was broke and everyone knew it would take years to recover. The menfolk worked hard at any job they could find and after work they went into their gardens or to their allotments and grew vegetables so that their families would have enough to eat. The fifties, especially the early fifties, were like the Great Depression. There was the relief and joy at having kicked Hitler right in his single, well publicised and highly musical testicle, (there is a rather lewd song about it) and there was light at the end of the tunnel (except for Hitler) but everyone knew that although the war was over the struggle to put it behind us would take some doing.

For the struggling workers there were panaceas, of course. A pint down the pub on a Friday night was one of the best anesthetics that a shilling could buy, especially when it was good Welsh beer, brewed locally. The other indispensable crutch upon which almost everyone leaned was a good old cigarette, and I have to admit having rather a fondness for them myself, at that time, at least, despite the fact that I was still a few years away from my teens and although, unlike Hitler, I had two balls, neither had yet dropped, either as a pair or singularly, so my smoking days had begun really early.

The 1950s were tough times, not as tough as the war years, obviously, but the shadow of the war still hung over us with an ominous menace that was, of course, heightened by the constant threat of some kind of Soviet-inspired annihilation, and we were sometimes informed of government polices such as staying indoors in the event of an atomic attack and hiding under a strong table which was so brilliantly helpful that it's giving me goosedumps.

The threat of atomic disaster loomed over everything and was as palpable as the real war that had all too recently ended. It was almost as if the war had just changed direction and we were no longer fighting evil hordes of goose-stepping Nazis but were now going to have to contend with evil hordes of goose-stepping Russians dressed fashionably in radiation suits. And, I have to ask, why do all fascist or communist regime soldiers 'goose-step', and what on God's Earth is a 'goose-step' anyway?

Absolutely everyone on the planet, including Hitler and Stalin, were perfectly aware that both geese and ganders do not goose-step, or two-step, or even side-step — they waddle! But then, I guess, it would not sound as threatening to read a news report that states, for example, 'One hundred thousand of Mr Stalin's highly trained troops, all appropriately attired in atom-bomb suits and armed with tons of radiation burn-cream, waddled down Oxford Street today, having landed yesterday at Hastings.'

The general public was being informed of all the dangers which might come our way as a result of atomic attack and the many things we were, or were not, to do. Closing all the windows and doors, for example, and drawing the blinds — gosh I'm sure that would have saved gazillions!

We were told to get into basements, if we had them, or head to the nearest subway, both of which were non-existent in the terraced house regions of Swansea.

To prevent being 'tossed about', (hilarious) — we were told to drop flat on the ground and then to hide our eyes in the crook of our elbows. Now, I'm absolutely positive that this government policy was actually either a tongue-in-cheek joke or a daydream some Whitehall bureaucrat had while scoffing custard-creams at morning tea. We were told not to 'loose our heads' — which, when not being used as a metaphor, would have been helpful, and after the bomb had 'burst', we were to wait a few minutes before going out to help fight the resulting fires.

It was as if we were still dealing with the Nasty Nazi Blitz!

Yes, the fifties were actually all about finding oneself in a world that had just come through the wringer of the war. Now, as a boy, I knew rather a lot about the conflict. I bought all the comics. Herr Hitler featured in many of them and there were very strong rumours, largely generated by the comic-book writers, I believe, that Adolf had survived the war and scarpered with his bitch Blondie and his new wife Eva. I was always confused about which was the Alsatian and which was the bitch. If the comics were to be believed then Hitler was living somewhere in South America where he was in the process of cloning Eva and the bitch and himself and creating a master race of Latino goose-steppers. Hollywood later made a movie about it starring Gregory Peck. I was always a little sceptical of this concept. I didn't know very much about South Americans apart from the fact that they had rather naughtily killed John Wayne at the Alamo, but I had a lot of trouble imagining thirty-three million cloned storm-troopers wearing sombrero helmets, especially when they would all look like a combination of Adolf, Eva Braun and Eva Peron with a toothbrush moustache.

My father ran a grocer's shop which was quite a jump from his previous work at a toy factory owned by two German brothers. It's rather a curious reflection on life that he had gone to work for the Germans having only just come home from fighting the little blond buggers in the Western desert, although, to be fair, these brothers had been refugees from Nazi Germany.

However, life as a 1950s grocer's boy had its compensations. The first, of course, was the abundance of sweets. Most lads of my era were rarely able to enjoy any sweets but my life was filled with gob-stoppers, sherbet lemons, bullseyes and sticky cakes that accidentally-on-purpose got crushed and couldn't be sold to the general public because all the strawberry jam had squished into the fake cream making it look as if the bun had quite recently committed suicide. Nobody would buy them but I didn't mind at all.

I was a grocer's lad and everyone treated me like royalty. At least all the kids did — well, most of them. There were some who stuck to me like poo to a shoe because they knew I had a bag of Licorice Allsorts in the pocket of my baggy shorts. Then there were the bullies who didn't know the meaning of good sickening sycophancy and would try to bash me to get at the Allsorts, or my packet of fags, but they could rarely do that successfully because I was as fast as a dust-mite at a carpet beating. The streets of St. Thomas, where we lived in Swansea, were as hilly as buggery, and pushing and pulling a heavy grocer's barrow up and down them made me spectacularly fit. My legs looked like lollipop sticks but were a blur when I ran. I was like The Flash. I could run the socks off most of the bullies, gobbling sticky humbugs while I did so and flicking them the Fickle Finger of Fate — an interesting if somewhat naughty gesture I'd discovered on

Mr Moran's television set which occasionally showed programs other than snow.

My father was the only person in the street to own a car which in those days was almost cause to claim royal blood. It wasn't much of a car — just a van really, bought secondhand. Yet to me it was like having a Rolls Royce. It would be parked outside our little corner shop, emblem of wealth and prosperity. I would just sit on the stone wall and look at it, pretending I was Prince Charles. It would be quite nice to have blue blood, I reflected, and wondered if the residents of Buck Palace really did have blue blood running through their royal highness veins. Probably not, but it would be great to waft around with an air of gracious superiority smelling slightly of cucumber sandwiches and Corgi poo.

The main problem I had with being royal was the fact that they kept shooting things that really didn't want to be shot. Deer, for example, pheasant, grouse, sick corgis and, had the opportunity presented itself, the occasional Russian spy masquerading as a royal art curator. Even as a boy I had a real passion for not shooting animals. I did own an air-rifle, bought secretly for ten bob by saving my pocket money, but I literally never killed anything with it apart from a fly I was unlucky enough to hit as it landed on a bottle of Tizer pop in our shed. I was astonished when it just dissolved into a little blood-blot on the bottletop. I felt awful. I *had* aimed at it — true. But it was just a fly, for God's sake, and about ten feet away. I never in my wildest imagination believed that I would actually *hit* it.

I loved animals and did not want to kill them for any reason. I did eat meat. It was the fifties. Not to eat meat would have seemed so outstandingly loony that I would have had to undergo brain scans or something equally as malodorous. Have you ever seen the brain scanners of the 1950s? They looked as if they had been invented by Picasso when he was totally off his head on *Sangria*. I know because I suffered from frequent migraines as a child and was ordered to have a scan to see if there were any brains at all beneath my skull. By the time I was hooked up and ready to go my head was completely swathed in rubber cups, wires, springs, lever-arms, tubes, clips, straps, needles, oxygen masks, probes, domes and about a million tiny clamps that looked suspiciously like clothes pegs. And that was just to have a brain scan! So I ate the meat, at least a little of it, and shovelled the remainder into a soggy pocket to be disposed of later in the back lane. Mostly though, I convinced my mother that I was having one of my famous potato days. Good for the brain, I told her. Created more white cells. Good for growing boys to have white cells. Too much dead animal with all the dead blood cells it contains inhibits the growth of healthy white cells in little boys smelling suspiciously of fags and really strong Polarmints.

Thus my meat consumption was greatly restricted while the rest of the family happily snacked on turkey, lamb, tongue, pressed beef (whatever that was), potted fish-paste, corned beef, spam, tinned crab, smoked kippers and something called suet pudding. Spam was always the mystery meat. You didn't know if your fork was going to reveal a mashed pig's bladder or a goat's testicle. It was like some kind of lucky-dip from hell. Corned beef was interesting too. On cold days it came out of the rectangular tin with a slow sucking sound and fell on the plate looking like a builder's block of fat and flesh shredded by high explosives. However, in summer it poured out of the tin like some kind of fatty glue that unfailingly reminded me of donkey diarrhoea.

Instead of dead animals I usually tucked away the equivalent of a Mount Everest of hot chips followed by slabs of bread and butter. Not quite vegan, but getting there. Actually I never knew what a vegetarian was in those days. Had I done so I would have scratched my head and looked stupidly perplexed. I don't think anyone had heard the term in the 1950s. If suddenly I had gone down the street proudly proclaiming myself to be a vegan I expect the bobbies would have picked me up and locked me into one of their Tardis police boxes. Even today vegetarians are considered to be people strangely transfixed with boiled cabbage and boring salads who appear to live their lives in some kind of hazardous mayonnaise daze.

I felt that killing animals was one of the worst forms of bullying imaginable. My father trained me to bone the bacon in the shop so I was often up to my knuckles in salted pig. I'd whip out the ribs with a bit of string. That was the most efficient way. It left the bacon on the animal and not on its bones. I saw death up close, and one of our frequent customers who lived down the street, used to come in as regular as clockwork to scrounge free bones for her soup. But I saw the eating of corpses as taking bullying to a whole new level because those being bullied were not sufficiently alive to be able to protest. Was it just me or was an overindulgence of fags going to my head? I only mention all this because I am an ethical vegan and being a vegan in a world of carnivorous people is a lot like being an alien.

Not that I have anything against aliens, apart from the fact that they look as if they would smell like mud-wallowing crocodiles, or possibly wet voles, and appear to spend rather a lot of their free time carrying out rectal probes on non-alien Earthlings — usually small Earthlings wearing socks with their sandals. If you think I'm joking check out this statistic. It's real. One person in every fifty now living in America has claimed to having been abducted by aliens. If that number is correct then we are already in the middle of the biggest alien invasion since the Mayans arrived by spaceship a few thousand years ago. You may not believe me but in later years I actually met one of them, a Mayan-alien I mean, and wrote a magazine article about him. He claimed to having come from some planet about a million light years away and I have to say that he did look somewhat travel weary.

A recently released *Defence Intelligence Reference Document* titled: (*Anomalous Acute and Subacute Field Effects on Human and Biological Tissues*) even states that known contact with U.F.O.s had resulted in sexual encounters with aliens that had left at least one woman pregnant. The document actually lists the biological effects on humans of U.F.O. sightings and contact. The report states that U.F.O. sightings have been known to leave witnesses with radiation burns, brain problems and neurological damage.

Being a veganalien (I just made up that word by the way) doesn't happen overnight. It takes time. It was years before I finally realised that I didn't actually belong on this planet. I remember seeing someone in the movies saying, 'Stop the world I want to get off'. It was funny. But for me it was kind of real. What if I were able to get off the world? I would really have liked to get off Earth even if it were just for a holiday, like a fortnight at Butlins, but of course it was just fantasy. The reality was here. Grounded by Earth. Lost in the anonymity of the masses. Blended into humanity. I felt different, I did different things and thought differently but looked just like any other member of the human race apart from ears that stuck out like a shag's wings when it's sunning itself on a seawall. That's the bird 'shag', by the way, not the shag tobacco one can still buy in exclusive tobacconists, and definitely not the other shag, the one that flashed immediately to your mind the moment the word popped out, although in my time I've seen one or two of those on seawalls as well.

I was a bit of a loner as a boy. It just worked for me. There were rather nasty teddy-boy gangs to be avoided and steering clear of them was an obvious necessity because they had a penchant for carrying cut-throat razors, knuckle-dusters, or leather strops in the pockets of their shiny teddy-boy jackets. Being alone meant that I could quietly duck and hide when I saw them coming or run like buggery. I don't think it was cowardly. What small boy of nine or ten would face up to a gang of youths of fifteen or sixteen armed with enough sharpy hardware to open a small barber's shop? I became a phantom. No one could ever find me. I'd be hiding in an old bomb-shelter behind the fish-and-chip shop or in the men's bogs, a small brick building up by the bowling green which usually had its toilets completely bogged up with a yellowish sludge of poo and soggy, government-issue toilet paper. That's why it was called a bog. It stank like Stalin's underpants. The tiny loo was surrounded by thick vegetation which provided really excellent cover if I had to dash out of the back window in my endeavours to escape being roasted alive or chopped into little bacon strips by razor-wielding weirdos with alarmingly long sideburns, drainpipe jeans and crepe-soled shoes that were known universally as 'brothel-creepers'.

The St. Thomas area of Swansea where Tony lived as a boy.
Kilvey Hill can be seen behind the row of houses.
— Tony & Lensie Matthews collection.

Sometimes I'd climb to the top of nearby Kilvey Hill and sit among the stone ruins of an old windmill knowing that from that vantage point I could see for miles in every direction and also look below me to the long slopes of the hill as they descended to the town and bay beyond. If anyone was coming in my direction I could easily hide among all the white stone ruins or scarper in the opposite direction where there were boggy marshes and streams with secret trails among the quicksands which only I could navigate safely and where anyone pursuing me would be swallowed alive by the mud and digested by voracious mudcrabs with an acquired taste for teddy-boy meat. Actually I'm exaggerating a little about the quicksand, it was just a boyish dream, but it gave me the satisfaction of a deliciously hideous power that only I possessed and I fantasised about whole bunches of razor-wielding brothel-creeping teddy-boys covered with slimy mud as they sank deeper and lower into the sludge, crying for their mummies like the nasty little twits they were. There would have been a significant social upside to this quite delicious carnage, of course: all that mud would probably have helped the bone-dense idiots get over their chronic chaotic acne.

There was an old iron-ore quarry on the hill, vast in circumference with tall man-made cliffs all around which had been cut by hand by dismally paid Victorian labourers wearing cloth caps, hob-nailed boots and sweaty neckbands. They were gone now, of course, long in their graves, which, conveniently, were situated just down the side of the hill in the Danygraig cemetery where all the tombstones could easily be seen from the quarry. Sometimes I'd sit up there among the rust-coloured rocks and look down at the singularly depressing cemetery and wonder if the labourers had also sat here where I was sitting, eating their lunches perhaps, looking down at the forest of stone crosses and wondering how long it would be before they too were there. Somehow it gave me an earthy sense of mortality. It brought home to me that when we die the world goes on as if it never misses us. Here was the quarry, dug by hand. It was still here a hundred years later but the hands that had dug it were stilled forever. It was all so ominously final. It brought death closer. It made the constant teddy-boy threat seem even more real and deadly.

I'd sit alone in the quarry for hours because people tended to stay away. Perhaps it was just the melancholy of the place or perhaps it was the oft-told story of the disaster that had apparently occurred there and the ghosts who were reputed to haunt the site. According to legend, a group of Victorian quarrymen had been killed while excavating a tunnel, digging out iron-ore, and that the bodies had been buried so completely by the rockfall that they had just been left where they had fallen, deep in the heart of the tunnel. The tunnel could still be seen but I'm not sure if the story of the bodies was true. It didn't matter. In death or legend they were still serving their purpose of keeping all the teddy-boy gangs away from the site and as a burgeoning introvert in fear of my life that suited me perfectly.

In the centre of the quarry was a huge pond of rainwater, collected over the years and now filled with reeds, weeds, rusting bicycle remains and old prams. I spent endless hours alone there netting tadpoles and peeing on the thick clusters of gelatinous frogspawn which had the interesting effect of making it look like lemon jelly with currents.

There were all kinds of loners in St. Thomas during the 1950s. At least that's how it seemed to me, and perhaps I moulded myself on them a little. This was the post-war decade and the war was still having an impact on society generally and individual lives in particular. Lots of women had been left widows. Men had sometimes been left widowers. Swansea had come in for its own blitz bombing and many people had been killed. Shortly after the war my sister and I had lived with our parents in a tiny terraced house in Manselton, Swansea. Psychologically the war was still with us, it was a part of who we were. It filled us with fear for years afterwards. My sister recalls waking after having nightmares that the Germans were coming to take us away and she would run, crying, down the landing to our parent's bedroom seeking comfort and reassurance. I was only about as tall as a pint of bitter but I already loathed all greasy little Nazis.

I should mention in passing that the term 'Nazi' has a fundamentally ridiculous background about which few people know. We have seen in more recent times how the growth of neo-Nazi organisations grew dramatically and became far more emboldened after the installation of a certain president as the failed Spelling-Bee King of America, but it's unlikely that all those brain-dead swastika-licking heroes of National Socialism actually realise that the very term 'Nazi' is a colloquialism for 'blithering bloody idiot'. It originated from the term 'Ignz', a common Bavarian name, normally associated with people such as uneducated labourers, and 'Suzi', a German abbreviation for socialism, and was first used by German propaganda minister Joseph Goebbels in a pre-war pamphlet. It didn't go down too well because basically it brought together the two names which typified someone who was a brain-dead peasant from the corn-shuck sheds of lower Bavaria. After that initial publication and contrary to everything you see in Hollywood movies the term was never used again in Germany during the war. It was the 'N' word. I expect that Herr Hitler had a few rather nasty saliva-spraying sentences to say to Goebbels after the publication of the pamphlet because it made every *Sieg Heiling* little twit on the planet look like Charlie Chaplin in his brilliantly comic film, *The Great Dictator*.

The 1950s was a rather grim time; economic recovery from the war years meant heavy taxation and a shortage of money so not everyone was dancing to Lonnie Donigan's ridiculous skiffle group. Whoever would have thought of making musical instruments out of used tea-chests, broom handles and string? Shows you how poor we all were.

Loners lived on the terraces. Some of them were road-workers or park-keepers. Most of the men were ex-servicemen, some of the women had also served during the war. One or two of the men were thieves who usually ended up in Swansea prison, a grim grey-stone edifice down near the gasworks and soccer field. One oldish man I came to know was employed in laying bitumen. He virtually lived in a tent which was comprised of a steel pole framework supporting a large sheet of ratty, tar-stained tarpaulin.

His name was Dirty Bertie, mainly because he didn't wash very much and therefore ponged like freshly-turned gravesoil. He moved his tent around all over the neighbourhood as work demanded, laying bitumen by day with the work gang and sleeping at night in the tent, ostensibly in order to stop little Anthonys from traipsing all through the newly laid bitumen but in reality, I think, because he had no other home to go to. He would light a coal fire in his little brazier on the pavement and warm his bum there, or his hands, turning like a rotisserie until he had toasted himself sufficiently. He would then sit on an old wooden stool and light his pipe while brewing black tea in a black kettle, or warming up baked beans. It was a simple, lonely life and suited him perfectly.

Being a loner myself I came to know Dirty Bertie quite well. In fact it was Bertie who taught me how to smoke a pipe. He used any kind of tobacco he could obtain and that included picking up fag-ends on the pavements, breaking them open and emptying any remaining tobacco into a small leather pouch he kept in his bitumen-stained waistcoat pocket.

When I first tried to talk to Dirty Bertie it was the middle of winter. The night was bitterly cold and I was drawn to his glowing brazier like some massive moth draped in scarves. He wasn't particularly interested in talking to me and told me to go away, although his exact phraseology was slightly more robust than that. But I persisted. Perhaps I recognised a fellow loner, and eventually, over a period of a week or two, I found myself sitting beside him on the pavement or hovering around the brazier, emulating his movements as he tried to keep himself warm. It was during one of these nights that he offered me his pipe and I took it cockily because I'd been smoking for yonks and thought I knew how to handle tobacco. However, I was in for a nasty surprise. Smoking cigarette tobacco from a pipe is, apparently, very different from smoking cigarette tobacco from a cigarette. Add to that equation the fact that the tobacco had already been half smoked by half of the men of St. Thomas, had been sitting in the rain, or the sun for God knows how long, had probably been peed on by half the dogs in the neighbourhood, and you will begin to understand that within five minutes I was kneeling at the foot of a lamppost mass-producing what navy sailors rather descriptively call 'pavement pizza'. It wasn't a pretty sight. In short, I'd never been so violently sick in my life.

After that I refrained from taking a puff of Dirty Bertie's often offered pipe. I think he only offered it because he'd never laughed so much and wanted a repeat performance but I was far too canny for that. I've never touched a pipe since nor have I scavenged used dog-ends to smoke even though writers are usually so poor that by comparison an aged pensioner is the equivalent of a Wall Street trader with a *Maserati Grancabrio.*

Dirty Bertie remained, apparently forever, on the St. Thomas landscape, moving from here to there as necessary, his little canvas shelter appearing on street corners, in laneways and on pavements in what seemed to be a rather confused and seemingly unplanned or uncoordinated series of roadworks that never appeared to end. When one road had been successfully laid or relaid another would begin the same process with Dirty Bertie always on the lookout for errant boys or vagabonds from Danygraig intent on finding anything that might easily be lifted and sold to the dockers or pawnbrokers. Dockers were like jackdaws. Tools were always being 'liberated' as there was a constant market for them.

Dirty Bertie was something of a legend. At times he would sit at his brazier chewing pieces of bitumen as any normal person would chew gum. He loved it. He was careful not to use bitumen that had already been laid, but would break off a piece of the black, tar-like substance from the sacks in which it was supplied. They were like cement sacks and just as heavy. I tried it once but didn't like it much. It had almost no taste and when it had warmed up in the mouth it chewed just like bubble-gum but its flavour could have been improved with a hint of sugar and spearmint.

Bertie might have been a rather old man, at least by my young standards of the time, but he was still full of fire and fascinating stories. He'd sit there beside me, his mouth full of baked-beans or semi-masticated bitumen, and tell me about the deadly dangers of being a nightwatchman. Sometimes he carried a piece of lead-pipe to protect himself against the depredations of the teddy-boys who had proved themselves to be particularly light-fingered and were not in the least constrained when involved in petty thefts. They would come onto the work-sites at night, carrying petrol-cans and rubber-hoses to syphon fuel from the road-rollers and earth-movers, or even to steal the wheels from trucks, at times. If disturbed in these criminal activities by some rather annoying nightwatchman they were perfectly willing and capable of using rather a lot of violence. It was just their way, and Bertie was well aware of that. In fact I think he was justifiably frightened of them. I know I was.

Old men seemed to be everywhere when I was a boy and they mainly looked like lonely old men. I like to be alone but I wasn't sure that I wanted to be as alone as they seemed to be. For some reason quite a few of them had goitres — bulbous growths on the sides of their necks that looked to me to be terrifyingly terminal. They were veterans of the First World War, some of them, and I wondered if the growths had been caused by living for years in wet trenches, fighting those rather unpleasant Huns, or drinking cheap French wine in the village *estaminets* or possibly as a result of kissing rather naughty French girls who hadn't brushed their teeth properly.

One of these old buffers was a creaking veteran and as I had been having nightmares about the war since I was a very small child (terrifying nightmares — bed wetting stuff, I should add) I had a kind of empathy for him although he didn't look like a bed-wetter to me. He would sometimes come into our little corner-store for five Woodbines, his pension not apparently stretching very far, and take away a packet of salted butter and a small tin of Fray Bentos corned beef. That seemed to be just about all he ate, along with some bread and potted fish-paste, and I'd shake my head and wonder why he still thought corned beef was edible when he had probably been force-fed it in the trenches of the Western Front. Fish-paste too for that matter. Sometimes when he was flush with a new pension payment he'd buy Gold Flake tobacco and a packet of cigarette papers and would be smoking cautiously for days, as if he didn't want to annoy his goitre too much.

I never discovered his name but I liked him a lot. He shuffled rather than walked and I had the distinct impression that he might have been gassed during the war. I don't know why, but that was always the way I imagined gas victims to have walked — bent forward slightly, as though attempting to preserve the air in their lungs, eyes on the ground, knowing that they will soon fall on it, and looking for the safest place to do so without too much injury.

I'm not sure why I felt that I had any kind of affiliation with this old soldier. I was stupidly young and he was tragically old. What could we have in common? He always wore a long, khaki army greatcoat that came down almost to his ankles. He even wore it in summer. It had voluminous pockets into which he would stuff his loaf of bread and tins of corned beef before shuffling up the hill towards his little bedsit in the basement of one of the houses up near the top of Jersey Park. As he walked, his corned beef tins clanked comfortingly. On Remembrance Day he would wear a poppy in the lapel of the coat and he'd be a bit tipsy. But he loved his home-rolled cigarettes. His fingers were stained the colour of old oak. I don't think I ever said a word to him but he would look at me and give me a heavily whiskered half-smile, revealing nicotine-stained teeth that were actually darker than his fingers. I felt a bit uncomfortable about that smile. It seemed to say, 'You will be me one day.'

Perhaps being a recluse wasn't such a good idea after all!

Yet there were strange people all around. Dirt-poor people who had nowhere to live. Hermits and hobos, the one a willing participant in poverty and the other a victim of chance, ill-luck or post-war economic depression. You'd see them in the parks or sleeping in shop doorways. Some pushed those old fashioned perambulators along the roads, seeking work, everything they owned in the pram. They would wash themselves, hesitatingly and only occasionally, under the taps in the parks, stripped to the waist in summer but rugged up in winter and not even bothering to wash behind their ears mainly because the water in the park taps had turned to ice. A quick lick was all they needed after the ice had melted a little. I wasn't very keen on becoming one of those people either. I liked being alone, certainly, but the thought of having enough dirt between my toes to grow King Edward potatoes did not strike me as being a particularly good way to live. I was also not very fond of scavenging for leftover fish-and-chips in a garbage bin behind the pubs in Wind Street. No thank you. You could never be quite sure who'd been sick in the bins. If I was going to be a loner, I was going to do it on my terms and I was going to make sure that if I ever had to sleep rough there had better be a good chippy close by.

Speaking of chippies: my favourite place in the world at this time was an old Anderson air-raid shelter situated in the back garden of a small set of shops facing Kinley Street. The garden was lavishly overgrown with weeds and resembled something from a post-apocalyptic world, which it may well have been had all the thousands of similar Anderson shelters in Britain failed miserably and Hitler had walked in to become the king of England and, of course, the defacto mayor of Swansea.

Almost everyone had an Anderson shelter in their garden during the war years. They were inexpensive to install and really consisted of a large hole in the ground, dug by hand, of course, and then covered with a sheet of corrugated iron bent into the shape of a U. It was then possible to jump into the shelter at a moment's notice should any of Hitler's really unpleasant Bavarian peasants with jackboot fetishes pop over in an appropriately named Fokker to bomb the living poo out of anyone unfortunate enough not to have installed an Anderson shelter when they'd had every chance to do so.

The shelter behind the shops was my secret place and I would go there simply to be alone. There was a permanent puddle of really grungy water in the bottom of the shelter which ponged a bit, but I didn't mind because there was a nice earth shelf I was able to sit on and smoke my illicit fags while reading a *Beano* comic or a Biggles book or possibly even the illustrated version of *Robinson Crusoe* which I loved. I should mention at this point that there really was a Robinson Crusoe, by the way, although he was not a castaway. Daniel Defoe actually pinched the name from a tombstone in a graveyard when he was hiding after the failure of the Monmouth Rebellion in 1685. He wrote the book in six months using Robinson Crusoe as its main character, and a nanosecond later became immensely rich from it which only goes to prove that grave-robbing comes in a variety of forms and that little Welsh, history-loving twerps in dilapidated bomb-shelters can sometimes be infuriatingly well read for their age.

The only indication that there was ever a little Hobbit in residence at my subterranean hide-away were the clouds of cigarette smoke that came from the shelter on regular occasions and must have looked as if Thomas the Tank Engine had actually taken up residence.

One of the really major advantages of my hermit-hole was the fact that no one ever came into the garden so it was perfect for the budding recluse, but even more importantly, my father had rented both the shops that stood in front of the shelter and in one of them had opened a very successful fish-and-chip shop. Now it has to be said that no young lad could have wished for more — a dad who not only owned shops selling lots of sweets and squishy cakes, but also a shop selling hot chips! I was in heaven. I'd sit in my bomb-shelter, safely tucked away from any stray explosives that might be falling from an altitude so ridiculously high that they were still on their way down since 1944. While waiting for the loud bangs to start I'd enjoy the heavenly aroma of chips frying in boiling oil, contemplating the delicious crispy saltiness of them. Naturally, I could not simply go into the chippy and demand a free sixpence-worth. My dad would not have been amused as he was trying to teach me the value of money but that didn't prevent me from going on the scrounge, especially when I was sitting all alone in my personal private protection against Hitler's butt-ugly bomber pilots and my tummy was beginning to growl like an air-raid siren.

Now what every young boy knows after visiting any chippy is that the lady cooking the chips would often use a kind of miniature pool-cleaner to scoop out any bits of potato or batter that had fallen off during the cooking process and would then tip these scraps into a small stainless steel compartment at the side of the deep-fryer so that they could drain and be disposed of later. In our chippy there was never any need to throw this culinary treasure into the rubbish-bin because I would always present myself at the shop at *precisely* the right moment when the deep-fryer had recently been scooped and all the little bits of delicious batter-detritus were still crispy and hot. In effect, I was a mobile rubbish-bin on two chopstick legs. The deep-fry lady, whose name was Mrs Arnold, would see me coming through the door just like a starving hermit begging for a few scraps and would knowingly tip all the golden bits into a grease-proof bag and hand it to me with a wink and a shake of salt. In the blink of an eye I would be back in my Anderson's bomb-shelter, thumbing my nose at the ghastly imaginary Jerries, and deliciously munching slightly over-cooked golden batter with a crunchy joyousness that surpassed even a freshly lit fag.

God, life was good!

Another of the most isolated places I haunted like an owl-eyed ghost-child was a row of derelict terraced houses that had been requisitioned by the city council because a new roadway was scheduled to be constructed where the houses stood. The row of houses intrigued me because it was like visiting an old Wild West ghost town but without the six-shooters, broken-wagon wheels or Clint Eastwood. In fact it was all pretty mundane: grey, bleak, dead and abandoned, but it was also completely deserted and that suited me down to my little white ankle socks.

Even when occupied, these had been grim, grimy, poor houses constructed sometime around the middle of the 19th century. Many of the streets in the region had been named after battlefields or prominent personalities of the Crimean War: Raglan Street, for example, or Inkerman, Balaclava or Sebastopol Streets, that sort of thing, so it was likely that the houses had originally been constructed around the late 1850s, just after the war. Even then, when new, they would have been depressing, but now, about a hundred years later, abandoned, leaking, with falling slate tiles and rotten window frames they seemed to be half alive and half dead. They existed in a kind of twilight world. Like me, they should have been half invisible, as if passing from one time dimension into another.

The row of houses had intrigued me since they had become abandoned but I had never plucked up the courage to investigate. They looked so forbidding with the windows broken or boarded up, doors hanging off hinges, and rather naughty graffiti scrawled on the walls including some rough depictions of Marilyn Monroe of which she probably would not have approved. The street was full of rubbish and, quite evidently, tramps had been there, lighting fires on the broken pavements and using some of the old doors as fuel. Sometimes you could smell stale beer, piss and tramp-poo, because some of the rooms had been used as toilets and the pong could be a bit fruity at times, but that was only in some of the ruins and the smell went away after a while, as did the tramps, who moved on, apparently searching for other places to mark like stray cats.

I wasn't sure when the bulldozers would arrive to begin the work of knocking down the houses and for a while that uncertainty kept me away from the buildings because I wasn't entirely enamoured with the thought of being trapped under a pile of 19th century rubble like some really sad Dickensian character. However, after a few months, when nothing more seemed to be happening, I decided that it was time to carry out a thorough reconnaissance. Perhaps this could be a good place for a skinny little bundle of near-invisibility to nest for a while.

It was a Saturday morning, and drizzling with rain. I had planned my adventure with care. My school satchel was packed with a torch, a packet of five fags, (yes they did sell cigarettes in little packets of five) a box of Swan Vesta matches, my penknife (just in case I had to defend myself from any murderous tramps who wanted to pinch my fags) and a packet of Branston pickle sandwiches, wrapped in grease-proof paper. I'd told my mum that I was going to have a little picnic down at the beach and she never asked why I would want to have a picnic on a wet day. I was always doing crazy things anyway so I expect she didn't worry too much about it. Thus prepared for my great adventure, and wearing a duffle coat with the hood pulled over my head, I walked down Kinley Street towards the abandoned houses. I must have looked like Scott heading for the Antarctic but without the huskies, of course.

On any normal Saturday the neighbourhood would have been busy but now it was raining quite heavily and I had the streets virtually to myself. Alone again. Just what I liked. By the time

I reached the old houses I was soaked almost to the skin, my satchel was dripping wet but everything inside was still dry including my sandwiches which was fortunate because soggy Branston pickle tastes a little like frog poo and sadly I know that from personal experience.

I began my careful investigation of the derelict homes. Close up they appeared to be even more depressing than they had when viewed from a distance. I walked past one or two, tried the doors but they were firmly locked. I walked almost to the end of the street and came to a few abandoned shops, just the corner-store type of shops that had once been a grocer's or a butcher's, nothing very important. One of them still had some sun-faded posters in the window advertising pharmaceutical products and medicines. I peered through the grimy glass. It had been a chemist's shop and, as luck would have it, someone had already broken in through the front door, leaving it ajar. I gave it a push and it squeaked a bit on rusting hinges then suddenly I was inside a narrow, dark, wet passageway with sodden wallpaper hanging off the walls in strips. I pushed the door closed behind me, isolating myself in semi-darkness with grey shadows, and stood still, listening. I guessed that it might have been the sort of really creepy place that Adolf Hitler could have been using as a hideout so anything was possible. I was already imagining the stupidly huge reward I would receive for bringing in the world's most wanted moustache.

However, all I could hear was an occasional car on the street, tyres hissing on the wet road, and the running of rainwater in the rusting gutters and downpipes. A sudden feeling of foreboding came over me and for a moment I wanted to turn, open the door and scarper as fast as my invisible little feet would carry me, but I resisted the temptation, dug my torch out of the satchel and switched it on.

On my right was a doorway leading into what apparently had been the shop. The passageway, smelling of mould, stretched ahead of me into darkness. A few doorways opened on both the left and right of it. I turned and entered the shop. Surprisingly, the place still contained many of the original fittings — a long, ornate wooden counter ran along one wall and there were wire-framed stands and old cardboard display cases now bent with age and water-damaged because in places the roof was leaking and there were puddles on the wooden floor. The front of the counter had been glassed, but the glass was now broken and shards of it littered the floorboards, glittering in the light of my torch. I crunched over them, treading carefully, to look behind the counter. Kneeling down, I was astonished to find all kinds of medicines scattered over the broken and worn linoleum. Bottles of ointments, jars of creams, now covered in dust and mould and a huge box of glass phials containing a urine-coloured liquid with the words 'spleen elixir' printed on them. I wasn't actually too sure what a spleen was but I had a fairly reasonable idea that I wouldn't be needing any of the elixir for the foreseeable future.

I couldn't understand why all this had been abandoned. It was like one of those zombie movies you see on TV where a group of half starved people living in a post-apocalyptic world are scavenging for foodstuffs and medicines in abandoned supermarkets. I always like those movies because the fantasy is that all these really cool goodies are there just for the taking and you don't have to pay a brass razoo for them. The downside, of course, is that in the movies there is always some hideous zombie waiting behind the fridges or in the cool-room and he jumps out, bites somebody on the bum who then turns into a zombie and begins biting all his friends, although not usually on their bums, and they all end up eating each other raw which would be quite a depressing way to end your day.

I wasn't going to have that, not in a million years, so I took my penknife from my satchel, opened out the little wobbly blade and clutched it tightly as I continued my exploration while at the same time keeping a sharp lookout for any of the walking dead, especially if they looked even a tiny bit like Adolf.

I went from room to room. Everything seemed lifeless. Nothing lived there. Even the rats seemed to have abandoned the place. The people who had run the shop had evidently lived in the same building for there was a small lounge-room devoid of any furnishings, a dining room with some broken chairs, and a kitchen, completely empty now but with an old black stove in a hearth, its cast-iron doors hanging tiredly open. The only light came through a dirty window against which the rain was now washing in torrents. A steady drip of water was falling into the stove from a leak in the chimney. The water had gathered around the base of the stove. It had been blackened by the ashes of the coal that had once been used to fuel the cooker. Everything smelt of age, mould and dust.

At the back of the kitchen was a small scullery, also empty, but a twin set of basins held an old fashioned, knuckle-bruising wash-board. There was a toilet here too but the lead cistern and piping had been taken away for scrap, or stolen, and the ceramic toilet bowl was cracked. Someone had used it anyway. A tramp, probably. It didn't matter any more. Its happy little flushing days, testimony to its genius inventor and one of my superheros, Thomas Crapper, were now long over. (My other superhero is Henry Hook, by the way, but more on him later).

I climbed a set of stairs to the bedrooms. There were three of them, two small rooms and one slightly larger than the others, facing the street. They were all empty and hollow. I tried to imagine what they must have been like when full of furniture, beds, wardrobes and people, but although my imagination is usually pretty good, I could see nothing of the past there. The rooms were just shells of history. Perhaps it was because they were about to be torn down but the life of their history had faded from them. The house had given up its ghosts. Nothing existed there any more.

I went into another house, farther along the street, and it was the same. It was a little cleaner and there was a ragged armchair in the lounge room with its stuffing hanging out. I sat in it, looking out of the grey window and the rain towards a small garden, now completely choked with weeds. I sat there for half an hour, eating my sandwiches, trying to imagine the people, their lives, the families, the happiness, the sadness, all the anguish of living in these poverty-impregnated homes, but nothing would come to me. Everything was dead. I had thought that this might have been a good place for me to find quiet solitude, to hide from everyone when I needed to be alone, but in fact I felt almost haunted here, not by the ghosts of those who had lived and died in these houses, but by the terrible abandonment of them, the bleak dinginess. I realised that people had lived for years in these grimy homes, had gone through the terrible years of war, firstly, perhaps, during the Crimean War when sons and husbands would have been killed, then the Boer War followed by the terrible carnage of both World Wars. The people who lived within these grim walls, even during times of peace, would have had nothing more to look forward to than going to work every day, down on the docks, or in the factories, or the copper-smelting works, and then coming home to these small, depressing, rented homes full of poverty, hunger and despair. A life without any kind of future, from one generation to the next. It was all so ineffably sad. I finished my sandwiches and left, slinking away into the rain with the distinct feeling that I never wanted to spend my life like that. Whatever I did in the future would have to be brighter, more promising and infinitely better than living in a house that even ghosts refused to haunt.

Months later I went to school one day and the houses were still there, just as grim and depressing. When I came home that afternoon they were gone. The entire street had disappeared in a day. The wrecking balls and bulldozers had been at work. All that remained were piles of broken stones and slate, a few smashed toilet cisterns, broken window frames and a cardboard box full of spleen elixir. I was rather pleased with myself that I hadn't been inside the houses when the wrecking balls had begun their work. Had I been inside, Mr McLeod, my irascible maths teacher, owner of the largest conk on the entire planet, would have been waiting rather an unconscionable amount of time to review my always incomplete homework.

Within a few weeks even the rubble had completely disappeared as if someone had waved a magic wand. The entire street had been torn up, the ragged gardens had disappeared. It was called progress and I guess that was correct because no one could actually *want* to live in those grotty hovels with their stink of boiled cabbage, wet coal and rotting Victorian condoms that could actually be rinsed out after use.

I recall standing at the side of the road and looking towards the place where the houses had once stood. It seemed almost impossible to believe that the homes had even been there. In a way, this was my first practical history lesson. I had, in some small way, been a tiny part of that history, possibly the last person ever to enter them. I had explored the rooms of those houses, sat in one of them and eaten my lunch, but nothing now remained. All the evidence of their existence had been erased. My time in the homes was gone, just like all the families who had once lived in them, often for generations, and that history could never be retrieved. It proved to me that nothing is forever. Everything comes to an end and is then forgotten.

I think the demolition had been positive progress but I was a little disappointed that during the deconstruction work no one had actually dug up any mysterious bodies in the gardens sparking off some intriguing 'cold case' investigation. My adventure had fizzled into a depressing realisation of the grinding poverty the houses represented, but if a real life mystery had been kicked off, the entire escapade would have taken on the incredible dimensions of an Enid Blyton *Secret Seven* story, only in my case, quite obviously, it would have been a *Secret One* story or possibly *The Case of the Invisible Muppet.*

From the row of lost houses I progressed to an old cinema in Wind Street. It was called the Rialto. I actually found the cinema with a couple of other boys my age with whom I sometimes roamed the streets, largely for protection against the gangs, as there was greater security in numbers, but I often returned to the huge building alone because I'd set up a kind of little-boy nest in the old projection room. Access to this magical world of fantasy was through the back fence which was broken so I never had to damage it further; then through the long grass and weeds to a window that was also broken and lifted quite easily but with a bit of noise so I had to be careful that the workers in the brewer's yard next door did not hear me.

The Rialto was a place of infinite wonder. I had asked around — as much as a young boy could without arousing undue interest in my curiosity — and discovered that the cinema had originally been the Star Theatre, a low-set stone building with a big stage where thousands of plays and concerts had been performed over the years to the Victorian audiences of Swansea — at least those who had been able to afford them. Then finally the heyday of live theatre and vaudeville had vanished forever and movies were now the preferred entertainment medium with films from Fatty Arbuckle and Charlie Chaplin. (By the way, I should mention that Charlie Chaplin once entered a Charlie Chaplin look-alike competition and quite hilariously didn't win. After he died (in Switzerland on Christmas Day, 1977) his body was kidnapped and held to ransom for $600,000 which only proves that Swiss kidnappers can be comically imaginative).

It was almost inevitable that the Rialto Cinema should replace the old Star Theatre and for years Swansea audiences enjoyed all the old films we now see only on late night television, although, whereas we think they are boring and full of people with slicked-back Brylcreem haircuts and snotty posh accents and *Gone With the Wind* moustaches, the audiences of those days thought they were the most wonderful thing ever seen. And they were, at least up until that time, and the actors were legendary, apart from Stewart Granger, of course, who was a complete twerpy. At school, Granger bullied a young lad in a boater hat who subsequently became one of my friends. The lad later became an uncle to Hayley Mills the Academy Award winning actress who, many years later, was to write me a beautiful letter signing off with, '... Love Hayley'. I think every boy on the entire planet was in love with Hayley Mills. I adored her.

The Rialto cinema closed in March 1959 when I was just ten years of age and the owners had hardly abandoned the place before I moved in like a hermit crab in sandals. It's not difficult to imagine that I felt really at home in the hollow emptiness of this great old cinema with all the ghosts of its colourful past. It was almost as if I were predestined to nest here for a while.

For the uninitiated I should explain that a little-boy nest is usually comprised of old seat cushions (often smelling a bit of cat-pee), a few cardboard boxes to put things in and hide behind in case anyone should appear unexpectedly; a candle, a bag of sandwiches, lots of discarded toffee wrappers and some Superman comics. One had to be careful that the candle did not come into contact with the cardboard or other nesting materials because that could be tragic. I once burned down an entire nest I'd constructed of twigs and dry grass on a block of waste-land near our home. Fortunately I managed to survive the resulting inferno by scrambling rapidly out on all fours, but there were rather a lot of questions when I arrived home looking like a smokey version of Al Jolson, whose 'blackface' persona would last all of one nanosecond today!

For some really obscure reason I have always been attracted to huge spaces: old halls, abandoned warehouses and now this cinema in what was then one of the roughest areas of the city. (It's now something of an upmarket 'cafe' scene stuffed with overly expensive coffee shops which are patronised by trendy people who cut their hair on only one side, use Brylcreem hair gel on the other, and talk about trading in bitcoins but very sensibly never do).

Yet in my day Wind Street was rough. It was close to the docks and littered with really grotty pubs (one of which had a moth-eaten stuffed bear at the door), drunks, cheap Indian curry houses and a few ladies who dressed rather oddly and didn't appear to mind when the drunks began to kiss them, at times quite passionately, it seemed. Sometimes, I noticed, money changed hands but I just thought the ladies were selling cockles. Now I know that sounds rather rude but I should explain for the uninitiated unWelsh that cockles are a kind of rather sad shellfish dug from beneath the sands of Swansea Bay, boiled (alive) and served with salt and vinegar. Frankly I'd rather catch canine warts, but all the Wind Street drunks really liked them because they were, apparently, especially tasty after three pints and a quick knee-trembler. (Gosh that was rude, wasn't it?) I actually remember being offered a bag of cockles at school. The children would eat them with a safety pin. However, when I looked more closely at the tragic little thing, stuck like a butterfly on the end of a pin, I noticed (and I'm absolutely *not* exaggerating here) that a short string of boiled cockle-poo was hanging limply from the unfortunate creature's bum. That put me off cockles for life!

Clearly, Wind Street was not particularly salubrious. The drunks and the women who were *not* boiling cockles in their own excrement seemed to love it, but for little boys like myself it was a place where one went only if one were willing to step around the puddles of pavement vomit and risk a clip around the ear from any docker walking past who had a mind to backhand little boys just for the sheer joy of it. I tried to stay away from the place when the pubs were closing because that was the worst time of day especially when the cockles had been a bit off which sometimes resulted in projectile vomiting and at my height if you didn't have an umbrella that could be colourfully hazardous.

I think it was largely my imagination at work but I knew that *my* cinema (I had already taken possession of it, you see) had been in full swing during the war years. People such as my parents had gone there even before the war and countless numbers of amazing films had been flashing up on the silver screen. It gave me a feeling almost of belonging to the past, being a part of it, not only of the past of the cinema but of all the films and the amazing stories that had once been told through those films.

My cinema was a place of creepy seclusion, magic, adventures, romances and drama. Every second I was in the building sent a thrill through me, especially when I was alone and even more especially because I should not have been there. It was almost alive to me. There were still ticket stubs on the carpeted floor. The rubbish bins were full of mouldy drinking-straws and cigarette packets. The toilets still flushed. I know because I used them often enough although I had to take in my own soap to wash my hands afterwards. I was always a very good little boy like that. A proper little hygienist. It was a bit of an obsession. Had I ever been a super-hero like Spiderman I would have been called Soapman or something. Possibly Lifebuoy Boy.

I didn't know why the cinema had closed its doors. It baffled me. These were the 1950s and people were still going to the movies like lemmings going over a cliff. The silver screen was hosting stories such as *Ben Hur*, *The Bridge on the River Kwai* and even that hilarious masterpiece, *Der Fuehrer's Face* in which Donald Duck has a dream that he's being forced to work in a shell factory for the Nazis and things are so bad that when he gets poked out of bed in the morning at the point of a bayonet his breakfast consists of a piece of wood instead of bread and he makes coffee from a single bean which he's hoarded. His main course for breakfast is an aromatic spray that smells like bacon and eggs. At the end of the film a rotten tomato smashes into Hitler's face and forms the words 'The End'. The film was made in 1943 and I don't expect Adolf would have been all that chuffed when it won an Oscar for the best animated short film. He probably had a few film directors exterminated just for a laugh but I was still rolling around in the aisles fifteen years later when I first saw the film in all its gory glory.

All those old movies were so irresistible. Even so, my cinema had closed and now lay in mothballs, just waiting either for some wealthy entrepreneur to come along with a bag of gold to resurrect the magic and mystery of yesteryear or for some tiny twit with elephant ears to take over completely and run it as his own little theatrical empire.

I fantasised about that. I should have liked to have been a rich media mogul. It could have worked because almost everything needed to reopen the cinema was still there apart from the projectors. The screen was still in place and all the rich drapery and red stage curtains. The rows of seats were still there, at least most of them, as were the discrete lighting and popcorn counters. The dressing rooms were still intact although someone had pinched all the lights and mirrors. Even the Kia-Ora orange drinks tray was still there. Waitresses wearing skirts that were happily far too short would carry these trays around the cinema during breaks, selling drinks, nuts and chocolates. Another waitress would sell cigarettes or cigars or even pipe tobacco. In those days you could sit in a cinema and smoke like a bacon factory. This was the 1950s. At that time cigarette smoking emphatically was not a health hazard. It was healthy. At least that's what we were told and we were so gullible we'd believe anything. I guess it had something to do with the euphoria of having won the war. Even ten or twelve years later we were still blindly high on success.

Alone, silent, like some phantom of the opera but without the spooky mask or cloak, I would roam around the cinema, imagining the crowds of patrons coming in from the rain on a cold Friday night, after all the German bombers had gone home to have breakfast with Adolf. The screen would flicker a few times, the Wurlitzer music would start, the lights would dim, and suddenly a very young John Wayne would be right there on the screen in a super enormous cowboy hat, long before he had acquired his paunch and the impressive love-handles that gave him the incredible advantage of not allowing his gun-belt to slip down to his ankles just as he was about to exterminate a few really unpleasant Apaches who were, rather naughtily, second rate white actors in Apache fake face-paint.

I was in the cinema illegally, of course, and eventually found myself being chased out by a couple of really beefy bobbies with red faces (probably not face-paint) and quite beastly truncheons, but I'd done no harm other than to dream and live for a while in the golden past of Hollywood. For a few amazing months I'd been a director, screenwriter, critic, producer and tea-boy. My film budgets had been in the millions. I'd changed the world with colour, vision, music and words. Sadly, no one had noticed, or if they had they were not telling me.

After that the old building was more securely boarded up and not even a skinny little clapper-board holder like me could squeeze in. My days of movie dreaming were over. Sadly, the Rialto was later demolished. It was like losing a friend. Some person who evidently had no taste or sense of decorum later opened a German sausage eatery on the site. I mean, really: a German sausage cafe on the site where audiences had once watched United News newsreels of Spitfires happily shooting down Nazi bombers. I wonder if old Adolf would have popped in for a Gestapo banger. Oh no, of course not. He was a vegetarian. I almost forgot. And he was also (maybe) dead.

Life continued as normal. I loathed school which was a Victorian drudge, literally learning our times-tables by rote and using pens requiring ink-pots that were filled daily by the prefects. One of our teachers still wore a long black dress that she had probably worn at Queen Victoria's coronation. It was as if we lived sometime in 1856 and were expecting all the wobbling war wounded to be coming home from the Crimea after giving those really unpleasant Russian peasants a rather nasty thrashing. It was a staunch Catholic school and the days of zealous religious education were so hilariously ridiculous they actually kept me hanging onto my seat because I was laughing so much I thought I might have fallen off and broken an ankle or something. However, I was virtually ordered to become an altar boy at the local church. There were about a dozen or so altar boys serving the St. Illtyd's Church and I was pressured by the school to become one of their ranks.

I really didn't have much choice about being recruited into becoming one of God's little-boy-petals, but in the end I was grateful because my exceedingly brief and rather nauseating experience as an altar boy taught me one important lesson — that I always needed to be in some place where people were *not* looking at me. I discovered I loathed being looked at and it was impossible not to be looked at when one is up at the altar waving a great brass gongy-thingy full of smoky incense that makes young boys choke up and cough like camel farts right in the middle of Holy Communion.

The inevitable initiation ceremony into altar-boy-hood was less than charitable and involved having one's head ducked under water in a manky concrete sink for an interminably long time by several sniggering altar boys until one was almost drowned. I'm reasonably sure that someone had been pissing in the sink beforehand. This was considered to have been a badge of courage which I faced with some trepidation and came up spluttering and shouting in a most unholy manner and using words taught to me by a platoon of vituperative teddy-boys whose breath stank of onions and tobacco. Thereafter, however, I was ensconced into the brotherhood of chanting altar-servers and took my place at the altar, dressed in a little white cassock and stood, on the following Sunday morning, alongside my fellow nose-picking devotees. My cassock had been hanging on the back of the sacristy door for about ten years and smelled rather vilely of dust, stale little-boy, and ancient incense. The Mass was then given entirely in Latin so we didn't have a clue what was being said or chanted. However, we learned when to give the necessary responses to the priest at the appropriate times and when to dither about with a whole range of rather ghastly pieces of equipment that seemed better suited to a torture chamber in some medieval castle or the set of a Vincent Price movie: brass candlesticks and incense holders, silver crosses, wax tapers, pots, wine cups, and a cracked wooden box holding white wafers that were, apparently, little slices of Jesus, which, if true, would have been vastly interesting to any little boy wearing a grubby cassock with someone's else's dehydrated nose-pick still on it.

However, the role of altar boy did present me with one major problem. As I've said, I had discovered that I very much disliked being *looked* at! And there I was, standing before the entire Catholic congregation of St. Thomas, dressed in my little white virgin's cassock, looking ever so angelic, with people's *eyes* on me. I shuddered. *This I certainly did not like*! I was at a loss about what I could do. One can hardly resign from being an altar boy, the priest would think that I had 666 tattooed on my bum, or something. Resignation was out of the question. It would be against God; I would have failed in my duties to the Great Creator in the Sky. I worried about this for several weeks while suffering the agony of people actually *watching* me during Mass. Then I decided that if I were just a little late for the service, I would not be required. One can hardly go racing up to the priest in the middle of a Muttering Mass to apologise for one's tardiness. *Sorry Father, but I just needed to use the bog!*

Week after week I arrived at the church a few minutes too late to serve at the altar and when the priest finally confronted me about it I promised to make amends. However, I never did. I would sneak into the vestry ten minutes late, then creep around to the front of the church, touch holy water to my brow, (terrified of being struck down by a sudden bolt of lightning for not doing so) make the sign of the cross and take my place at the back where absolutely no one could see me, apart from God, of course, but that went without saying.

Here, seated in the rear pews, behind the towering backs of adults, I could ponder on the meaning of it all. I was considerably confused as to the meaning of the Virgin Mary and her Immaculate Conception. What was a Virgin, exactly? I asked myself. Was it her Christian name. Was she actually Mrs Virgin Mary, the wife of Mr Joseph Mary who lived at 33 Carpenter Lane, Nazareth? And as to the Immaculate Conception, for a while I thought this was a kind of ceramic pot in which they placed babies to wash them before the Three Wise Men were due to arrive with all their gold, frankincense and myrrh.

And what was myrrh, anyway? Or frankincense for that matter?

~~~~~~

As I have briefly mentioned earlier, I lived for fourteen months with an aunt and uncle at Taunton, Somerset, and although they loved me like a son, those were months which I was forced to spend largely alone because all the other boys in the rather posh street where we lived (the street was actually called a 'close') thought they were a cut above my social position in life, principally because I had drifted in from one of the terraced houses of coal-stained Swansea with all its rough-and-tumble dockers, sailors, cockle-women and factory hands. My Welsh accent didn't help either because it made me sound as if I were either about to break into a song or break wind. It didn't really matter which. Best to be a loner, I finally calculated.

Taunton was a completely alien place to me. I was more used to the dirty city with its coal dust, coastal tramp steamers, carbon black works and the ruins of copper factories where the owners, just as a sideline, naturally, and for a bit of fun, I expect, had, during the 19th century, made copper bangles, known as manillas, which had been purchased by English slave traders. The manillas had then been transported to Africa and used as trade goods to buy slaves who were subsequently transported
~~~~~~

to America to be sold, on auction blocks, like Michelle Obama's great-great-great grandmother, Melvina, who had been sold at the age of eight and was bearing a white man's child at the age of fifteen. I've always thought it strange that slaving currency had been made just down the road from where we lived. Somehow it seemed almost impossible that scruffy Swansea people who lived in scruffy little terraced houses without any inside loos were connected to the African slave trade. Perhaps a manilla made by my great-great-great grandfather was the one used to purchase Melvina for the cotton fields, and if so it stands to reason that it was the Matthews family alone that had put Michelle Obama into the White House. Stranger things have actually happened — Elvis dying on his toilet of eye-popping, heart-fragmenting constipation, for example, when he wasn't even wearing his blue suede shoes. Now that was *really* strange.

Thankfully, in Taunton all my slaving days were left behind although they had market days in the town centre where everyone brought their produce for sale: pigs, apples, honey, sheep. It was a revelation to me as I thought that apart from slaves all those things grew on trees. Taunton was a rural town and I was delighted to hear absolutely everyone speaking with a deliciously rural accent. They all sounded so wonderfully 'farmer's gate' — all clotted cream and strawberry jam. It was so fruity it almost tasted of apples and gooseberries. I just wanted to put a piece of straw between my teeth and scuff some cow-poo onto my shoes. I needed to blend. It was all part of the Great Invisibility Plan.

Across from my aunt and uncle's house was a narrow stretch of woodland where I could hide effectively. It was the perfect place for an invisible boy. After school and on weekends I could usually be found somewhere in the woods. I was like James Fenimore Cooper's 'Chingachgook', quiet, cunning, running silently on handmade moccasins (actually sandals without socks as per Aunt Ethel's directive) and with a razor-sharp hunting knife in hand, ready to strike at a moment's notice. My knife was, in fact, a flat piece of dressmaking wire which my aunt, who made her own clothes, had given to me as a substitute, astutely realising that a little boy with a real hunting knife might actually do more damage to himself than the Mohicans he was so cunningly hunting.

At the bottom of the woods was a beautiful stream that was always running. I'd sit on one of its grassy banks and pretend to fish or sail little bark boats downriver, imagining that one day they would end up somehow in China or Jerusalem, I wasn't sure which as my geographical knowledge was not exactly top-notch. I once sent off a note in a boat that said something like, 'Help. Kidnapped by people who look like Red Indians. Please pay ransom of ten million dinars as soon as possible because my aunt is cooking chocolate cake this afternoon.' I don't know if my cry for help ever managed to raise any alarms but for all I know the constabulary of five counties could have been out looking for a little Welsh boy with curly hair who was famously prone to emitting gaseous eruptions. Apparently I was never rescued and perhaps there was a very good reason for that.

Aunt Ethel, didn't believe in working class people, even though her father, my paternal grandfather, had been a coal-trimmer on the Swansea docks. Auntie Eth had the very good fortune to marry a man with infinite patience and understanding, for, at times, she could be slightly challenging to live with, God bless her. Uncle Don had also been able to raise himself from the ranks of a common private, becoming firstly a captain in the British Army during the Second World War and later a successful business manager. But my life with them was one of boyish solitude, especially after my sister, who also lived with us for ten months, returned home to live with our parents in Swansea. That's when I really started to become invisible.

I was an 'expert' on birds, having read *The Observers' Book of Birds* about ten thousand times. Armed with enough knowledge to have been able to pass a bachelor's degree in avian studies, and even knowing that puffin chicks are known as pufflings (which I thought quite lovely), I'd spend all my spare invisibility in the woodland or roaming the farmers' fields hunting down thrushes' nests or robins' eggs so that I could see how the nests were built and hopefully watch a chick or two actually being hatched. Other children robbed the nests of the eggs so they could 'blow' them and place the resultant empty shells in little cotton-wool displays, but all I wanted to do was to watch the nests and kill all the boys who were killing the eggs and maybe put *them* on display in little glass cases with handwritten identification cards stating something like: 'The flightless lesser-red-headed Brian McSimons. Nests on a couch in a council house. Eats lawn worms and is known not to mate for life. Identifiers: Brightly spotted bum. Beak red, especially during the cooler months.'

I guess I was a pint-sized invisible conservationist, possibly the only one on this planet, which made me an outcast and I really liked that rather a lot. At last I had something to be smug about and because I was almost completely transparent not a soul could see me being smug. How perfect was that?

Auntie Eth was a product of the Edwardian era when the very word 'vegetarian' had yet to be invented. Meat was the central core for just about everything Auntie Eth cooked. Without something dead on the plate then a meal was not complete, she reasoned. It therefore became really difficult for me to find anything that I was happy to eat, especially as Auntie Eth made a Nobel Prize winning chocolate pudding and would unconscionably hold it to ransom should I not eat all the food on my plate beforehand, including, of course, everything lately deceased.

Like the late Queen Elizabeth, Auntie Eth had a corgi (naturally) which was an excellent vacuum cleaner for my unwanted meat but I had to be particularly careful as feeding a dog at the table was, apparently, one of the worse crimes known to humankind. Stuffing sliced beef into my hanky rarely worked because it was usually covered with gravy and when I shoved it into the back pocket of my little shorts it looked as if I'd had some kind of embarrassingly unfortunate accident.

Breakfast was always soft boiled eggs which I loathed because they looked and tasted like bubonic mucus, especially when they had been boiled for only three minutes which Auntie Eth considered perfect timing. To me they looked like jellyfish with yellow fever. Lunch was often chicken broth or ham that had been cooked to buggery in a pressure cooker. The reddened flesh fell away from the bone and looked like a human thigh from some rather unfortunate plump person who appeared to have been boiled alive like an oversized Swansea cockle. Our evening meal, which both the British aristocracy and Auntie Eth called dinner but the rest of the world called tea or even supper, was usually something like boiled potatoes with roast beef or lamb chops or pork chops or even, at times, chicken or fish. God it was agony! On one occasion there was roe and for a few startled seconds I thought Auntie Eth was going to serve up boiled oar or something equally as unusual, but then my uncle explained that roe was actually fish eggs and they would be served on brown-bread toast. That was the moment I knew that I had to do something dramatic to change the world forever. I went to bed that night believing that I was slowly being turned into a human cemetery where fish babies were being sacrificed on little square altars of burnt Hovis.

For those of you who have never heard of Hovis I should add that this was a deep brown wholemeal bread manufactured, apparently specifically, for little old ladies with bowel problems — or at least that was the general impression I had, because only little old ladies with bowel problems bought the bread from our shop in Swansea. If someone came into the shop and asked for Hovis the general assumption was that they were ... oh you get the drift!

Auntie Eth was actually rather a good cook and one of her specialties was the humble chip. She and all other posh people on the planet called them french fries but we down-to-earthers from Swansea referred to them simply as chips. I attempted to convince my aunt that I could and would happily live on chips for the remainder of my life and that she shouldn't bother cooking any more dead animals for my consumption, but she was having none of it. 'One cannot live on chips alone, Anthony,' she told me haughtily, sounding, upon reflection, just like Maggie Thatcher, and the conveyor belt of murdered animals, great and small, furry and feathered, egged and unegged, kept churning out of her little kitchen like a dog-eared funeral procession. Auntie Eth's corgi, Zella, just got fatter and fatter and no one could understand why, although the fact that it was always sitting at my feet beneath the dining room table might have been a reasonable clue. Eventually it died, probably of cholesterol poisoning, and I felt a little guilty until I realised that I would not have my very own four-legged garbage disposal unit readily available beneath the table. My fear and trepidation were soon assuaged, however, when the first corgi was replaced by another, younger and very much slimmer model, at which time I made it my sole quest in life to fatten it up as quickly and as surreptitiously as possible.

My uncle was a menswear manager for the Taunton Co-operative Society and it was a pretty big job because he had about ten or twelve menswear shops under his control through the southern counties and therefore we used to travel rather a lot when he'd have to visit them to do audits and other business stuff which was far above the pay-grade of a wing-nut like me. Still, it made for a jolly good day out with my sister and also Auntie Eth at my side, striding confidently in her fur coat made from a thousand dead foxes. We'd end up in towns like Tiverton, Honiton, Wells, Minehead, and other areas where we would have the day to spend exploring while waiting for my uncle to complete his work. It was always frightfully embarrassing being with Auntie Eth on these occasions as she walked haughtily along like some kind of kinky Canadian beaver-trapper in furs and high heels. However, no matter how much I protested she would never relinquish her fur coat. This was, of course, during the rather tragic days before activists very correctly began throwing tins of red paint over anyone brave enough to wear dead animals in public.

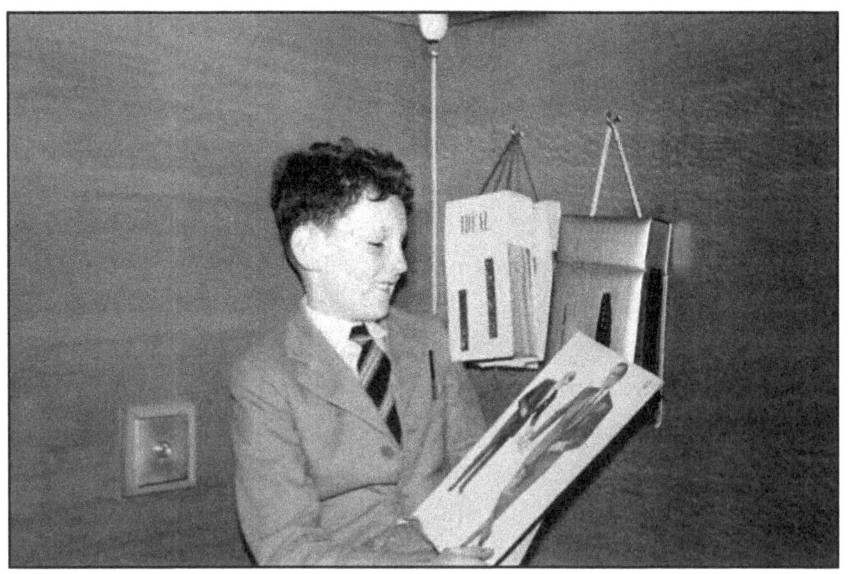

Anthony 'Tony' Matthews during the period when he was living with his aunt and uncle in Taunton, Somerset.
His uncle, Don Bearne, managed a large menswear business for the Co-operative Society.
— Tony & Lensie Matthews collection.

The treat of the day was usually morning tea at some really posh little tea-shop where exceptionally tiny sandwiches with the crusts cut off would come on plates decorated with something called garnish. I never actually realised that the garnish was just for looking at and couldn't understand why I was admonished for grabbing all the bits of parsley and lemon slices and sometimes even really thin slices of pickled cucumber that had been placed onto the plate just to make it look pretty. After the sandwiches had been scoffed (actually I was the one who did all the scoffing while Auntie Eth and my sister daintily nibbled) then came the enormous tiered cake-plate loaded with chocolate éclairs, pink and blue cup-cakes, sticky-buns and other dainties specifically designed to drag a little boy's eyes out of his tiny skull. All this heaven would be washed down with pots of steaming tea to which I would add huge spoonsful of sugar so when the morning tea was over I would be so stuffed I could barely walk and would begin wobbling again.

After that, however, the day usually took a darker turn when the two ladies with me went shopping, usually for feminine trinkets, hats, gloves, petticoats and stockings and the afternoon would stretch out to about 1.5 million light years and become so boring that I would fall asleep and topple from the shop-chair where I had been ignominiously parked like a pot-plant to wait patiently for an aeon. At times it was necessary for me to try to hone my invisibility skills because I discovered that if Auntie Eth was looking for me, then she wasn't shopping and therefore I wasn't being bored out of my brain so that was always a good result. Looking for an errant, near-invisible vagrant tended to distract Auntie Eth from the lipstick stands or rolls of cotton, often resulting in shortening the shopping expedition and prompting a return to the beach or park where there was always a perfectly splendid ice-cream man to be queried very minutely about every single flavour he had for sale.

Failing that ruse, and if I could stay awake long enough, Uncle Don would meet us for lunch and even if we'd only finished morning tea an hour earlier I would generally find the courage somewhere within me to force another three thousand calories or so into my tummy, especially if they consisted of hot chips with tomato sauce. Auntie Eth would never have a tomato sauce bottle on a table, of course, because that would have been so manifestly working class. Therefore the waitresses were told to bring the sauce in a little bowl with a spoon so that it could be transferred with the necessary decorum to my plate. I was never allowed to eat the chips with my fingers nor dip a chip into the tomato sauce. Chips were meant to be eaten properly with a knife and fork and the sauce placed onto them with the knife and only one chip at a time was to be placed into little boys' mouths. After completing the meal the knife and fork were to be placed together on the left side of the plate to indicate to the waitress that she was now allowed to clear the plate from the table. Napkins were to be rolled and placed on the right side.

One was not to pick one's teeth with one's fingers. Little boys' knobbly legs were never to be crossed when seated at the dining table nor were hands or elbows allowed on the table.

Now you can see why I needed to hide rather a lot.

~~~~~~

Back at Swansea after fourteen months in exile at Taunton was like coming back to another world of grime, coal and grinding industry. I had also changed so much, even in that short time, that no one could understand me. Gone was my lovely Welsh accent, replaced with a soft Somerset/Dorset burr that came largely from my Uncle Don, but it was more than that because Auntie Eth had been determined to teach me how to speak properly like some posh boy from Eton. Which was all well and good but when I returned home after being at Aunt Ethel's Really-Posh-School-For-Little-Muppets all the other boys in rough and tough St. Thomas thought I'd been replaced by an extraterrestrial who somehow looked exactly like me. I was a complete alien now to all those I had known before leaving for Taunton. The fourteen months with Auntie Eth had proved effective in driving out all the little horror in me. I was a born-again Prince Charming. I was so polite it was positively sickening. My table manners would not have been out of place at Buckingham Palace. H.R.H. would have approved. I could have received a knighthood for sycophantic politeness. I ate grapefruit with a tiny little fork, for God's sake! Have you ever seen *anyone* doing that? I tipped my soup bowl *away* from me and never *ever* put my knife in my mouth because to do so would have meant literally the end of the known world. Either that or I would probably have cut off my tongue which would also have been quite unpleasant.

I remember standing in the road on the day I arrived back in Swansea with a gaggle of my old friends clustered around me. They literally stood wide-eyed and listened to me with their
~~~~~~

mouths gaping in awe. Young Anthony Matthews had gone away to Middle Earth on some great adventure, and this strange little Hobbit sounding weirdly like the Baron of Bumhollow had returned in his place. It actually scared them.

My cultural tastes had also changed. Now I was deeply into Elgar, Chopin, Beethoven and Dvorak. I was able to speak a little French, just enough to get me into trouble should I ever actually use my scant knowledge of that incomprehensible language, because Auntie Eth had a French tutorials record collection and I'd listen while she played them. Together we would laboriously imitate the phrases and laugh at each other when we found it impossible to pronounce words that were clearly unpronounceable unless you were standing at a corner *pissoir* in Paris with your willy hanging out for everyone to see.

My cultural exchange at Taunton had been unforgiving. It had been full on. I was even able to make pretty little rose flowers out of self-hardening clay, mainly because Auntie Eth liked to sculpt flowers and paint them and put them on the mantelpiece, and she taught me how to do it because I had little else to do having read the print completely off my *Observers Book of Birds*. Yet I dared not tell *anyone* in Swansea about my newfound clay-flower talent because my reputation as a tough St. Thomas grocer's lad would have been irrevocably in tatters and I would have been bashed by teddy-boys until I resembled a plate of soggy corned beef.

I now knew when to speak in the company of adults and when not to speak (which was most of the time). I knew that polite little boys just sat quietly on chairs, knees modestly together so that their tiny testicles did not peek out from their tiny shorts and horribly embarrass everyone present, particularly Auntie Eth. I knew that if little boys did speak at all they always thought deeply beforehand and only added to the conversation if they had anything particularly intelligent to offer — which, for me, was almost never. I was even reluctant to ask to go to the loo which at times caused my face to go pink and my eyes to bulge a little by which time the symptoms were becoming obvious to everyone and Auntie Eth would notice that something fearful was brewing and quickly tell me that I was excused and not to forget to wash my hands using plenty of soap and not leave drips of pee on the floor. Not that Auntie Eth would ever have breathed the word 'pee', of course, she would just say, 'And Anthony, *do* be careful, there's a good little boy.'

I returned to Swansea as if I had suddenly floated down from Mars. My younger brother who had remained living with my parents failed to recognise me. I was a stranger.

I found solace alone on Kilvey Hill which in those days was still quite wild. The land was almost completely bare of housing with just a farm or two here and there. Right on top of the hill was a tiny stone cottage surrounded by stone walls. To me it seemed like something from my history lessons of the ancient Celts or maybe of Saxon times. The cottage and walls were tinted green with lichen. Running through the tiny garden was a clear stream of water that actually bubbled to the surface right there in the grounds, coming up so clear and cool it seemed to cry out for someone to drink it, especially a skinny boy with knees like conkers and a thirst like a Swansea docker.

The house was owned by a little old woman whom I called the Water Witch. I have no idea of her real name. She was bent with age and wore an old Welsh shawl so threadbare it looked as if it had been made in 1649 to celebrate the rather nasty topping of King Charles I. Her face looked to me like an oversized walnut. It was sun-browned and creased with age. She lived alone, totally shut off from the rest of the world. I never once saw her go beyond the walls of her garden. She had a few chickens and a dog, I think, for company, but never welcomed visitors, preferring to be left alone. I thought she was marvellous. I called in one day, walking cautiously through her broken-down gate and along the garden path towards the cottage. The garden, as such, was non-existent; it was comprised almost totally of weeds interspersed with a few cooking-apple trees and some gooseberry bushes. I had been looking thirstily at that lovely spring of water that bubbled up among a scattering of rocks very close to her back door. For a while I stood there at the door, hesitating to knock. The Water Witch was a slightly forbidding sight. There were actually a wart or two on her face and a few impressive moles and I worried that maybe she boiled young boys alive. Who knows? I turned, a tremor of fear running through me and was about to run when the door creaked open (it had to creak, didn't it?) and the old lady was suddenly standing there looking at me as if I were an oversized dingleberry.

'Well,' she said, frowning, eyes quizzical. One of her moles was wobbling. Honestly, I almost peed myself.

I politely doffed my school-cap just like Auntie Eth had taught me. 'Do ...do you think I might have a drink from your spring, Missus?' I stammered in my best Welsh/Somerset/faux-Etonian accent.

She stared hard. I think she was attempting to dissolve me with her eyes. There was an awkward, lip-chewing silence as if she were trying to make up her mind. Vaporise me or boil me in oil? Did it really matter which?

Finally she turned, shuffled back into the darkness of her coal-smoked kitchen, and returned a few moments later with, of all things, a pewter beer mug. She handed it to me without a word but nodded towards the spring. I took the mug, thanked her, and dipped it into the spring which literally ran past her door. The old woman did not move. She just stood there, dark eyes watching as I raised the mug to my lips and drank. That was about the sweetest water I had ever tasted. It was soft, clean and cold and didn't even taste of mud or cow's pee, which was a major plus. I drank every drop, then politely rinsed the mug in the little pond that always formed around the spring and handed it back to the old lady, thanking her as I had been taught. She took the mug and closed the door without a word. I heard the latch drop back into place and her footsteps on the stone floor.

That was the first time I had met a real recluse and I loved her. The Water Witch was everything I had dreamed a reclusive hermit to be: old, sharp-eyed, dried up by years of sun and toil and with gnarled hands that looked like the claws of some prehistoric flightless bird. I wasn't very fond of the warts, moles and liver-spots though. They were a little challenging.

I returned regularly after that and she always knew I was coming. Was that some kind of prescience, I wondered, or did she sit in a little rocking chair by her coal fire staring out of her sooty window to watch for the arrival of visitors who never visited — apart from me of course? I only ever said hello, thank you and goodbye, and I always rinsed the pewter mug before handing it back to her. She never said any more words to me either.

One day I went for a drink and the Water Witch was gone forever. I suspected that she might have been just another grave down in Danygraig cemetery. Either that or she had been kidnapped by aliens. I literally was never sure which. After that no one lived in the old cottage. I'd still go there for water. It seemed the right thing to do. The pewter mug was long gone but I'd just cup my hands into the cool spring. I know it sounds like something from a Wordsworth poem, soppy as crap, but that old lady gave me my first taste of what it might be like to live alone on top of a remote hill surrounded by mist, grass and ancient walls.

In my family there was also the equivalent of the Water Witch. Her name was Aunt Sarah. I don't actually know very much about this old bird but she quite fascinated me because her living room was decorated with corpses.

Now I know that sounds rather weird and although I am prone to exaggerate slightly when making an important point I assure you that everything I say about Aunt Sarah is true. She lived in a small terraced house in one of the bleaker areas of sooty Swansea.

The house was grey, cold, unfriendly and quite terrifying for a young lad used to the more gentile surroundings of Auntie Eth's little country estate with its two corgies (one dead and buried under the roses and the other now rather too plump). Aunt Sarah was a jolly but rather crumbling old soul who had been born in 1424 or thereabouts and had the immense wrinkles to attest to her great age. Her eyes were colourless. All the colour had leached out of them at around the time that Captain Hardy had rather reluctantly snogged Nelson.

Aunt Sarah was stout, in a bent and shambling sort of way, but still active. When I first went into her house I was completely flabbergasted (and I never use that word lightly) to discover that from the whitewashed ceilings a number of butcher's hooks were hanging and on these hooks were numerous sides of bacon. There were so many dead pigs in the room I thought for a moment that I'd accidentally stumbled into some kind of hideous Victorian meat-works. I couldn't take my eyes off the swinging corpses, all sliced into neat halves like something you would see in a movie about mad serial killers. It was truly horrifying. With a little boy's eye for detail, especially when it comes to the macabre, I noticed that at the bums of each of the pigs the tails had not been sliced perfectly in two. Whoever had cut the animals in half had sliced them in such a way that the tails had been left on only the right-hand side of the bacon. I only mention that because it proves how a boy's apple-sized brain is able to suck in an incredible amount of detail when confronted with dead things.

The pigs were just hanging there without heads or feet. I'm not too sure where the feet had gone but the answer to the mystery of the heads, or at least one of them, was quickly found in a pot on the old coal stove with a wet snout sticking out above the level of the boiling water. Aunt Sarah was making pighead soup with split peas and it looked suspiciously like orc snot.

Meanwhile the sides of bacon were swinging around in the breeze. There were still clusters of pig-bristles on the cured skins. My tummy began to feel a bit wobbly and I didn't like that very much. The stink from the cooking head wasn't helping either.

Aunt Sarah did not seem to mind that she was living with all these dead creatures. I could never figure out why she needed to have quite so much bacon hanging around the place. Obviously she liked a rasher or two in the morning with her fried eggs, but really, this was going a bit too far.

I was there on one occasion with my sister, Marna. She was equally as mystified over the bacon farm and tried to ignore it as much as possible. She decided to go out to the tiny sliver of land at the back of the house which, in terraced houses, was comically called the garden. Now it comes as no surprise that old terraced houses in Victorian Swansea had been constructed without any thought to the installation of sewerage facilities. Veterans of the Crimean War who came to live in them apparently never needed to poo. Wasn't that a neat trick? At Aunt Sarah's home the business end of human plumbing was precariously taken care of in the form of a brick loo at the back of the house that contained a wooden seat over a pan toilet. It was a rather unpleasant arrangement because when the pan was full it was necessary to find somewhere to put all the plumber's waste that had been deposited over the previous week. Aunt Sarah had a really good contingency plan for this eventuality. She placed it around her gooseberry bushes.

Now my sister, at that time, enjoyed a good gooseberry. They were just sweet enough to be pleasant and just sour enough to make you feel not too guilty for gobbling about a thousand of them in one sitting. So there she was, enjoying a jolly good munch of Aunt Sarah's greatly gratifying gooseberries, when she noticed with sudden horror that she was standing in 'fertiliser' which turned out to be Aunt Sarah's perfectly preserved personal plumbing. Marna has not eaten a gooseberry since that day and I really can't say that I blame her.

Yet Aunt Sarah was an inspiration despite her rows of swinging corpses and her overly green but somewhat pongy gooseberry garden. She lived alone in happy seclusion, an inspiration to all budding recluses. She was the end of an era. When she passed, the likes of Aunt Sarah would be seen no more. She eventually died after falling from a chair, I think, and injuring herself so badly that she never recovered. What she had been doing standing on a chair at the age of about 209 is completely beyond me but it's just possible that she had been up there with a boning knife slicing off a few rashers for her bacon-butty breakfast. It would have been just her style.

In fact we had rather a lot of potty old aunts so perhaps seclusion and peculiarity runs in the family. One of these oddities was Aunt Beatrice, known simply as Auntie Beat (a sister to Auntie Eth), who had the uncanny ability of being able to talk to dead people. To a boy of just ten years this was a pretty impressive feat and when I heard of these astonishing capabilities I simply couldn't wait to learn more. Actually Auntie Beat's whole family was rather interesting, including her son-in-law who was a prison warder in, I think, Newport prison. He once allowed me to hold his prison-issue wooden truncheon and that really impressed me too because I figured that you could crack some really serious walnuts with that on a Christmas morning.

However, to return to Auntie Beat's really cool party trick of holding intelligent conversations with the late dearly departed. She was a skinny, wizened old woman with faded but questioning eyes who lived literally in the pencil-like shadow of an enormous factory chimney in a suburb of Swansea with the somewhat unfortunate name of Cockett. If a boy came from Cockett he would attract a plethora of rather disparaging nick-names such as the Cockett-Rocket or the Sprocket from Cockett, and others that were far more impolite, inferring at times to the size of one's penis, which could be quite disconcerting for a young chap.

I didn't particularly like talking to people when they were alive but I would have given up my much loved fags for an entire month just to be able to speak with someone who was actually dead. I mean really, how cool would that have been? Sadly, Auntie Beat was never able to tune into anyone in the next world that I might have wanted to talk to, although I had a great longing to talk to Henry 'Harry' Hook.

Now I realise that most people would probably be mystified as to why I would want to talk with a man who never became famous and who was probably unrelated to Captain Hook the pirate. In fact few people had ever heard of Henry Hook but I was an avid reader and Hookey was one of my all-time heroes.

Private Henry Hook had won a Victoria Cross by rather frenziedly digging his way through the infirmary wall at Rorke's Drift while a bunch of really unpleasant Zulu warriors had been prodding him in the bum with their splendidly pointy spears. What a story old Hookey would have had to tell me! I bet he hadn't been able to sit down for an entire week. His actions, however, saved the lives of eight soldiers in the infirmary so everyone thought he was a bit of a champ.

Yet it's interesting that even someone like Henry Hook, with his hard-earned Victoria Cross, should largely be forgotten and ignored by future generations which is why I wanted to have a jolly good ghostly chin-wag with him because I'm fairly sure he would have been really pissed off about what happened next.

After the 1879 Anglo-Zulu War and his discharge the following year, Hookey was given the incredibly stupid position of 'Inside Duster' at the British Museum. Can you believe that? This really demonstrates that you can win a much coveted Victoria Cross and be the object of adoration and respect by the entire world but the English Government really couldn't give a toss.

And not even *that* illustrious job had come easily. Poor old Hookey only got the post after considerable intervention by a man with the really unfortunate name of Gonville Bromhead (which I always thought would have been a splendid name for a door-to-door brush salesman). Bromhead was the swaggering officer who had been second-in-command at Rorke's Drift, (ably played by the dashing Michael Caine in the subsequent film [whose real name, by the way, is Maurice Micklewhite, so you can see why he changed it]). Support for Hookey had also come from the Prince of Wales (not Charlie, of course, because he wasn't around in 1879). So it took two really influential people to get Hookey his magnificent job as a flunky duster.

These days anyone who wins a Victoria Cross receives film proposals, marriage proposals, stupidly huge book advances and spends months doing podcast interviews. V.C.s also get paid to do toothpaste commercials where absolutely everyone has been surgically implanted with Donny Osmond's teeth.

However, for Henry Hook I'm sure it wasn't all doom and gloom or shaking the hands of Royal wannabes. He was probably enormously pleased with himself when he was subsequently promoted to the incredibly stupid position of the Keeper of Readers' Umbrellas.

Now you can understand why I wanted to talk to him in the afterlife. I imagine he would have had rather a lot to say about all that!

Chapter Two

The Many Dilemmas of a Youthful Alien

What is it like to grow into an alien? I really had no idea. When I had first returned from my sojourn in Taunton with Aunt Ethel, I was placed into a relatively posh private school which immediately set me apart from all the other young boys in St. Thomas. It wasn't actually all that posh — not in the Eton or Rugby class of schools which were reserved for particularly posh knobs, but Clevedon College was posh by Swansea standards. To go there meant that one was, basically, a bit of a gopher.

I wore a posh school uniform, travelled on the bus every morning right across the city, and was educated in a way that was largely denied other boys, most of whom went to the usual state schools and wore no uniforms at all. Most were dressed in jeans with pockets specially designed to carry flick-knives, brass knuckle-dusters and pornographic postcards sent home by their rather naughty sailor brothers in Malta.

I even had to attend elocution lessons which I immediately called 'electrocution' lessons because I knew that if anyone in the St. Thomas neighbourhood discovered that I was being taught how to speak 'proper posh' I'd be roach-squished in five seconds flat. St. Thomas was not a place for the fainthearted. To survive there, little boys had to learn how to run really quickly so that the street-gangs of teddy-boys from Danygraig, armed with knuckle-dusters, stood no chance of catching up to them.

The elocution classes were, of course, Auntie Eth's brainchild and she alone hatched the entire diabolical plot. What would have been the point in spending fourteen long months in expelling the lilting Welsh dragon from my accent only to have it return as soon as I went home and started mucking about with all those rough-and-tumble little-boy horrors from St. Thomas? Oh no! That was never going to happen. Therefore, the quest for a proper posh accent was launched in the same way that the *Titanic* was launched, and down the slips I went.

My sister also came to elocution lessons but it was all frightfully embarrassing because I was the only boy in the class, the remainder being little girls in pigtails and pretty frocks. In my grey school shorts and stork-transplant knees I felt as out of place as a gravedigger at a baptism. Each Saturday morning I would have to attend class and the 'electrocutioner' (I just invented that word by the way) a fearsome lady with a grey bun in her hair, would steam Titanically into the room with the greeting: 'Good morning ladies and gentleman,' with particular emphasis on the final singular and an eagle-eye on me. I'm perfectly sure that she could swivel her eyes independently like a chameleon lizard and watch me continuously while also watching the girls recite impossibly posh verses from *Hiawatha* or inane tongue-twisters such as: 'Red leather, Yellow leather', rapidly repeated.

Now if *anyone* was even slightly inclined to becoming a youthful recluse and introvert then an experience like that would just about clinch it!

After a few weeks at 'electrocution' classes I could speak like Prince Charles but with a slightly Welsh-ish/Somerset-ish accent that made me sound like Lord Lucan gargling Spanish olives. It would have been splendid had I been walking corgis in Hyde Park but in St. Thomas a speech impediment like that was downright hazardous. We were taught how to enunciate our vowels and would chant little quotations such as, 'Put a proper cup of coffee in a copper coffee cup.' It didn't make a whole lot of sense to me but by the time I'd chanted that about a million times I could enunciate my vowels like mad. When the lads of St. Thomas asked where I'd been on Saturday mornings I'd blandly tell them that I'd been enunciating my bowels. They had no idea what enunciating meant and thought I was having some rather messy toilet troubles.

Today clever psychologists call that 'deflection'. I was just happy to get out of being smashed like an avocado.

Anthony 'Tony' Matthews
Photographed when a student at Clevedon College, Swansea.
— Tony & Lensie Matthews collection.

School generally was okay apart from the lessons in trigonometry, geometry and algebra which made me wish I'd remained in Taunton. I stayed away on those days, not bothering to attend the very expensive lessons that clearly were driving me literally insane. I'd leave home for school in my posh little uniform with a brown satchel over my shoulder and if I knew that any of the maths subjects were on the timetable I'd get off the bus when it reached the centre of town and catch the bus to Mumbles, about four or five miles away.

Mumbles is just as it sounds: a small Welsh village right on the sea with the waves mumbling over rocks and sand around a beautiful, old, whitewashed lighthouse that stood at the end of a series of small rocky outcrops accessible at low tide but cut off at high tide. On the farthest island, where the lighthouse blinked, were concrete fortifications constructed as gun emplacements during the war years. The guns were long gone but the fortifications were the perfect place for a young alien on the run from school to seek refuge, solitude, and a place to scoff soggy tomato sandwiches.

Anthony 'Tony' Matthews at one of his favourite haunts as a child. The Mumbles lighthouse can be seen in the background.
— Tony & Lensie Matthews collection.

It was here, really, that I discovered how much I liked to be alone. I could walk out at low tide and spend the day on the islands, isolated by the sea and rocks with gulls for company.

I had to be careful to watch the tides. The bay was shallow and the tide came in quickly. If I failed to pay attention I could have been trapped out at the lighthouse for hours, unable to get back to the mainland, and there would have been hell to pay had it been discovered that I was wandering alone among the rocks and heather rather than learning the Pythagoras theorem at school. Fortunately I was never trapped by the tide.

When it was impossible to get out to the lighthouse because the tides were too high at the wrong time of day I'd spend my time roaming around the shopping area of the city, or the crowded markets, poking my nose into shops or stalls or sitting in a cafe for hour upon hour with a plate of baked beans on toast, stretching out the meal by eating one single bean every two minutes. I think I must have set the *Guinness Book of Records* record for the longest time taken to eat a single plate of baked beans: four hours, sixteen minutes and forty-three seconds, but that included a cup of coffee as well and stirring in three spoons of sugar as slowly as humanly possible. Eating my beans so slowly gave me time to ponder about beans generally because I'd read somewhere that the preservation of food in tins had been around since the early 19th century which was just as well because otherwise baked beans could never have been invented and I just about lived on them.

In fact I wasn't alone in my fascination of the humble bean. Almost the whole of Britain was gobbling them down as if the national economy depended upon them. The American economy certainly did because the Yanks had invented the baked bean to feed their troops during the war years. The bean-plague had quickly spread like a big lumpy tomato-saucy tide. Britons were now eating more than ninety-five percent of the entire world crop of baked beans which in turn would have added significantly to global warming through a massive balloon of human farts hovering over the country like a huge greenish-bluish cloud of beany gas. It was really rather ghastly when you stopped to think about it, as I did, because when you spend a lot of time alone in a cafe eating beans you begin to think about a lot of really peculiar things like how beans are sealed in tins in the first place.

So I checked.

Historically there had been a major problem with tinned food. The genius who had come up with this crazy idea of putting food into tins had never actually thought of how to get it out again so that it could be eaten. Some kind of Einstein *he* must have been! It took until 1858, another forty-eight years after tinned food had been invented, for another crazy genius to come up with the tin-opener, by which time, of course, everything tinned up to that time had long passed its use-by date. Now you see what I mean about thinking too much about these things.

Meanwhile, in the cafe, the bottle-blonde waitress kept giving me a really weird look as I slowly ate my meal, bean-by-bean, as if she suspected that I was suffering from a sudden attack of gastroenteritis or something equally as messy and she was the one who probably had to clean the loos afterwards. Firstly she asked me if the beans were all right. An hour later she asked if I'd like the plate warmed up which was actually quite nice of her and I accepted because that would take more time. An hour later she looked around suspiciously and asked if she was on Candid Camera. Another hour passed and she asked if I suspected the food might have been poisoned by the Russians. When I eventually finished the last bean and looked at her triumphantly, smacking my lips in grand appreciation, she twisted her own heavily lipsticked lips ironically and asked if I'd like some dessert. I told her that I'd really felt like a small plate of Black Forest gateau with cream but only if the cream was fresh and not that synthetic sugary muck squeezed out of a tube that looked like a plastic cow's nipple. She said that as I appeared to have more than enough time on my hands she'd send over to Berlin to see if she could get some good old fashioned German cake and while that was coming she'd phone Cornwall for the clotted cream. I suspected that she was being slightly sarcastic so left her only threepence tip.

I began slowly drifting inwards. I attended school every day that I did not have maths and did well in every other subject, especially English, literature and history. Yet I was already pulling away from the rest of the planet, discovering that another world existed out there that did not include rather bothersome people who spoke in mathematical riddles and that it was really just a place where I could be me, alone with my crazy thoughts, deep inner discussions and the recitations of *Hiawatha* we'd been forced to memorise during our endless and hugely embarrassing 'electrocution' classes.

I liked to keep to myself. I was beginning to understand that being alone was actually something positive. It gave me space and time to think. In all this time I was never once lonely because I just loved being by myself. My seclusion was certainly depriving me of some of the personal contact that would have made me more adept at social interaction, and I now realise that, but it never bothered me. I wasn't interested in gossip or unimportant issues. People called me shy but shyness had absolutely nothing to do with it.

As I grew older things began to change. Girls had a lot to do with that because suddenly I found that I rather liked the look of them. They were soft, pretty, cute, and had bums. I'd *never* actually noticed that girls had rather pleasant bums before.

Girls were, apparently noticing me by this time too. I must have been about thirteen when a girl in my class asked if she could be my girlfriend. This came as quite a shock, largely because I had never actually noticed her before, or at least not very much, and I wasn't all that keen on being her boyfriend because her bum was not as nice as many of the other girls and I thought that was probably quite important. She was disappointed, of course, although I tried to let her down gently.

Time passed and I could feel the alien inside growing inexorably. Not only was I inherently different but the angst of teenage agony made me feel like I was almost betraying myself. One half of me wanted to head off into the wilds of Kilvey Hill, or the clifftops of Mumbles but the other half was becoming increasingly interested in girls.

Gower, a beautiful peninsula to the west of Swansea was where I began to find real happiness in solitude. I'd catch the bus down to a small village called Parkmill about eight miles from Swansea which was a wild place inhabited only by one shopkeeper who ran a small roadside store and also a few villagers, some of whom came for holidays or weekends. Parkmill is one of those ancient Welsh hamlets, the type you see in TV series like *Larkrise to Candelford*, but more earthy. The people were real, not television actors. You could tell because they had pimples and sometimes smelled of cigarettes and stale beer and occasionally they would fart while standing next to you at the bus-stop which could be a bit disquieting on a hot, windless day in summer after they had been eating a lot of fishy cockles.

But Parkmill was a place steeped in history and I loved that. You could almost smell the bones of those who had once lived there — providing you weren't standing in the bus-stop shelter at the time, of course. A small rivulet passed through the village. It was called the Pennarth Pill and if you knew where to look you could find the ruins of an old chapel. (This is now sounding all so pathetically Wordsworth isn't it?) On the foreshore were the ruins of a Norman castle, probably built at the time Robin Hood was coming home from the Crusades, but more on him later.

At times I would go to Parkmill with a couple of other boys who liked the adventure of the place but in reality I preferred being alone because it was a wild and seemingly haunted hamlet full of the ghosts of the past. I could almost imagine the ancient cave-dwellers here and in fact there was, and is, a prehistoric megalithic burial chamber in the valley, a 'long barrow' as it is known, testimony to the region's antiquity. The burial chamber had been built about six thousand years before my rather insignificant arrival. The time difference between then and now was of considerable interest to me. Six thousand years is a lot of water under the bridge. Even those awful Roman chappies with their dreadful little stabbing swords and rather girly togas had thankfully come and gone during that period.

I wondered if those ancient megalithic people with all the precognitive abilities attributed to their seers had ever predicted that one day a little boy with koala ears would be seated on the grass in front of their burial chamber contemplating where their bones had long ago rotted and turned to dust. I wondered who they had been and if any of them had been named Anthony. I found that all those long years acted as a kind of time-bridge between us. In a way it linked us. They had stood exactly where I now stood. Time didn't seem to matter any more. It was almost as if they were with me. I didn't tell anyone this, of course. There was a place in Swansea where they put strange boys with lunatic hallucinations and it wasn't very pleasant — or so I was told. They gave a treatment called enemas there and while I wasn't too sure what enemas were, exactly, I knew they had something to do with giving little boys' bottoms a jolly good rinse out with soap, water and castor-oil and for some unfathomable reason I didn't really fancy that.

During the periods when I was alone at Parkmill it seemed to me to be another world. The valley was uninhabited. The megalithic burial chamber sat in the centre of the valley with rising hills on either side. These were heavily wooded and hid a series of caves that had once been the dwellings of ancient man. When I went there with friends we'd play around, fool about and cause a lot of boyish noise, which was fun, but when I went there alone it was completely different. The act of being alone drew in the sides of the limestone valley and heightened the silence and the sounds of birds and running water. I'd wade through the shallow river and hike up through the forest to the Stone Age valley. I'd camp alone in one of the caves and imagine that the souls of the long dead cavemen were close by, watching as I heated my tins of baked beans on a camp fire.

These were special times. They were not fun, as were the visits I made with friends, they were solitary, quiet times of reflection. I know that all sounds far too serious for a young lad of thirteen years and perhaps 'reflection' is too strong a word but I did have time to think, to ponder where my life was heading without any knowledge of trigonometry or algebra. I thought that I may have been completely stupid but then I reflected that not everyone had to have a maths degree, and being ignorant of the finer points of calculus wasn't the worst crime in the world. I'd get by. I could always be a dustman and live in a council flat. Lonnie Donegan's dad did! (Have any of you actually *heard* of Lonnie Donegan?)

My cave-dwelling days were incredible. I knew that during the megalithic and neolithic periods the bodies of those old cave-people had probably been stored in some of these ancient caverns for a while until being moved down to the valley floor to be laid to rest in the burial chamber. I'm not sure why they did that but it intrigued me to think that perhaps they couldn't stand the parting and delayed it for as long as possible. Of course that would have made the caves a bit pongy. It's funny, but we don't often think about Stone Age man having families they loved and cared about, protected, fed, felt joy and sadness with, and eventually grieved over when they died. At school we'd learn the basics of them but we never really *thought* about them too much. They were just rather hairy people with bad teeth who used bones as clubs — not a bit like Fred Flintstone who drove a really neat roller-stone car. It almost seemed as if they had come from a different planet. We never thought about who they were, how they lived, how they loved or what they called their children. Did they name them after their grandparents as we often do, or perhaps give them names later in life when they had achieved some kind of significant prominence such as Great Beaver Hunter or Pansy Picker or even Pees in Golden Arc, a bit like Native North Americans? Being alone in the ancient caves where they had lived all those thousands of years ago brought me closer to them. I could almost smell the smoke of their cooking fires although that was probably just me heating beans.

I'd explore their burial chamber with keen interest. The bones had long since dissolved into nothingness but their ghosts were there, I felt sure. They never really frightened me, even when I was alone at night, because I felt a kind of kinship to them. It was almost as if time had stood still. I was time-travelling.

I even discovered a real pterodactyl fossil in a tiny cave next to the large cave where I usually camped and was thrilled by the sight of the ancient bones now turned to stone, the wings, the massive beak and all the ribs in place, standing out in sharp relief in the light of a rolled up newspaper I was using as a flaming torch. I was actually with a couple of other boys when I found it and had crawled into a narrow cave for a dare. It was an immense adventure. We'd either forgotten to bring battery-operated torches or our batteries were depleted so a rolled up newspaper had to do for illumination. I crawled forward on my belly, hardly enough space to wiggle along, and finally, after a few metres, the narrow passage opened to a broader cave and there, in the light of my newspaper torch, was the intensely beautiful fossil. It was one of those truly breathless moments that you never forget, no matter how long you live. 'Try not to crawl through any old caveman poo,' giggled my companions from the entrance to the cave. I was hardly listening. I couldn't take my eyes off that astonishing fossil until my newspaper torch burned so low that it singed my hand and I dropped it to the ground where it immediately went out. I crawled laboriously back through the passageway to the sunlight and open air. I was gasping for breath but my skin was tingling with excitement. I had stepped into prehistory and returned safely to the present. It was like using a Disneyland time-tunnel. That fossil had come into existence about sixty-five million years before I had popped out of the egg. I had seen something that might never before have been seen by human eyes. I felt a real sense of adventurous discovery — like Enid Blyton's *Secret Seven* solving the greatest mystery in the entire planet.

When I was alone in my cave, which was most often, I'd sometimes sit outside and transform myself into Neanderthal man, strip down to my Y-fronts and with a wooden spear go hunting for food — mastodon or monster snapping turtles or, more realistically, tins of wild Heinz baked beans, mainly because they were the easiest to trap and I already had a really good Boy Scout tin-opener which had cost me two bob in the Swansea markets.

At the top of the valley was an old cottage that was completely irresistible to a hermit-in-waiting. The two-storey, red-brick building had been abandoned to the elements decades previously. The gardens were choked with weeds and overgrown trees. A deep well at the rear of the home was still full of water, cool and clean, but the boards that had been placed over it for the sake of safety had long since rotted away and fallen in. An old tin bucket with a frayed, sun-bleached rope was lying in the weeds close by.

I'd first discovered the cottage with two other boys some weeks earlier and had helped the owner to strip out the old interior walls in return for being allowed to camp on the stone floor. But this was a place I simply could not resist. It was completely isolated, almost forgotten by the world. I returned alone when the cottage was empty, cold and still. It was a perfect place for a little ghost-bat of a ghost-boy to visit. There was something about this cottage that drew me back to it. It was a ruin, the roof was in tatters and the building was basically a stone shell which smelt a bit of the tramps who occasionally slept there. A few really disgusting mattresses were scattered on the floors.

They stank of old piss, stale wine and cigarette smoke. There were also some stains on the mattresses that didn't bear thinking about. I'd light a fire in one of the fireplaces and heat my beans while ruminating about all the families who had once lived within these walls, had loved, argued, shagged, raised children, struggled to survive, and finally died — family after family, each knowing little of those who had gone before them and nothing of those who would come in the future. To me it was like looking through a window into the past and I knew that I was able to do this only because I was alone in that ancient cottage, quiet and reflective. When I had been there with the other boys a few weeks earlier I had been unable to connect with the past, but now, with the flames of the fire my only illumination, I was able to go back in time and almost become a part of who they had been.

My time in Gower and Mumbles and also up on Kilvey Hill taught me one thing. I liked being by myself. Being alone gave me a chance to speak quietly to myself without being interrupted by others. I'd sit and ask myself if this solitude was strange, unusual or even right. I'd also ask myself if other people liked being alone and if so would they also talk to themselves? Was I normal or was I just a weird little twerp with incurable mental pimples? For a while — years actually — I thought there must have been something wrong with me. Was my brain going rusty? Was I allergic to people?

When at school I spoke to no one about my growing interest in seclusion. No one would have understood anyway. I tried to fit into everything that was going on, although sports were a challenge and I found that I would rather sniff goblin farts on a regular basis than play any kind of competitive game where the incomprehensibly ridiculous object of the exercise was to get a ball into a net or make more 'runs' than someone else or to run faster than some lanky chap with legs that appeared to be about five yards long and made him look like one of those really intense spiders you find unexpectedly in the corners of your wardrobe.

My father may have been a bit of an introvert, quiet, thoughtful and intelligent, but he definitely wasn't a recluse or hermit. He was a businessman who was out there meeting people and doing what he could to earn enough to keep his family together. He was also sports mad and his intense love of soccer left me gasping to understand why. I just couldn't figure out why anyone would actually want to sit in an overcrowded football stadium with about ten thousand screaming individuals all of whom smelt strongly of beer, cigarettes and pork pies. Not that my father smelt anything like that, of course, in fact he had season tickets to the Swansea Football Club's executives' section although how he came by those is a mystery he took to his early grave. He also never screamed at football matches which said much for his self-control because it was quite obvious that he would have loved to let go and barrack for the team, but decorum prevailed, at least during the one football match that I attended with him after he had bribed me with some Mars bars. I think he had always dreamed of taking his son to the footy but alas I was about as interested in soccer as I was in advanced trigonometry or the parliamentary speeches of Enoch Powell.

I was a big disappointment to my father, at least in that respect, as I think he would have wanted me to become the next Stanley Matthews (no relation by the way). Most people today have probably never heard of Stanley Matthews, known as the Wizard of the Dribble, (which, as a double entendre, might be a bit of an embarrassment), but to soccer fans of the 1950s he was a megastar and they hadn't even invented the word at that time. Stan was the Sean Connery of the footy pitch. Better looking than Engelbert Humperdink, faster on his feet than Roger Bannister, and more humble than Mahatma Gandhi, Stan Matthews was the ideal sporting idol, worshiped by all young aspiring soccer stars.

But alas, not I.

My father worked hard to influence me to change my ways. He made me join the school soccer team and bought me a pair of soccer boots and the team uniform so that I could play on the weekends in the local park. The team jersey had horizontal stripes of black and amber and when I was running hopelessly around the soccer field trying to work out which was my goal and which was the enemy's, I'd look *exactly* like a large bumble bee that had suddenly been stung on the penis by a real bumble bee. It was a sight guaranteed to draw press attention so in the end the team dropped me because they feared that I might either run myself into a paediatric coronary and die right there during the game, or, far worse, actually boot a ball between my own team's goalposts which would have been so embarrassingly horrible that absolutely *everyone* on the team would have had a coronary except me.

Sport was for team players, not for lonesome little Hobbits. I wasn't competitive; I disliked any kind of tribalism except when it involved *National Geographic* photographs of ladies in some distant parts of the South Pacific Islands who insisted on running around completely topless. For me that's when tribalism became quite interesting. Playing sports also meant that there would be spectators because that's what sport is all about, but being looked at by a bunch of strange men wearing plastic macs, standing on the side of the footy field, was just about more than I could possibly endure because I really hate people looking at me especially when I look like a bee with a stung dick.

Trying other tactics my father bought me a pair of boxing gloves and a punch-bag, the sole result of which was a couple of sprained wrists and an interesting case of near concussion when the bag sprang back suddenly and hit me in the head with the force of a Mohammad Ali right hook. I was seeing stars for hours.

Then came the gym sessions at the Y.M.C.A. designed for me to fit into the athletic youth of the day. My first and only day at the gymnasium was hellish because there was a huge amount of noise with kids screaming, instructors shouting, the continuous shrill of whistles and the soles of rubber gym-shoes shrieking on wooden floors. Bodies were bouncing thunderously on and off wooden horses, parallel bars and judo mats, creating a perfect storm of choking, week-old body odour that wafted over me like the pong of an old fridge that had gone mouldy. (Most people took a bath only once a week and apparently used the soap rather sparingly). I was ordered to climb a rope right to the ceiling which was about fifty feet high and when I got half way up I fell off and almost killed the instructor standing below who ended up with head contusions from my new gym-shoes which can be a brutal weapon when attached to the feet of a reluctant sports star plummeting dramatically to earth at precisely sixteen feet per-second — per-second.

I could never understand what the attraction was to balls. (I'm not actually talking about testicles now). It seemed universally necessary that if you were human, then, like a kitten chasing after balls of wool, it was absolutely vital to chase after soggy leather balls on a soggy soccer pitch or whack little round balls from cricket bats or even smaller white balls from a number 5 iron. Not even the tiniest sub-atomic nanoparticle of that made any sense to me.

I should add that a typical story about the stupidity of men chasing after little balls is amplified by the saga of the Darlington Football Club, the members of which bought fifty-thousand worms so that their waterlogged pitch could be properly irrigated. Sadly all the worms immediately decided to drown themselves in despair. They probably hated football too. The burning question I had to ask when I later read this story was: who counted out exactly fifty thousand worms in the first place and what would have happened had the phone rung and he or she had lost count? It didn't bear thinking about.

Sport made no sense to me. I would rather sit beneath a tree and read a book or think about Raquel Welch's impressive frontal bumps or, more realistically, I suppose, the same kind of bumps that had somehow magically manifested themselves on Susan McWilliams — almost without my realising it.

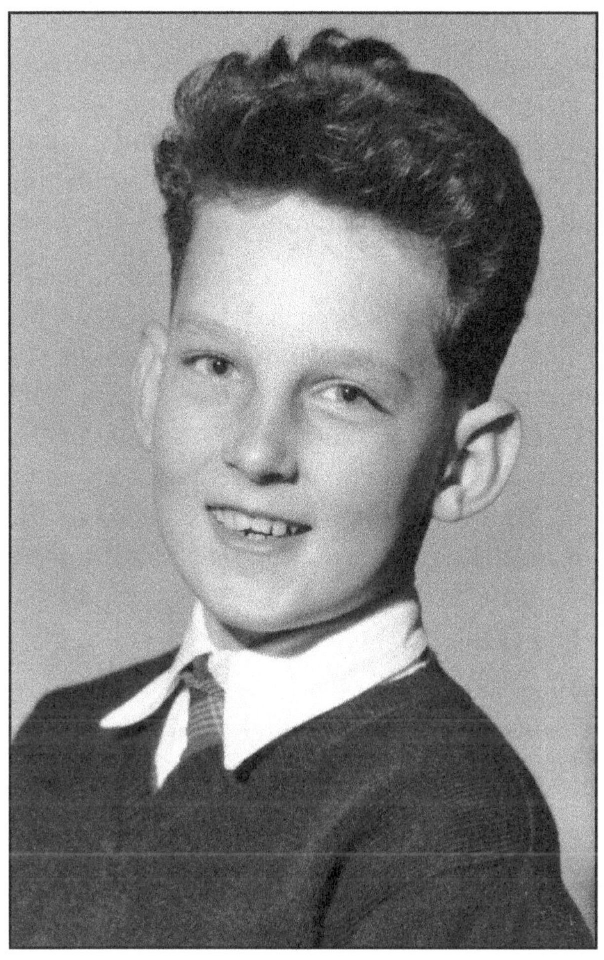

Anthony 'Tony' Matthews
Unlike most other boys, Tony was never interested in sporting activities and preferred to be sitting alone beneath a tree reading a book of Dylan Thomas poetry.
— Tony & Lensie Matthews collection.

Susan was in my class at school and I thought she was rather spiffing. She had that quiet, reflective, super sensitive and intelligent look about her — the sort of look that appeared to promise a soft and thoughtful personality. I thought we could be friends. I'd sneak glances at her in class but she would never look back at me because she was always beavering away making notes. She seemed to be endlessly studious. She was also pretty, in an Ashley Judd kind of way, and when I eventually drummed up the courage and asked if I could take her to the pictures she immediately agreed which astounded me so much I almost peed myself which I expect Susan would have found a little confusing. I was so excited I couldn't eat for two days. My mother thought I was coming down with something.

I prepared carefully for the grand event. Polished my shoes, slicked my curly hair until it curled no more, and wore a clean shirt that did not have any yellowed frogspawn stains on it. Then I stood waiting outside the Odeon cinema one Saturday afternoon, nervously clenching and unclenching my sweaty teenage hands and wiping them down the sides of my jeans to dry them off. And I waited and waited and after a while I waited some more until two hours had passed, the film was actually over, it was getting dark, Susan had still not arrived and my jeans needed to be put into the spin-dryer.

I decided that being alone was better than that. Susan may read this book one day, now in her granny-years, no doubt, and realise suddenly that while young, ex-curly-topped Anthony Matthews had been nervously pacing up and down outside the Odeon, she had been doing much the same thing outside the Palace, or the Rialto, although probably not with sweaty palms. I'm guessing it was just a mix-up for we neither mentioned it again and hoped somehow that we had both simply forgotten the date that never was.

As I grew older, dealing with people became a little more difficult because in reality I didn't actually want to have too much to do with them. Teenage parties were the worst possible experiences for me. By the time I was fourteen, parties were the only places where one could meet girls and as my experience with Susan McWilliams had clearly demonstrated, I'd found that they actually interested me in ways I was still trying to understand.

This was the era of the Beatles. *Love Me Do* and *Twist and Shout* were on everyone's lips as the mop-topped boy-band began their meteoric rise not only to eternal stardom but also to strange Hindi prophets, Yoko Ono and an LSD dream that would soon manifest itself into *Lucy in the Sky With Diamonds.*

A rather odd looking singer, for want of a better description, was also making headlines, not only because his voice sounded like gravel being poured into a council cement mixer but also because he had a face that looked astonishingly like a badly constructed stone toilet from the Emperor Claudius period. His name was Mick Jagger and for a while at least he and his equally stone-faced and completely mossless Rolling Stones were serious contenders for the kind of fame being bestowed upon the strangely misspelled insect quartet, but could never really hope to catch up to them in glassy-eyed, weeping, star-bound, bonkers, knickers-throwing adoration. The Beatles were undoubtedly Number One.

Everyone, including me, wanted to look like a Beatle. Girls were throwing themselves on the Beatles like skydivers throw themselves out of Cessnas. Would they do that for little Beatle clones from St. Thomas, one pondered? Tailors' shops and department stores were churning out sharp suits with drainpipe trousers and rounded collars. No one had ever seen a round-collared suit before John, Paul, George and Ringo appeared suddenly on stage wearing them. The girls' screams on national television on the night of the Beatles' much hyped live performance had almost completely drowned out the appalling off-key singing. No one was noticing anyway. The screams were for the mop-top hair cuts, the round-collar suits and the impossibly tight trousers which displayed three skinny little Beatle-bums to perfection. The fourth Beatle-bum, by the way, belonged to Ringo but you couldn't actually see that because, as the band's drummer, he was always sitting down.

Winkle-pickers were the shoes of choice; they were another part of the indelible Beatles persona. I managed to get one of the last pairs in a Swansea shoe-shop. They cost my father the amazing sum of six pounds. All the boys were also attempting to copy the Beatles' haircuts but it was impossible to get my curly hair to look like a pop star's so when I walked down the street in my drainpipes and winkle-pickers I looked absolutely nothing like a Beatle but rather a lot like a toilet brush with painfully ingrown toenails.

Teenage parties were full of Beatles lookalikes who actually looked nothing like the real Beatles and a lot like ordinary teens with pimples. Boys and girls had magically assumed Liverpudlian accents. The girls, of course, were copying Cilla Black (whose real surname was White, by the way). Have you ever heard a Welsh teenager attempting to emulate a Liverpudlian? It's not only hilarious, it sounds like somebody desperately holding in poo after having accidentally swallowed a jumbo tube of elephant-lax.

People were changing their names to John, Paul and George but not so much to Ringo because that would have been too weird. Dogs, pet rabbits and even goldfish were being named Starr, Harrison or the Ringo Gringo. Cakes were being called Lennon Lemons or McCartney Macaroons. It was nuts. I loved the songs but all the craziness was sending me mental. At one of the very few teenage parties I attended I found I was again hiding in a cupboard beneath the stairs. None of me made sense, not even to me. All my atoms had been Beatleised. I was no longer Anthony Matthews, the grocer's boy from St. Thomas. I was now a pathetic synthetic pop star who couldn't even play a guitar or sing. Not that it mattered a lot. I was reasonably sure that none of the girls with splendid bums wanted a pseudo-Beatle with shag-ears and ingrown winkle-pickers.

Parties have always meant mixing and mingling but none of that was ever for me, even when I was a teen and parties should have been an ordinary part of my life. Birthday parties, anniversary parties or parties to celebrate religious festivals were all events I could never imagine attending because of the thumping music, brightly coloured balloons that make your eyes ache, and the orange-flavoured punch into which people were dipping little glass drinking cups right after they had been slobbering on them.

The one or two parties I did attend as a teen were disasters. Dancing at parties is one of the strangest human rituals I have ever encountered. Dancing in winkle-pickers is even more ridiculous because every time you move your feet you stab somebody, hopefully not the girl you're dancing with because that would really stunt any chances you might have entertained of snogging her. The danger of doing irreparable harm to other people on the dance-floor was actually intensified because, firstly, people were looking at me and the inevitable wobble factor had kicked in, and secondly my winkle-pickers were so outrageously long and pointed that they had the rather unpleasant ability to act like wheat-scythes, mowing down anyone who came within a few feet of them. When I asked girls to dance with me they didn't usually look at my face before making a decision. They didn't have to: they were already either seriously wounded or in the act of dodging the twin prongs that were threatening to murder their ankles.

Winkle-pickers also had another quite important design fault. When seated on a stool my pickers would be sticking out from the footrest in a particularly menacing fashion. Lighting was often deliberately poor at parties or dances (largely so that you could convince yourself your partner was gorgeous when in fact they usually had blackheads) and therefore it wasn't difficult for people carrying trays of drinks to stumble over the elegant elongated points and spill pints all over the floor. It was messy, soggy and expensive, especially when one had to buy new rounds to replace the spillage.

In the end I decided that being a Beatle look-alike was probably not worth the effort. The entire enterprise had failed spectacularly. Not one single member of the opposite sex had even for a moment considered ripping off her panties and throwing them at me.

Party noise is another irritant to loners and hermits. As a teenager the popular songs of that period were slightly boring but at least they were songs. They had voice, tone, feeling. There was almost a warm colour to them. Herman's Hermits wondering about love and life on the Mersey and Roy Orbison rabbiting on about a house in New Orleans which he knew for a fact was a rather insalubrious place of ill-repute stuffed to the rafters with the kind of women John Wayne would politely have referred to as saloon gals. The house was called the *Rising Sun*, and probably catered for all the Japanese tourists with really interesting names like Shit-zo.

Music said something in the sixties and said it in a way that mattered. But it all changed spectacularly for the worse. Now it's all 'gangsta' rap and hip-hop — whatever that actually means, and parties don't sound like parties any more, they sound like rather unpleasant drug-fuelled misogynistic messages of sexual impotence and the kind of language that's deliberately used to threaten and intimidate. Sometimes I hear it in cars going past my house and all I can pick out from the tidal surge is, 'Pimp my bitch' or 'Slam your whammy in my mammy' or words to that general effect which has to say something really important about those who write the 'lyrics', and I use that term very loosely indeed. I mean really! These guys are so hilarious they actually fit shiny hubcaps that spin *backwards* on their SUVs. I'm completely confused. What does it all mean? And why do they all seem to sing about people who are having sex with their own mothers?

The composer Dvorak, who was himself influenced by Afro-American and Native North American music, once said that the future of music would be dominated by the 'Black American' sound and he was right. Jazz, soul and reggae were all powerfully influenced by Afro-American or West Indian music trends but Dvorak could never have imagined in his most fevered dreams what Afro-American 'music' was about to become. Can you imagine a Dvorak libretto beginning with something like, 'I'm gonna touch ma cock, go round da block to fuck ma Glock ...' I mean, really!

Now I know you think that I have used the 'F' word gratuitously here but I assure you that it's all quite innocent and above board and not naughty at all. Rather than being rude I'm really being geographical. It might surprise you to learn that there is actually a village in Austria called 'Fucking'. It's true! I suspect that the area has a higher than average road accident statistic because the region is often under snow and ice and when one comes to a road-sign stating, for example: 'Fucking, 10 km', it would be almost a natural reaction to floor the accelerator immediately, and on snow that could be quite dangerous. I expect they have other rather interesting road-signs too: 'Welcome to Fucking', for example, or, 'Fucking Detour, please follow the signs', or my favourite: 'Fucking scenic drive — caution required when icy'.

Speaking of ice, winter could be a particularly trying time for a young alien stranded on earth in the 1950s and '60s. Anyone who experienced a winter in Swansea at that time will know exactly what I'm talking about. I always loved snow but most winters were just ice, cold, rain and gallons of snot. The watery light faded from the grey skies at around 4.30 in the afternoon and didn't resurface until about eight o'clock the following morning when the light would be about as weak as cold candle wax. Rain was not intermittent, it was constant. Everything was permanently wet. Houses had a characteristic pong of mouldy blankets and soggy washing. Pavements and roads were hazardous and nobody bothered to take a bath because it was too cold, so when they took off their heavy overcoats the B.O. rose from them like marsh mist. That, by the way, was usually when all the bollocks scratching went on.

Going to school was awful. I'd walk to the bus-stop in the dark and rain and huddle beneath a yellow florescent streetlamp while waiting for the bus to arrive although it was always late, particularly when it was raining more heavily than Niagara Falls during spring thaw. There was, of course, no bus shelter. That would have been too intelligent. Once on the bus, however, I'd climb to the upper deck and scrunch down into a seat that had already been soaked by the previous occupant. Almost everyone would have a cold, or the flu, so the coughing, sniffing, nose-honking into a manky-hanky and misdirected sneezing sounded just like pneumonic plague had suddenly broken out.

The windows of the bus were usually running with snotty condensation from the steamy breath of all the sick passengers and I couldn't help looking at the dribbles on the panes of glass and imagining that my eyes were 1000x magnification microscopes and I could see zillions of tiny bug-eyed microbes in the drops of moisture that had recently been sneezed with happy abandon over everyone on the bus including me. It was like an advanced warning to beware of an incoming Covid pandemic.

In short, winter was really shitty — at least until it snowed.

I longed for the snow. When it finally came, winter became, for a while at least, not just bearable but really quite pleasant, especially if you liked being alone and didn't mind freezing your balls off.

The children and teens would come out of their soggy, coal-smoked houses, of course, to build snowmen, using carrots as noses and penises, some of which would be pointing hilariously upwards, and to throw snowballs at each other, but it only lasted for a short while because snow is bloody cold at the best of times and soon all the snowmen were abandoned with their vegetable erections still intact and the kids went back indoors to toast their feet by the coal fires so that they could suffer the agonies of instant chilblains.

I, on the other hand, headed for the snowy hills. In particular, Kilvey Hill, the rising mini-mountain that stood behind our home. Kilvey Hill was a fairly solitary place even in normal times but when covered with a thick layer of snow it was like walking through an Antarctic landscape but without the penguins, of course.

Actually, to the uninitiated, and from a distance, I could have been mistaken for a rather tallish penguin. Dressed in my blueish duffle coat with the hood up over my head and flapping my mittened hands to keep them warm, I could easily have resembled a large Emperor penguin, particularly when I was wearing my daffodil-yellow polo-neck.

This was during the 1950s and early 1960s, before developers had dreamed up their evil plan to construct houses on *my* hill, and the entire wilderness was as solitary and remote as it had been for millions of years. The old stone cottage where the Water Witch lived, the ruins of the ancient windmill, the Seven Sisters quarry where the iron-ore workers apparently lay buried in their rust-coloured cave-grave, comprised the only human intervention on the hill, apart from a pig-farmer down near the cemetery but like me he was such a recluse he'd become almost translucent and I had trouble finding him one day when I discovered three of his pigs roaming the streets of Danygraig and had to drive them home. As a vegan I regret that now. I didn't think that I was also driving them towards their eventual deaths. I should have pignapped them and given them a permanent home in our back garden with Sammy our tortoise who had been acquired specifically to eat all the snails that rather maliciously kept eating my mother's rhubarb plants. (Sammy, by the way, will be featuring as a 'character' in one of my upcoming novels).

Kilvey Hill when covered with snow was a paradise for anyone wanting to get away from the cruel world where everyone coughed on each other and asked if they could borrow a hanky. All that could be seen on the hill was a sea of pure white, marred only by the Charlie Chaplinesque footprints of a skinny, almost mythical and usually invisible boy.

Chapter Three

The Secret Seclusionist

Yes, I'm an introverted isolationist but while that really is a part of who I am, my need for seclusion was also deepened by an experience I had when I was between fifteen and sixteen years of age. I call it my year of living dangerously, after the Mel Gibson film, but in fact it was a year of horror which cemented my belief that human nature, while often good, can also be stupendously bad or stupid, and there exists in the heart of man a deep recess where, sadly, just about anything is possible.

My year of living dangerously deepened my need for seclusion. I realised that I didn't actually want too much to do with people because I had seen with my own eyes and experienced with my own body, often painfully, that there are forces of human nature that simply don't bear thinking about. My dangerous year had forced an isolationist withdrawal into myself that I welcomed because it was an intrinsic part of me, but it was also a bit of a shock to discover that I needed to isolate myself just to survive. During that year, and for a long time afterwards, I was mentally curling into a tight little ball of wire-wool just to protect myself — like a caterpillar when it's touched with the tip of a finger, only I wasn't quite so green and furry.

To explain all this I need to step back in time to my schoolboy days. After having missed so much of my maths classes, and finally being exposed as a habitual absentee from trigonometry lessons,

I was hauled out of my relatively posh school and put into a really awful Victorian era state school for six months where the only things I managed to learn were headbutting, swearing with an extraordinarily expressive colour and learning the ancient mysteries of 'metalwork' — a completely new and dreadful experience for me — which required my not falling into a vat of boiling steel because that would probably have been quite unpleasant too.

When I was a lad I was an avid reader. Books in our house were as common as fleas on a bear's bottom; they were everywhere and I couldn't have stopped myself reading even if I'd tried. I'd shut myself up and read all day and then again at night, even when I wasn't supposed to be reading any more. I'd use a torch and huddle beneath my blankets reading books like the *Famous Five* or the *Secret Seven*, *The Wishing Chair*, *Moonfleet*, *Robin Hood*, *Robinson Crusoe* and absolutely anything to do with Stone Age man or dinosaurs, largely, I think, because of my stupendous fossil discovery in the Parkmill cave.

One of my favourite books was *Just William*, by Richmal Crompton, originally published in 1922 and featuring a series of lovable short stories about a young boy named William Brown. William was always getting himself into trouble: running away from home and entering domestic service where he was able to create havoc among the entire household, or, in another story, William falls in love with one of his teachers with disastrous results. He even had an Aunt Emily who was just like my Auntie Eth and on one occasion William decides that he is going to be a writer and pens a story called *The Tale of the Bloody Hand* which contains so much appalling grammar that everyone falls about laughing. I loved William so much because he was naughty, cheeky, reckless, adventurous, rough-and-tumble and in a constant state of disarray — exactly the opposite of me. I was always perfectly mannered, well-behaved, unadventurous (to a degree) and hardly ever in a state of disarray except when I'd been forced into a corner by one of the Danygraig gangs and had to defend myself which I was always willing to do, although I really didn't want a broken nose because I'd seen a boy with one of those and the sudden gush of blood and snot coming from it had looked a bit like dinosaur afterbirth.

At this grotesque Victorian school I had been forced to take on one of the school bullies because that had been part of the boringly puerile initiations I'd had to go through, but another boy had tipped me the wink that the bully's Achilles Heel was his belly so when it finally came to blows one cold Monday morning behind the bogs in the bleak schoolyard I just kept my head tucked well down between my shoulders, so that my opponent couldn't break my nose to make me look like blended Dino, and then used his belly as a human punchbag, slamming into it until he could stand it no more and called for an unexpected truce.

I only mention all this rather violent drivel because the boy who had given me the inside intelligence became an instant friend who was also the exact opposite of me and every inch like the fictional boy William Brown. He showed me that it was okay to be different — he in his way and I in mine. It was he who convinced me that when we left school we should join the Royal Navy which in turn led to my year of living dangerously. It was the worst decision I ever made.

My year of living dangerously is important to this book because it hardened my resolve to be an isolationist. After that year I found that I did not like people very much and they had to work hard to gain my trust and respect — always assuming they wanted them in the first place, of course, which was probably unlikely. I was very young and impressionable. I knew nothing of the real world. I really did not know how to judge people for who they were, or to size them up, but the navy taught me one very important lesson. When weak, morally challenged people are given power, even a little power, then suddenly they have the capacity to become Dr Evil, mastermind of *The Spy Who Shagged Me*, who, apparently, was *really* bad.

I was fifteen. The date was 1 June, 1964. Along with a trainload of other really silly boys of my age I was sent to Shotley Gate near Ipswich where the navy ran one of the grimmest, harshest and most frightening training establishments known to humankind. It was called H.M.S. *Ganges* and not only did it scare me so much that my bowels seemed to seize up for about a decade, but it also scarred me for life. It was like stepping into another world, a world run by men who apparently loved the sound of their own voices even more than they loved harsh and usually needless discipline.

Ganges was a meat-grinder. Really stupid little boys went in one end. The handle was turned continuously for 365 days, and out of the other end popped curly bits of ground bones, meat, blood, fat, skin, gristle and poo. Actually, after a year at *Ganges* and their near starvation diet in which cockroaches and live maggots featured in plentiful disarray, there wasn't too much fat or poo, now I come to think about it.

When I first arrived at *Ganges* I thought, well this isn't too bad. The barracks looked clean and tidy and everyone was being really nice. We were taken into a large hut and given forms to sign which would bind us to the navy for the next twelve years. It all sounded quite simple and everyday. We'd be trained, be well paid for our services to the Queen or Good King Wenceslas or whoever was on the throne in twelve years time. We'd receive free uniforms, free medical, free underpants, and when we got a bit older all the girls in every port would be throwing their knickers at us just like they were throwing them at John Lennon and Paul McCartney. It all sounded really exciting. They were even going to show us free V.D. films just in case the knickers avalanche became a tad too overwhelming. I'd never actually seen a V.D. film before but it sounded spectacularly interesting. I wondered if any really famous actors would be in it. Just pretending, of course.

We all signed on the dotted line. What were twelve years anyway? We'd be so busy sailing the seven seas, seeing the world and fighting off all the gorgeous ladies we'd never even notice the passage of time. It would pass in the blink of an eye.

We signed the form. That was when the nice part of the day went out of the hut's little window. That was the very moment, the nanosecond my childhood ended and my year of living dangerously began.

Now that we were legally theirs, many of the trainers and also the naval police turned on us like famished wolves turn on sheep with broken legs. It was really quite unpleasant and I'm actually understating here for a change. For the next fifty-two weeks while under training we would be completely under their control and they did not need to pretend to be nice to us any more. The rotters didn't even offer us a cup of tea. They believed that a reign of brutality, fear, deprivation, semi-starvation, whipping with cane rods and other forms of rather unpleasant activities were the only methods that could possibly be used to hammer us down from normal, reasonably intelligent little boys to a physical and mental state where we would be simple automatons, doing everything by rote and in constant fear of brutality and mind-numbing testicle-scrunching punishment. I was just a wide-eyed kid with a penchant for Neolithic cave-dwellers and cheap fags. I didn't really understand any of this. Yet in *Ganges* I saw that man's inherent brutality to man lies just a titchy bit beneath the surface. I actually think that Stone Age cave-dwellers would have been rather more pleasant and I wished I'd had a time-machine so that I could go back to live in my Parkmill cave with Fred and Barney forty thousand years ago.

Most people are never in a position to see or experience what we were now going through. It requires a certain set of circumstances and they all existed at *Ganges*. To begin with you need people who are just ordinary men, not too bright, of course, who have just enough education and intellect to get them out of school and into any kind of menial employment. In civilian life they would probably be happy as bricklayers or street-sweepers or dustbin collectors but in the navy they were usually just low-ranking individuals who basically had been handed a licence to do what they wanted. There was a policy that the harsher the discipline the stronger it would make us and the more willing we would be to obey just about any order we would be given during our naval careers. It was a policy designed to instill fear into us and it scared the crap out of me, I'll willingly admit. I'd come from a gentle, loving, family home where voices had never been raised in anger but had now been thrust into the heart of an angry disciplinary poo-storm. I did not like it one little bit.

Everything about *Ganges* was so horribly evil it was almost hilarious. The whole place was run like some kind of deeply dark antithesis of a Monty Python circus. Even the characters were so evil they seemed somehow surreal. I spent that entire year in terror and never really understood why. Looking back now on the few photographs I have of myself at *Ganges* I can't help noticing that my face is frail with constant terror. My eyes are dark with foreboding. I look like a whippet about to be whipped — a mouse about to be whacked by a steel trap.

The naval police were particularly harsh. I'd never experienced such instant anger as I saw in them. Just ordinary family men most of them, but about as bright as Harold Steptoe's horse. The British military system seemed to breed people like that and there are loads of them in the agonising annals of British history.

If we even looked at someone the wrong way at *Ganges* we were punished, and it wasn't just a smack on the wrist with a ruler. We'd find ourselves running up and down a long steep hill for hour upon hour, a mattress on our backs, our laces taken out of our boots and deprived of socks so that after an hour our heels and toes would be stripped of flesh. Then we'd have to run for another few hours. In the rain it became an additional torment because the mattresses became progressively heavier. We would also be forced to run backwards with a .303 rifle held above our heads until we collapsed from exhaustion. That was more fun-filled entertainment inflicted upon us by our wonderfully clever and compassionate 'superiors' who called themselves our trainers. I wouldn't have minded so much but they actually enjoyed it. The look on their faces was priceless. I've seen a boy caned so badly that his skinny little bum wept blood. Boys committed suicide at *Ganges*. I'm not sure how many because the British Government still refuses to release figures, even under the FOI act. Some went insane. If you went nuts at *Ganges* they politely called you a 'basket weaver' and sent you to a remote place in the hills somewhere where your drools and your incessant gibbering wouldn't offend anyone.

I almost went mad just with the food. It was so bad we were eating sandwiches of brick-stale bread in which cockroaches had been trapped between the slices. I'm not exaggerating. There were thousands of cockroaches in the galleys (kitchens to you landlubbers) and the slices of bread, stacked together in huge wooden trays, were literally seething with cockroaches. Rancid butter was melted and painted onto the bread with a paintbrush. Bread-painting was actually one of my jobs. The tinned tomatoes and baked beans were often full of maggots so I ate rather a lot of Mars bars my father would thankfully send. We'd be forced to queue for food for hours, standing often in the dark and rain, sometimes the sleet, freezing, while waiting to be allowed to eat, or try to eat, what had been served up to us. For me it was hellish because I refused to eat the appalling meat they served which left me largely with powdered potato that tasted like Somali dishwater, and maggoty baked beans with cockroach bread. I lost weight like a River Kwai prisoner. Never fat to begin with, within months I looked as if I was suffering from something horribly late stage. I had a boil on my bum, caused through malnutrition, that was so large it looked like another bum. I was the only boy in *Ganges* with two bums. One white and the other as red as a Russian flag. I could hardly walk, let alone march, and one day the boil burst when I was painfully climbing a rope in the gym and the virginal little white shorts they forced us to wear, even in winter, suddenly looked like a surgical sponge some African witch doctor had been using to mop up rather obnoxious bodily fluid from a tree-bat-eating patient in the final stages of Ebola.

We did receive free dental but that was restricted to those who were addicted to pain, so not too many boys took up the kind offer. Our free medical check was restricted to free coughing while some bloke held our balls in the palm of his hairy hand. (This time I *am* talking about testicles). I'm not entirely sure what that was all about, but having one's bollocks fondled by some fat bald bloke with a stethoscope was decidedly unsettling.

There was a sickbay at *Ganges* but it was so useless that boys would only go there either to die or to be treated for constipation because apparently the laxatives were free and there was sugar in them so they tasted great. We actually didn't suffer too much from constipation because there was never really enough to eat to enable us to suffer from chronic bum-clog. We scrubbed floors with our shoe brushes, (even when we were patients in the hospital, as I can personally attest) scrubbed toilet bowls with our toothbrushes and climbed impossibly high masts with our testicles stuck like lumps in the back of our throats, or at least that's what it felt like at 140 feet with nothing to hold onto but a skinny rope that had been in place since Nelson's days and was about as rotten as the late hero of Trafalgar. In winter we froze almost solid. The winds coming off the river turned the ropes on the mast to ice. The mast was stuck into the parade-ground like some kind of enormous acupuncture needle, and when we were forced to climb it, it seemed as if we were going around the Horn in the middle of winter with a Force 10 raging.

Sadly the promised and much anticipated V.D. films never eventuated because suddenly we were considered too young to see X-rated scenes of silly little sailors who, having caught the clap in some overpriced Maltese House of the Rising Sun, were now having their penises closely examined by busty young nurses in uniforms that were considered to be slightly too short especially when their knees were getting a bit on the thick side. It was thought we might faint from pure shock.

We were given sex talks, however, and one thing I discovered was that gonorrhoea bacteria are actually the Charles Atlases of the microbe world. It has even been claimed that they are the strongest creatures on earth and are able to pull 100,000 times their own body-weight which is really impressive for something that spends its entire short life living in someone's rather irritated donger. I just thought you should know that for the next time you do a pub quiz.

Ganges was a place where everyone seemed to be 'basket weaving' on a permanent basis. I could see that ordinary people were capable of just about anything, given the right conditions and I don't think I liked that very much. Power breeds bullies and empowers corruption. Bullies were able to thrive at *Ganges*. It was a greenhouse for them. They flourished like Italian tomato plants standing in donkey-poo. Is it any wonder that I deepened my resolve to be alone as much as possible?

When I got out of *Ganges* I was as broken as a well-used Barbie doll. My youthful spirit had disappeared. I looked like one of those half-starved scarecrows you see in farmers' fields, haggard and worn with bits of mouldy wheat sticking out of its bum. It took me decades to return to life. I never really got over the *Ganges* maggots. It took me yonks before I could even look at a tin of tomatoes.

Anyway, that was my year of living dangerously. I starved and was brutalised but managed to survive by withdrawing even more deeply into myself to find any kind of happy seclusion away from the rest of the world.

Ganges was an especially unhappy time so I found myself asking the question: what was happiness? Is it all it's cracked up to be?

Are we able to fool ourselves by telling ourselves that we are happy, or even relatively so, when in fact that might not be the case? What does happiness really mean and can you fake it like an orgasm? Such deep thoughts for a puny young mind! I'd spent so much time being brainwashed and brutalised by the sorry little plonkers at *Ganges* that my head was still in a daze and I had no answers other than the fact that any kind of happiness could never come from what I had just gone through. And I had a moon-sized boil-scar on my bum to prove it.

I became what I called a 'secret seclusionist'. Nobody knew about it but there now appeared to be two of me. *Ganges* had forced me to separate the physical me from the inner me. The physical me would do everything I had been ordered to do, including all the punishments and to accept the brutality, when in reality I was buried deeply inside my own psyche like a steel ball-bearing, hardened by experience, impenetrably tough, so that no one could get inside. From there I could look out onto the world and separate myself from it. It was the only way to handle *Ganges*.

People tell me that I'm a square peg in a round hole. I don't fit. I never really have. Recluse. Vegan. Writer. Introvert. Hermit. Not exactly well placed in society to capture hearts, cut deals, make someone's day, be the centre of attention at a party or to bring light and laughter to the world. There is a clinical condition describing people who like to be alone. It's called, I'm told, 'social anxiety disorder', and while that's fine for people who actually suffer from that rather alarming problem it does not describe me or most of the recluses out there who live quietly somewhere within the hidden recesses of the world. I do not suffer from any disorder. I am not in the least anxious about being involved in any normal part of society. I have not even deliberately chosen to be who I am or live as I do because my way of life is so natural to me. *Ganges* just confirmed it.

I adore being alone. I resent having to live as others perceive how I should live. I do not like having to explain myself to others simply because what I do and how I live are different to how other people live. Alone, I do not have to ask other people to cater for my foibles. Being vegan is sometimes a difficult task because almost all those I know out there who are not vegan, have little or no understanding of what to do with a vegan when they visit. It's literally like an alien popping in for morning tea, expanding head-antennae and all that. Even worse, people begin to resent what they feel are unnecessary demands to provide for vegans. 'Damned old buffer, won't eat eggs! What's the world coming to?'

If I did suffer from social anxiety disorder then people might think, oh well, the poor old bugger's not right in the head so let's do what we can for the strange little sod and get rid of him as soon as possible. At least I would have the excuse of being not quite right in the head, but for anyone who has to put up with a reclusive vegan, we can appear to be annoyingly difficult to get along with. 'How long will this vegan things be going on then?' I've been asked, as if I'm just going through a teenage phase. A 'colleague' I worked with at a television station years ago, when told that I was vegan said, 'Oh you'll grow out of it.' He by the way was an inveterate bling-wearer with gold bangles on really hairy wrists. I'll be writing more about those later.

To be a recluse, of course, means that you have to be able to stay away from people even when you need to work. For most people who prefer to be reclusive that would be a problem, but I was lucky. My path in life was to be writing, and that alone gave me all the tools I needed to become a hermit.

I sometimes wonder how it was that I chose to become a writer. Was it because I just loved to write, to tell stories, or was it because deep down, buried within my psyche, I knew that one day I would want to resign from the rest of the world and that when I did so, then the perfect form of occupation and expression would be some kind of literary career? I still don't have the answer to that question and perhaps it's superfluous anyway, but the happy result is that I began to write more than half a century ago and I have been writing continuously since that time. I also found that writing was in itself a form of seclusion separating me from the people around me, setting me apart from my contemporaries, and that the more I immersed myself in writing the more seclusionist I became. I didn't even have to try. I became a recluse by default.

It all began in 1967. Having survived the trials, tribulations and torments of H.M.S. *Ganges* I was a young sailor serving aboard a leaky old destroyer that had been constructed during the Second World War. I was only eighteen but had already served for three years in the Royal Navy including twelve months in the pirate-infested waters of the Middle East, Red Sea and Indian Ocean so even at that tender age I was something of a veteran. I'd been part of the naval force blockading tankers from entering Beira in Mozambique after Ian Smith had suddenly declared independence for Rhodesia, and we had boarded Arab smuggling dhows armed with Nelsonian era naval cutlasses. It was all so deliciously piratical.

In August 1967 we were steaming down the Irish Sea in the middle of one of the most dangerous storms ever to hit the British Isles. We had recently finished guarding the Royal Yacht, *Britannia*, aboard which had been Queen Elizabeth and her son, Prince Andrew, when he was about the size of a pot of shrimp paste and had no concept that he would one day become embroiled in one of the world's most astonishing scandals.

Naturally Her Majesty had never spoken to me; I don't expect she even realised that she and Andy were safely in the hands of young, eighteen years of age, slightly post-virginal, pirate-fighting cutlass-wielding Anthony Matthews. I'm positive that she would have felt immensely safer had she realised that I was looking out for her.

Having completed our escort duties for the royal yacht, we'd sent Liz, with all her really interesting Alice in Wonderland hats and handbags, safely on her way to enjoy a glass of very expensive Madeira and a cucumber sandwich with a Welsh Corgi or two at Buckingham Palace. We were now returning south while fighting off this monstrous storm which was threatening to sink what then must have been one of the oldest, leakiest, crappiest ships in the entire British fleet. It was limping like someone's granny with bunions.

We were informed that this was a hurricane force 12 storm — the worst storm on the meteorological Beaufort scale, but later we discovered that it had been re-categorised and had made history as a hurricane force 13, completely off the scale. Ships were sunk, boats lost at sea, harbour walls smashed, and terrible damage done to beaches and other coastal facilities. I remember the storm well. Standing on the upper deck of the ship was almost impossible. Looking out at the waves I could see them rising up to the height of two or three storeys *above* the ship. We were actually looking up at the waves as they towered above us. The ship was rolling like a cork, being tossed all over the place, and we could do nothing except keep the bows into the waves and hope that somehow we would not roll over completely and end up like the *Poseidon Adventure*, largely because I didn't like the thought of hanging upside-down like a fruit-bat but also because I had a fairly natural disinclination to drowning in an upturned steel coffin and subsequently becoming eight stones, eleven pounds and six ounces of rehydrated mackerel poo.

I realised that to take my mind off the storm I would have to do something. I had been toying with the idea of writing a book for a while. Taking advantage of the navy's further educational system I had been studying externally through London University and writing loads of hysterical historical essays. It was a form of expression I found I enjoyed and thought that one day I might like to take up writing as a career. I decided, therefore, that to take my mind off the hugely dangerous storm I would begin to write my first novel. It would take the entire world by storm (as it were). I took a spiral-bound notepad and an old Bic biro from my locker, jammed myself between a bulkhead and the bilge pump which had the rather annoying habit of pissing constantly on my little camp-bed at night, balanced the pad on my knees and began to write my own version of *War and Peas.*

Actually I can't remember what the book was titled or even what the story had been but I seem to recall that it was about as interesting as watching the 1000th repeat of *Doctor Finlay's Casebook* and equally as irritating, especially when Janet was asking, also for the 1000th time: 'Och Dr Findlay, would yer no like a wee cup of tea?'

I weathered the storm and we came safely to harbour but the book did not thankfully survive. By the time I reached the fifth or sixth chapter, several months later, I had written myself into a corner of the plot from which it proved impossible to extricate myself without losing any more brutally masticated fingernails. The entire project was eventually consigned to the ship's aptly named garbage chute. It went into the sea along with all the galley waste where, no doubt, it floats today, somewhere off the coast of Ireland, a sea-smudged literary masterpiece just waiting to be discovered like some long lost message in a sun-bleached bottle.

Yet this one dismally unfortunate attempt to write did have a happy consequence. It set me apart from my colleagues in a way that I could never have imagined possible. Up until that point in time I had been just one of the lads. A bit strange, admittedly, because I was studying through London University, attempting to get a better education, and sometimes I'd like to go to watch a Puccini opera, which admittedly was a bit weird for a Royal Navy jacktar, but apart from that I was just doing what sailors usually do. Sail ships. Visit ports. Drink rum, and if the opportunity presented itself, to date as many pretty girls as possible.

Really! It was in my job description.

But now I became something else. I'd written a book, or at least I had attempted to do so, and people began to treat me as even more of a freak. It was *brilliant*! I was beginning to part myself from the world, only marginally at first, but the slight wedge was there, just a crack at that time, nonetheless it was real and I knew, deep down, that this was what I wanted. I wanted to be apart, not to be one of the crowd. I had suddenly discovered that I could be completely different and I liked the feeling a lot. Writing a book is something that has to be done as a solitary task. It has nothing to do with the much vaunted concept of teamwork. I found that writing my first book gave me a kind of solitude, even when living in a mess-deck crammed with about a hundred really noisy sailors all of whom appeared, for some unfathomable reason, to be waving their foreskins around like little rubber swimming rings. That's the one thing about naval mess-decks, they are always full of penises and it's really quite irritating.

Anyway, my attempt at writing a book meant that I could now legitimately go elsewhere on the ship in search of seclusion without having to have an excuse to get away from everyone. People began to understand that I needed to be alone for a reason. I was the plonker trying to write a book. I had discovered the magical world of seclusion and liked it.

I continued with my studies and a few years later became an engineering department writer. That placed me into a whole new world of seclusion because it meant that I had my own office on the various ships in which I served and was able to hide away in there without anyone disturbing me. By now I was in my early twenties and was writing more and more, mainly rubbish, I have to admit, like short stories about zombies or haunted villages, but my preoccupation with writing, coupled with having my own office, gave me the opportunity to lose myself. I perfected the craft of hiding on a warship which would be one of the most difficult places in which to hide oneself. A ship like that was home to hundreds of men and becoming invisible was almost impossible, but somehow I managed.

My office was my sanctum. As long as I did my work no one bothered me. I had discovered the first stages of invisibility. Experience would give me the knowledge and power to improve on that. My contemporaries thought I was a bit loony, but that was okay too. My seclusion was aided by the fact that I was keenly interested in opera and poetry, especially William Wordsworth (largely because he wrote about remote rural places, wild and almost completely bereft of humans) and Dylan Thomas, who wrote about colourfully crazy people. Other sailors on board my ships thought I was a bit nuts too and that was absolutely brilliant. Exactly what I wanted. Mission achieved. I had found my way forward.

However, many of my readers might have heard the old housewives' tale that touching a sailor's collar brings good luck. I'm not sure if there is any truth in the story but for some reason I was always having my collar felt (although not in the police concept, of course) so clearly I wasn't as invisible as I would have liked. I'd be standing at a railway station, for example, waiting for the 9.10 from Bristol Temple Meads to Plymouth and trying to pretend that I was actually covered with vanishing cream and therefore pretty much transparent to the naked eye, when suddenly, out of the blue, I'd feel a light touch on my collar. Actually, if truth be known, I quite enjoyed it. It was almost like giving a gift to someone in need. People need luck and if I was able to bring some their way then that was marvellous, even though I was shedding my see-through invisibility cloak in order to do so. I have to say that there was also another advantage to my generosity in dispensing good luck to all and sundry. Rather pretty young ladies would sometimes touch my collar *pretending* to be looking for luck when in reality they were looking for something else entirely. It was *brilliant!*

I definitely wasn't invisible then, by the way!

In March 1970 I flew to the West Indies via New York to take up a posting as an engineering department writer. It was an event that changed my life forever and gave me a spiritual home that will remain as a central core of who I am until the day I pop my clogs and reluctantly join the turf club.

At New York I flew from J.F.K. Airport aboard an Air France flight for St. Pierre, the capital of Martinique, one of the Windward Islands, where I arrived just after darkness had fallen. It was my first experience of a hot, spicy, scented, exotic West Indies evening, lit with dancing fireflies. My senses went into overdrive. Despite the fact that I was as broke as Peter Sellers after Britt Ekland had done with him, I was totally stoked to be in the Caribbean. I wondered if I might find a few Pieces of Eight which would have been helpful considering my perilously impecunious situation.

St. Pierre had once been known as the 'Paris of the West Indies', although I'm not sure why because there wasn't even a replica of the Eiffel Tower in sight. The city had been completely destroyed when the Mont Pelée volcano had erupted on 8 May, 1902. After the eruption, rescuers from a French warship had gone ashore to discover that of the forty thousand inhabitants who had been living in the city at the time of the eruption only three remained alive. Of these, two died of severe burns soon afterwards and the sole survivor, a loner and ne'er-do-well known as Ludger Sylbaris, survived because he had been incarcerated in a dungeon at the time. He'd been arrested the night before for street brawling. Not all loners are pacifists, it seems, but on this occasion his lifestyle had saved him from being fried alive sunny-side-up. Sylbaris must eventually have overcome his inherent reclusiveness because he later joined Barnum and Bailey's travelling circus and freak-show and became well known as the 'Man who had lived through Doomsday'.

If anything, the year I spent in the Caribbean deepened my need to become a Lone Ranger because the islands are beautiful and I really had to be alone to be able to absorb the immensity of their power. That's not to say that I was alone all the time, of course. I did have a few girlfriends. Yet I found my own deep seclusion in the West Indies; it was almost spiritual but in a way that had nothing to do with religion or God. This was me just finding a way into myself, somewhere really deep, where I'd never been before. I was like Dr Livingstone exploring the heart of darkest Anthony, not that it was particularly dark in there, I should add, more like misty grey and full of question marks which kept swimming around rather confusingly inside my pineapple-shaped head.

I loved tropical Trinidad. It was so hot my bollocks would boil in my y-fronts but that didn't matter. I loved everything about the island — the sugarcane plantations, the bright people with brown eyes, the sea tinged with rust stains from the mud of the Orinoco; the palms, the coconuts and the poetry. I would walk alone in the rain of the seasonal monsoons with a book of poems tucked safely under my raincoat and dream of the day I would return to write my own poems and books. I would sit in the palm gardens of Port of Spain, the island's capital, listening to the chatter of tropical birds and watch the other type of tropical birds walking past in miniskirts so brief they actually made one's eyes water.

Or maybe that was just the coconut rum.

Chapter Four

The Zone of Absolute Terror

I expect you've seen the movies where some dopey C.I.A. secret agent is recruited into the ranks of really weird psychic remote viewers and from a secret location in a shipping container in the Nevada desert is able to watch Putin taking care of his morning fundamentals in a top secret underground toilet at the Kremlin. It's all very hush-hush psychic spy stuff and I should stop writing about it now because I think I'm being monitored by MI6 and possibly the KGB or whatever they presently call themselves. Have you noticed, by the way, that secret agents are always easily spotted in a crowd? They're the ones with what appear to be little expandable 1950s telephone cords hard-wired into their ears. Presidential guards have them too. Someone should tell them that it's such a giveaway.

My experiments into remote viewing were, strangely and surprisingly, reasonably successful and I thought for a while that if I could do this I might be able to get away with living a full and enjoyable life just seated in my little studio and tuning into whatever the rest of the world was doing without actually going anywhere or seeing anything in real life. I was never particularly interested in participating in anything that involved real people. When confronted with a situation involving actual humans, all I really wanted to do was to press 'Esc' on my keyboard.

In all the time I have been writing books or making documentary films it's been necessary for me to front up to the podium and talk to some quite large crowds. When I say large, any number over five for me is always terrifying, but at times I've been speaking to several hundreds which instantly places me into what I call, the Zone of Absolute Terror, or ZAT for short. Book launches are a major ZAT. They are particularly bad because they have usually been booked well in advance which allows weeks, or sometimes even months, for the dreaded ZAT factor to grow like a death-cap mushroom.

To begin with I am able to manage my ZAT like other people manage the thought of going into labour or having a testicle surgically removed. They know that they have to do it but put it off for as long as possible, usually because they don't like needles. (I'll be talking more about doctors' surgeries in a later chapter and would advise anyone with an aversion to fainting writers to skip that section). I do that with my ZAT. I push it to the back of my mind and pretend that it doesn't exist. That works for a while but, as Launch Day looms, so the ZAT factor in the fold of my cerebral cortex begins to grow like a Sicilian olive on a well-watered tree. Soon it's the size of a kiwi fruit and then a Granny Smith and suddenly, two days from the launch speech itself, it's the size of a medicine ball and my tiny cone-shaped head simply isn't large enough to contain it all. That's the point when the ZAT starts to spill down my head, over my shoulders, and invade my chest cavity making my heart beat like Ringo's base drum, then on down to my tummy and lower intestine where ZAT has been known to churn the bowels like a butter-maker.

My legs now begin to wobble, not only when I walk but also when I sit down. The knees begin to knock together like muffled castanets. They sound like castanets because my knees are uncommonly skinny. I thank God I'm not wearing shorts or they would be much louder. Tension builds up in the neck and I begin to worry about getting lockjaw. How is it going to look if I walk on stage to say my opening line of: 'A funny thing happened to me on the way to this book-launch' and all that actually comes out is the first word as lockjaw suddenly sets in? I'd be standing there looking as if I'm trying to catch native bees in midair and absolutely *everyone* would be able to see at least down to my tonsils.

I once launched a book with a crowd of about three hundred people most of whom had been avidly emptying bottles of gratis Chardonnay for the previous hour while I had been plucking up enough courage to get up on stage. Finally, after being pushed there by my beautiful wife, always supportive, I delivered a rather lengthy speech followed by a reading that went for about a dozen pages. It took an hour. When I had finished there was such a sudden rush to the loos that I thought there must have been an earthquake or something and everyone was running for cover. I actually looked rather apprehensively at the roof to see it had begun caving in. The hall cleared in about ten seconds which is pretty impressive considering there were only two exit doors and six toilet cubicles in each of the ladies and gents. You could hear the groans of relief. I could almost see the newspaper headlines the next day: 'Author literally pisses off readers at book-launch.'

Once the rush was over, the book signing began and, to be fair, I did sign an astonishing number of books that night. It was a great success. People were coming up to the signing table and eagerly shaking my hand. I just hoped fervently that they had all washed their hands after the Great Pee Exodus had finished. This was pre-Covid, obviously, and hand-shaking was still legal.

There is an art to public speaking, at least that's what I'm told. It ranks up there among the other arts such as painting distorted faces, Picasso-like on canvas, or writing great literature about a bunch of really hungry people living in snowbound Soviet gulags. The art of making a speech is just as important but it's an art-form that can only be mastered through experience. Many people spend their lives attempting to become the centre of attention. Give them the opportunity and they would be up on that amateur dramatics stage happily absorbing foot-light illumination as if it were a collapsing galaxy.

Introverts are not like that. We are the masters of disguise. Introverts actually make really good secret service agents because they are rarely seen or heard and do rather a good job of wafting around silently in the dark or in shadows. In fact one of the lesser known really interesting elements of my life is the true story of when the C.I.A. hilariously attempted to recruit me for a top secret mission at Lake Tanganyika somewhere in the deep jungles of Africa surrounded by quite small men with very large teeth they had laboriously sharpened to points with the sandpaper from Swan Vestas matchboxes. I know I'm prone to slight exaggeration but for the life of me, apart from the Swan Vestas, this is all perfectly true. Had I accepted the mission, and being British, I guess the C.I.A. would have allocated a double-oh number with the same kind of licence to kill that one generally finds on the back of Kellogg's cornflakes boxes. I expect that rather than a real Beretta I would have been issued with one of those totally believable rubber pistols they use in Hollywood blockbusters.

Anyway, in the end I didn't take the job because the C.I.A.'s dental plan sucks and at the time I was in need of some serious fillings. Additionally, I wasn't too keen on some of the tactical requirements. British agents, for example, were taught how to use their own semen to manufacture invisible ink which I guess would have been acceptable until reaching one's dotage, and being confronted by a great-grandchild eager to learn how democracy had triumphed over the Evil Soviet Bear, the child would almost certainly have been rather astonished and possibly disappointed to learn that Uncle Joe Stalin had lost the Cold War as a result of a few jolly good wanks.

I have to say that it's not easy being a hermit. Everyone thinks you are about as crazy as Picasso's underpants. (Picasso, by the way, when not involved in his prolific womanising, was also a recluse. He once stated famously: 'Without great solitude, no serious work is possible.')

People don't usually understand what a hermit is. There are lots of misconceptions. To lead a hermetically sealed life of the traditional hermit it would be necessary to run off to a pine forest somewhere, build yourself a log cabin, dig a nuclear shelter beneath its planked floor and stock it with vast quantities of baked beans, gun-oil, toilet paper and, of course, rheumatism cream because if the North Koreans or the rather irritating Iranians or the Chinese or Putin's mad bunch of stonebrains manage to launch a hailstorm of intercontinental ballistic missiles, it's likely that you will be shut away in your little bunker until your bones are creaking like a haunted house and a big tube of Deep Heat might come in really handy.

The reality of the modern hermit in a Facebook world is nothing like that. One does not necessarily have to live in a cave with ghost-bats and eat fungi for forty years to qualify as a card-carrying hermit. These days hermits are generally just recluses, like me, who live in towns and cities, who own houses or apartments and go to the shops every fortnight to buy their hugely expensive organic veggies and fruit. Actually I order my supplies online and then hide when they are being delivered. You *can* live alone. That's the traditional environment, just solitude. But these days many recluses like myself are married. Some even have children, but it is necessary to understand that recluses desperately need to be alone.

I live in a nice house close to the sea and my wonderful wife largely protects me from having to expose myself too much to the world. (That's not the rude 'expose' by the way and I don't even own a plastic mac).

My home is modern, bright and airy although some of the neighbours are so noisy they sound like South American Howler Monkeys. If I go to the shops, which is now about once every five years, my camouflage generally keeps me out of the high visibility zone and I never willingly talk to anyone, although in 2019 which was the last time I was in a food-store, I was coming out of a supermarket with a bag of organic bananas and a chap looked at me, rushed over and shouted, for absolutely *everyone* in the supermarket to hear, 'I know you. You're Tony Matthews the famous writer.' Well, stuff me! — I'm so unfamous I hardly recognise myself in the mirror but here was a chap who'd evidently seen my phizz on the back of one of my books and the bugger had some kind of photographic memory to match his electronic megaphone voice and now absolutely *everyone* in the entire shopping complex was turning to look askance at me!

I mean really. I could have done without the bananas.

My wife, Lensie, God bless her little cotton socks, usually does the talking, the communicating, the telephoning and, occasionally, the shopping because she knows I don't like dealing with people, especially those with tattoos of Justin Bieber on their arms or men with home-made lobe-expanders in their ears. For some really weird reason the ear-gongs make them look as if they are about to settle onto a ground-nest and begin laying eggs. I'm not entirely sure why that image comes to my mind every time I see some hairy bloke with dinner plates in his ears. Perhaps it's because their ears flap like mad as they walk.

Apart from people with photographic memories, if I'm seen at all in public it would be a bit like catching a glimpse of a ghost, or a wide-mouthed frog. Neighbours have absolutely no idea what I look like and I think that's really excellent. Just last night, at around seven o'clock. I went to close my front door when out of the darkness the shadow of a man loomed. I peered into the night and he suddenly introduced himself: 'Hi. I'm your mower man,' he said. The mower man had been looking after our lawn for at least eight years and in all that time had never seen me, not once. Success! The invisibility shield really works, at least when I'm wearing it.

A few months ago a neighbour stopped my wife, Lensie, and said, 'I never see your husband. Is he still alive?' Now, I've never actually been presumed dead before and it's a really interesting experience, like someone finding your clothes neatly folded on a lonely beach and pondering who they might belong to while shading their eyes from the sun and looking expectantly out to sea in case there is the body of a little Welsh vegan floating tragically face down in the surf.

Being a quiet recluse is not a disease, although hermits and recluses are generally the odd ones out; the one person in a crowd who does exactly the opposite of what everyone else is doing. It's all a part of not being a member of a pack or a team. Sports are often abhorrent to introverts because they generally require 'team effort', and that term does not exist within the vocabulary of almost all recluses unless the sport is solitaire. If people are madly rushing to the left to see what's happening at a traffic accident, for example, I saunter off to the right and look at a few flowers growing at the roadside or sit on a bench humming a few bars from a Chopin nocturne (a fellow introvert, by the way). If everyone is looking up at an eclipse of the sun, I'm looking down at my shoes to see if I've stepped in any poodle-doo. There is a built-in magnetic rod in me that pushes me in the opposite direction when I'm in close contact with people of the same magnetic pole. They say that opposites attract and it's true, but put the positive ends of two magnets together and they will force themselves apart. That's me, at least magnetically speaking.

Had you ever noticed, before the onset of Covid 19, the varying body language signs of people who live in the country, mostly away from other people, and those who live in cities, constantly close to others? The city people (who are often extroverts) when shaking hands would generally stand very close to each other, almost nose-to-nose in some instances. They were often so close that when they shook hands their arms were pointing rather alarmingly towards each other's crotches because there was not very much space separating them. On the other hand, people who live in secluded regions (who are often introverts) shook hands completely differently. They stood well apart and shook hands from a distance, arms stretched out straight in front of them, and after they released their grip they usually took a step or two backwards because they knew that they were already invading the personal space of the other person. Recluses, of course, are even worse than that. They never shake hands with anyone because they are always alone, and if they did they would probably have to have counselling and even then have plenty of access to antibacterial gel or Glen 20. Everything has changed now of course. Nobody shakes hands any more. We either *namaste* each other politely or elbow bump which is apparently quite safe because you can't pick your nose with your elbow unless you have cave-like nostrils like my old maths teacher Mr McLeod.

Actually it's here that I have to make an astonishing admission which most people will probably never understand. I have never once in my entire life felt lonely. The truth is I have no concept of the feeling of loneliness. I just can't imagine what that means. When I was young I would hear people talking about how lonely they would feel at times; it was almost an agony to them. They missed being with people and loathed being alone. When I was alone I tried to imagine how that felt. I'd analyse my own 'aloneness' to see if it somehow matched what others had been telling me about their experience with loneliness, but none of it made any sense to me. When alone I felt alive, free, happy and deeply thoughtful, even when that solitude went on for some considerable time. I tried hard to get lonely but all I felt was an intense happiness that there was no one else around to spoil that pleasure. So how wacky is that? I rather thought of myself as an old lighthouse standing on some precipitous rocky promontory overlooking a heaving sea, alone with the elements, but with purpose and direction. It was where I was rooted into solid rock and where I belonged. I knew that this was different to what most people felt when alone, and although I tried to understand their loneliness I could never quite feel what they were apparently feeling when alone.

Actually there have been a number of recent studies completed on loneliness and solitude and experimental psychologists have spent years trying to figure out if solitude might actually have significant benefits in our lives. One of the first things they have discovered is that solitude means different things to different people. I could have told them that years ago and saved a ton of cash in research grants. What I felt about solitude was completely different to what other people felt, so for me there were no surprises there. After years of study psychologists have been unable to come up with a single definition of solitude other than to state that if you are feeling alone then you almost certainly are alone. I'm not entirely sure why it has taken them so long to figure that out. Yet there are people who are not introverts who like to be alone, that's a proven fact. It satisfies their inner needs for a kind of secret seclusion which recharges their batteries and occasionally that even goes for colourfully dressed extroverts who ring your doorbell every fifteen seconds to see if you want to go out to gatecrash parties and steal hearses for joyrides. Yes, at times even *they* need to be alone.

However, most people don't understand the concept of solitude. For many (and this is a proven fact recorded during a 2014 study into solitude) a large percentage of people tested would prefer to give themselves an electric shock rather than spend just fifteen minutes alone. I should add that the shocks were more of an annoying little tingle than the kind of a tongue-cindering instantaneous blue-bolt you would unhappily expect to receive from a power-grid transformer or your dodgy toaster.

People generally have a number of opinions of those who are introverts. They either believe that introverts are rude, or overly shy, eccentric or haughty. Generally speaking, not one of those is true. Recluses are usually caring, kind, aware of the needs of others, especially animals, and are uncomfortable and feel awkward and alone in crowds, but rarely, if ever, uncomfortable or lonely when alone. Come to think of it we would probably make rather good scarecrows. Actually, there have been cases when posh people in really huge stately English mansions have hired 'ornamental hermits' either to scare people away or because it was a fashionable thing to do. Perhaps recluses should copy the idea and place human scarecrows in their front gardens to scare everyone away too. I'm not entirely sure if it would work but it appears to have been splendidly successful for the British aristocracy.

For those who have been fortunate enough to evade all the highly popular death duties and retain their 3000 bedroom mansions, the thought of having a lot of riffraff like us wandering around their grounds and frightening the bum-feathers off all the peacocks is positively ghastly. Chambermaids are usually too busy emptying elaborately decorated antique piss-pots in the mornings to be utilised shooing away unwanted working class visitors, so the odd figure of a really odd ornamental hermit dressed like an ageing Beatle in mouldy winkle-pickers might well do the trick.

Actually the ornamental hermit profession (yes it became a kind of profession) was rather more complex than the very simplified story I've introduced here. Like today, when the world universally can be overtaken with really silly crazes, which keep extroverts entertained for countless hours, the well-heeled, well-to-do knobs of Victorian England, and even earlier times, experienced a weird cerebral phenomenon and decided that it would be a rather bang-on fizz-whizzer to have a load of fake ruins constructed in their back yards. The English aristocracy was founded upon tradition and history, and it was felt that if one didn't have any 16th century ruins on one's estate then something was drastically missing. It didn't feel right. Suddenly builders were not constructing rows of new cottages for the workers but found themselves instead beavering away at building ruins: 'old' windmills, chapels, abbeys, priories, anything that might once have been really old but had now 'fallen' into disrepair. It was a jolly good talking point while attending posh, floppy-hatted garden parties, and the aristocracy, at least those who didn't have *real* ruins on their estates, could compete with each other by showing off their new *fake* 'ruins' and then building more just to be one up on Lady Chumpy or Lord Longneck. It had all started as a bit of a giggle but soon became quite serious, although the knobs who had *real* ruins on their estates rather tended to look down their noses at those lesser mortals who were building new-old ruins on theirs. The British upper class being a toffee-nosed lot, you can quite understand that they would be a bit miffed.

Added to this fad of building fake ruins, one bright spark decided that it would also be a jolly good wheeze to add a fake hermitage where a fake hermit could be installed to make all this impressive fakeness look more real. Crikey I'm getting dizzy now. The idea caught on like a dose of measles. The hermitages varied in design but were mostly basic constructions without any facilities that would give only the barest of comfort to any person silly enough to agree to live in them while pretending to be a hermit. You might think that no one would be quite so daft, but in fact people were queuing up to be employed as hermits. The reason for this is that the aristocrats employing them were stupidly wealthy and were offering up to six hundred pounds for seven years of service which was a small fortune in those days, especially when the hermits' duties called for nothing more than wandering around all day doing virtually nothing but looking bored, dishevelled and dirty.

As you may understand from this, not too many of the ornamental hermits were real hermits. In fact they were about as fake as the new old ruins. Their duties were simple. Firstly, they would have to be seen by guests visiting the estates, so the whole concept of a real hermit went straight out of the door, plus the fake hermits were under strict instructions about what they could or could not do, which would have been anathema to most real hermits who are usually pretty independent and like to do just what they want. The fake hermits were not allowed to wash nor could they cut their hair for seven years so that they would look and smell sufficiently scruffy to pass for the real thing. While that may not have been too onerous, they were also forbidden to shag the parlour maids which was always a bit of a problem and quite a few of them were sacked for just that reason. Despite these quite obvious staff problems, by the mid 1700s almost every major estate in England featured its own resident 'hermit'. They were usually fed a meal from the house each day; some were given books to read from the estate library, if indeed they could read, which was unlikely, while others were given music lessons if they were so inclined.

Today you can still see ornamental hermits in gardens everywhere; they are now made of stone or Chinese plastic (if they're the really cheap ones from the super stores) and are called garden gnomes, which, by the way, were first invented by another vegetarian, Sir Charles Isham, who thought they might attract real gnomes to take up residence in his flower beds. How crackers is that? There's no record of his plan having succeeded but it certainly led to the unhappy practice of gnome-napping which I've seen firsthand, having once interviewed a woman for a national magazine story whose gnome had been ignominiously kidnapped and a ransom note sent for its release. When she first contacted me to tell me this story I thought she was having a laugh. I had to check the calendar to see if April had suddenly arrived. But it was all true. She refused to pay the $50 ransom and the gnome finally found its way home by itself, so it's quite possible that it was simply a case of self-kidnapping. That's another true tale, by the way, but I'm full of idiotic stories like that.

Yet how do recluses survive without losing their sanity in a world where social contact is as close as the next keyboard stroke? One would think that living in an environment where people can constantly be in contact with each other would, to an introvert, be about as irritating as those really cheap plastic toilet seats that have a tendency to stick to your bum when you stand up, especially on hot days in the sub-tropics. In fact, the reverse is the case. Real people, flesh and blood people, have to be dealt with on a personal level. It requires facial expressions, sometimes not always genuine. Face-to-face encounters require empathy, tact, diplomacy and delicacy. In fact, for recluses it's the face-to-face encounters that are the most difficult. Electronic communications are far simpler and less challenging. Emails are a breeze; even Twitter is manageable if you can squeeze any kind of meaningful information into 280 characters that doesn't make it seem as if you have to rush off to the loo as a matter of some urgency.

Facebook for hermits is not so useful as there is far too much information about you out there and the site harvests your soul in the kind of way that you sometimes see in old movies where some poor American schmuck has sold his soul to the devil in exchange for three wishes — one of which usually includes a wish for more wishes which is not a bad idea when you come to think about it. Facebook generously gives you just one wish — connectivity. They then take not only your soul but also all your Instagram pics and your mother's favourite collection of naked baby-on-the-rug pics and keeps them literally forever while sharing them hilariously with the rest of the world. It's not actually a good bargain, especially when you can right-click on the photo and find similar images all over the web that might not be you but actually photos of Trump, for example, also naked on the rug, although that would only occur if both you and Trump had look-alike bums that Google could digitally match. Even so, it's a completely terrifying thought.

Then, of course, there's the issue of when you apply for that high powered job requiring tact, skill, diplomacy, sound judgement and insight (such as a drive-through attendant, for example) and when you go in to do the interview some really overfed, individual with heavy jowls and burger grease on his/her chin slyly swivels his/her computer monitor towards you and you see a photograph of yourself sitting on a little pink plastic potty beneath which is a handwritten caption, no doubt placed there by your mum in 1952, which reads something like: 'Anthony's first potty session'. Now, if that ever happens to you, I think I can guarantee that you will not be getting the job, even if it is just handing out paper cartons of paper food to paper people at a *papier mache* takeaway.

This is the age of narcissism. One has only to look at political events in the good old U.S. of A. to realise that. I recently saw a television documentary on narcissism and it was frightening. Not being a psychologist, I have struggled somewhat to understand precisely what the term narcissistic actually means — clinically that is. I probably still don't fully understand the condition but listening to the firsthand accounts of narcissistic people and their victims I have come to realise what a danger to society they can be. One woman in the program related that her husband was so narcissistic that given the opportunity he would have hounded and pressured her to commit suicide just so he could have enjoyed that intense feeling of power he had over her. There is a word for people like that and it is far worse than 'plonker'. I'm not sure if narcissism is on the rise, I'll leave that to the statisticians with little round National Health glasses to figure out, but it is certainly out there, alive and well, hovering over us in the workplace, the home, and in our recreational endeavours. Given that the phenomenon is so widespread it could well be time to consider what lessons might be learned from the reclusive introvert.

People say that recluses are too inward thinking, that they are so self-absorbed they have little time for anyone but themselves. In fact that is the exact description of a narcissist and the exact opposite of an introvert. Let's think a moment. In Greek mythology Narcissus drowned because he couldn't stop looking at a reflection of himself in the water. I actually know a few people who would probably do exactly that. This is now the age of the selfie! The religion of Me has arrived. Selfie is now a recognised noun. It became the 'word of the year' in the *Oxford English Dictionary*. It's difficult to imagine what Longfellow would have thought of that. Wordsworth would probably have thrown himself into one of his eternally babbling brooks.

I recently bought a new mobile phone, not to phone people, of course, because literally I would never do that. I bought it so that my wife can send me a text when she discovers to her ongoing consternation that I have accidentally-on-purpose become invisible once again and she doesn't know where to find me. I only mention the new phone because I notice that it has a new super-duper 'beauty-mode' built into the selfie camera. Automatically it actually takes out wrinkles, bags beneath the eyes and spotty skin, leaving one's face at least ten years younger than reality. How narcissistic is that? Not only are we being encouraged to fall completely in love with ourselves, the Chinese geniuses who design these phones are actively working to make us think that we are all perfect, even when we are, in fact, about as saggy as Hermann Göring's bum.

How many of those 'funny' videos have you seen on television of people walking along, completely absorbed by their mobiles and then bump into a lamp-post or get run over by a number 33 bus or walk off the end of a marina quay? I saw a news report on television when a woman walked over the end of a dock-wall and drowned because there was something in her text message vastly more interesting than her life. I don't know if anyone has calculated how many selfies are taken every year, probably about the same number of White House staff that Trump fired during his terrifyingly awful term in office, but it's a fairly clear indication that we are totally in love with ourselves in a way that even Narcissus would have envied. Can you imagine what *he* would have been like with a mobile phone complete with beauty function?

They are now making mobile phones out of highly polished stainless steel so that we can look at the reflection of ourselves when we are not otherwise engrossed in taking selfies. One phone company has brilliantly invented a phone capable of taking a photograph of someone else while at the same time taking a photograph of ourselves taking that photograph. I know. It's maddeningly confusing. Why on God's green earth would we want to take a photograph of ourselves taking a photograph of someone else. It's like being caught in a really hilarious Fatty Arbuckle film.

Introverts, however, are not in love with themselves. Most do not particularly like themselves but have to put up with what they have got unless they have the good fortune to own a phone with beauty function.

Recluses are intensely private. We would stick a 'Do Not Disturb' sign on our foreheads if we thought we could get away with it. I've been looking for the opposite of a 'Welcome' front door mat which is, of course, a 'Please Piss Off' mat. The problem with that, is that it would attract even more attention thus completely cancelling out any perceived benefits. We certainly do not advertise what we are doing, unless it's promoting our latest book, which is perfectly acceptable to tweet and is required practice by the publishers anyway. At least that's serving some kind of purpose. On the other hand it is not difficult to find tweets online of people informing the world that, for example, they've just been to the loo in the restaurant where they are having dinner and that there is no toilet-roll. It's completely up to the minute bog-drama. It's life imitating Reality TV. Now I ask you: was the Internet invented so that we could avoid the embarrassment of visiting the cubicle where the toilet paper had been rather annoyingly kidnapped by aliens?

Society worships winners, fame, wealth and those who construct electronic monuments to their own success and glory. I know of at least one former American president who does just that. Social media sites have become shrines where devotees prostrate themselves with 'likes' and 'follows' and 'friends', but it's all so false, it's like powdered eggs or that quite ghastly ersatz coffee made famous by Adolf. Nothing has real substance in the electronic world of self-love. It's all just a mirror image, an illusion, the ghost of reality. We become lost in the fantasy and in so doing we face the very real danger of forgetting who we actually are.

The world does not really understand seclusion. Unless you are a monk, or Robinson Crusoe, or possibly Tom Hanks and his marooned volleyball, 'Wilson', (which was later sold to a lonely investor for an 'eye-watering' figure) no one even wants to know why people prefer to be alone. Seclusion is for nutters, yet the very act of seclusion attracts almost unwarranted fascination. The more recluses seek their seclusion, the more people want to know why, and then to delve into the lives of those who prefer to be left alone. For the recluse it's a rather irritating phenomenon because people seek them out to ask the eternal and really annoying question: Why? Yet all the recluse wants is to be left in peace with the bees, their organic tomatoes and a book of Dylan Thomas poems.

Surveys have demonstrated, however, that recluses are high proportionately on the list of creatives. They are deep thinkers, slow to make decisions, preferring to weigh up all the possibilities before acting. They are safe people. Many are writers, artists, sculptors, film directors and architects, all fields of creativity that require really deep concentration at a level of creativity that few people experience in their lifetimes. J.D. Salinger, author of that American classic *The Catcher in the Rye*, was one of the world's most famous recluses. He shunned the limelight completely but his intense seclusion only made him even more famous.

He was the mystery figure everyone wanted to know. Salinger once remarked that while he was physically *in* the world he was not a part *of* it. He did not want to conform to the world's values. He made a provision in his will stipulating that when he died he did not want to have a funeral service because people would be there. I'm not having a funeral service because only two people would attend anyway.

Albert Einstein, Bill Gates, Steven Spielberg, Abraham Lincoln, J.K. Rowling, Eleanor Roosevelt, Mahatma Gandhi, Meryl Streep, Frederick Chopin and Barack Obama all rate highly on the list of well known introverts. Contrary to the modern trend of team effort, pack activities and even creation by committee (as many screenplays are written), Steve Wozniak, the co-founder of Apple and himself an introvert once stated: 'Work alone. Not on a committee. Not on a team.' Wozniak's words echo those of British author and philosopher Aldous Huxley who had earlier advised: 'The most powerful and original a mind, the more it will incline towards the religion of solitude.'

All that just makes me sound like a right plonker and that I'm just colouring the drawing-book by rote to claim that introverts are all really intense, interesting, and hugely intelligent people. That's not exactly true because some introverts can be rather strange and even nasty people, the kind who live in wet woodlands and shoot deer just for pleasure, for example, or who own chainsaws in Texas. Yet the truth is that most introverts are harmless, quiet, thoughtful people who are just seeking solace in solitude.

A classic example of this kind of person is a gentleman who recently became internationally known as one of the world's most astonishing and committed hermits after it was discovered that at the age of nineteen or twenty he had driven into a densely wooded area of Maine where he abandoned his car and walked alone into the forest taking with him only the barest necessities of life including a small nylon tent and some supplies. From that moment he simply disappeared for twenty-seven years. He set up his camp among thick trees in a region known as North Pond and apart from one hiker who saw him fleetingly, like Big Foot, no one ever knew that the hermit was there. He was later arrested by the Maine police and when questioned as to why he had disappeared into the woods he replied rather interestingly that the 'gravitational force' on his body to be alone had been so strong that he had been unable to stop himself from adopting a purely separate lifestyle and totally shunning human contact. In all that time he did not light a fire because he thought the smell of woodsmoke would attract undue attention, and in a region of the United States where temperatures can plummet to -20 degrees C. that was an astonishing commitment to the maintenance of his seclusion. This gentleman spent much of his time reading books (which he stole, along with food and other basic necessities from local cabins), walking to keep warm, and thinking. Not once during those long years was he bored or lonely.

Another extremely solitary hermit, whose name is withheld in order to respect her privacy, lives in a lonely cottage in a remote region of Scotland. She claims that solitude is the only place where she can find what she describes as an 'ecstasy', and says that all her senses are heightened by being alone. Sensory experiences are far more acute: taste, touch, smell, and even her hearing are heightened. She has experienced auditory hallucinations such as choirs singing in Latin which she could 'hear' coming from another room in her cottage. She believes that solitude and silence can be hugely beneficial and states that the art of practising silence should be important attributes to be discovered and learned as a child because such attributes can be hugely positive and can help us deal with stress and other challenging events in our lives.

It's also interesting to note that many recluses want nothing from life. They wish to leave nothing behind. After they die their preference is that no trace of their lives remain. They shun social media electronic footprints and require just a completely anonymous nothingness — invisibility for eternity.

It may surprise many people to learn that the well known revolutionary Che Guevara was also an introvert, although not, of course, a hermit, and he certainly left a well known imprint on human society and history. It hardly seems probable that a gun-toting rebel whose face now adorns about a trillion sweaters around the world would have preferred to hide in a remote South American leper colony (which he did for a while during his medical student days), but Che actually shunned publicity and preferred to remain as invisible as possible. Just look at some of the photographs of him with Fidel. Che looks like he wants to disappear in a major puff of cigar smoke — just as magicians' assistants do on stage. His face is famous but in reality he was the master of invisibility.

David Letterman, Daniel Day Lewis and dozens of other well known celebrities are also recluses. Bobby Fisher, the hugely talented but highly controversial American chess champion was so reclusive that he spent his last remaining years as a wild-haired, slightly nutty recluse in Iceland which was about as far away as he could get from normal civilisation.

The world is a pressure cooker. It is constantly attempting to make us conform, to be the same as everyone else. Friends pressure us to join Facebook. We tattoo our bodies with strange symbols that no one can actually read or understand. I've seen tattoos on athletes which are supposed to be symbolic and mystically oriental spells calling down luck, fortune and power. However, the tattooist was almost certainly having a jolly good giggle and the smudge of ink on the back of the athlete's neck is probably Tibetan Morse code for something like: 'My Husband Farts in Bed', but it doesn't matter because the tattoo is *really* artistically expressed and nobody can read what it says anyway. Conformity such as found in mass tattooing is just another illusion of safety, team inclusion and hunting in the pack, but I find that pack-clustering is really the enemy of creativity. To create, it is necessary to be yourself, your undisturbed, quiet, silent, deepest self, and that often comes with seclusion and at least a degree of non-conformity.

It's interesting to contemplate just what on earth is going on in the head of an introvert. If one is to judge us by the standards of ordinary people we could be considered completely nuts, which is okay because many of us are vegetarian or vegan and nuts form a major part of our diet. There are lots of obvious advantages to being a vegan but what could possibly be the advantage of staying well clear of everyone and locking yourself in a little cabin, cave, or boat, switching off the news completely and living the life of an impoverished version of Howard Hughes?

Well, in reality, there are many.

The first and obvious feature of being a recluse is that you probably won't be able to work for anyone because you will be in hiding somewhere. That's not entirely true because in these days of ever-increasing internet speeds it's possible to achieve some remarkable feats at home such as printing out a full-sized 3D aircraft carrier and emailing it to the Department of Defence. I'm just kidding, of course; if you did that the reels of printer-plastic would cost you a mint. However, the opportunities of working remotely are growing exponentially and we have seen a massive growth in that since Covid 19 descended on the world like some medieval pestilence. Yet for those without the requisite high level IT skills, working from home in your chosen profession as a small business is really the only alternative when one is a recluse. The advantages of this are wonderful. The hour-long commute to the office in the city through toxic clouds of exhaust gasses would be a thing of the past. Commuting stress levels would disappear completely so you'd save tons on Zanax and there is strong medical evidence to demonstrate that long-term stress can lead to dangerous medical conditions such as heart disease and really nasty cases of athlete's foot where it looks as if your toes are peeling like 1950s wallpaper in Croydon.

In effect, abandoning the daily commute has achieved success on multiple levels. Fuel consumption drops dramatically as does wear-and-tear on the car. The planet is less polluted; people can breathe more freely and other commuters have one less car to deal with in their struggle to push through the unending traffic jams. You also don't have to eat your breakfast donuts behind the wheel while attempting, not to successfully, to sip coffee from a paper-cup that's so super-heated it's in the process of permanently erasing your fingerprints.

Another advantage of working from home is that you don't have to get dressed every day. No more collar and tie or smart frock. (I love the word 'frock'. There's something deliciously fifties about it). I'm a writer who lives at the beach in the sub-tropics. What do I need clothes for? No, I don't write in the raw. Nor do I wear a frock. With my 1940s body not only would that be obscene but it might frighten the possums away. I wear just shorts and a shirt from which the sleeves have been cut in order to demonstrate to anyone who might call unexpectedly that I have a magnificent set of arm muscles. (My wife is now howling with laughter and I can't blame her because if the absolute truth is to be told my arms actually resemble knitting needles with wire-coat-hanger elbows).

I am my own boss. No one is looking over my shoulder to see if I have the next sales projection ready, and, apart from publisher's deadlines, I rarely, if ever, have to conform to time schedules which is a great relief.

When I first landed like a Martian in Australia in the early 1970s (I really did feel as out of place in this strange land as an alien), the only job I could find after weeks of struggle (and also of some starvation) was as a door-to-door salesman selling electrical goods to people in country towns. It began as something of an adventure but I soon came to dislike the work and proved myself to be the world's worst salesman because I had a massive amount of trouble walking up that garden-path to knock on a stranger's door — especially when many of them greeted me with that rather interesting Australian sobriquet: 'Piss off, ya bloody Pom'.

The one thing that brief exercise taught me was that the best salespeople are extroverts and that weedy little Martians should, firstly, plan ahead before arriving on a foreign planet and, secondly, to provide sufficient funds for themselves so that they are not forced to take the kind of employment that leaves them standing half-way up a garden path suffering from a sudden onset of lock-knees.

I'd come home at night, dig out my $11 typewriter (made in 1926) and bash out some inane short-story about zombies, or something, while being deliriously happy to be back where I belonged — seated alone at a desk while my mind was actually elsewhere — usually somewhere in a completely different time or dimension where zombies or time-travellers lived.

Some time ago I completed one of those really naff tests to see what level of introvert I am. I can hear you saying, 'Holy crap, dude, you don't know already?' The test asked a load of questions such as did I prefer to speak or write; did people tell me that I was a good listener; was I a risk-taker; was my best work achieved when I was on my own and did I spend far too much time thinking about Kylie Minogue (Actually I'm just kidding about that last question although the answer is probably yes). After I had run through about a thousand questions I found that not only was I at the extreme end of being classified a recluse and introvert but that every reclusive introvert in the entire world would want to vote me as their president for life! I felt quite regal for a while, in a lovely isolated kind of way, of course.

There is probably a bit of the introvert in all of us. How many times have you been to a dinner with friends who have just talked on endlessly, getting a little tipsier and louder as the evening has progressed, until you've reached a stage where you haven't been able to stand it any more and you've just longed to get home, have a nice hot shower and sit quietly in a chair with a hot cocoa or your favourite teddy? If that's you then it's quite possible that there is an introvert lurking in there somewhere. I don't have a teddy any more, by the way although I sometimes write in my pyjamas. (It's 9 p.m. and I'm doing that right now, actually).

People can be an annoying presence and we all need a little time to ourselves. That's the introvert seeking to be let out. Actually, not that many of us are extroverts. The pure extrovert stands at the far end of the scale. You can easily recognise them. They are usually in everyone's face. They are annoyingly boisterous. They like thumping music. They steal chips from your plate and dance to hip-hop which in itself is an indication that they need to undertake Hermann Rorschach's 'inkblot' test to see what exactly is going on inside their heads.

Most of the world's population is comprised of people who would probably be known as ambiverts. That's someone who is nicely, comfortably and sensibly in the centre of the two extremes between extrovert and introvert. They are mainly tax collectors or people who work in the aged pensions office. No one person is the same; we all have different degrees of introversion or extroversion, it's just that people like myself prefer the far end of the introversion scale to anything else. It's a place where everything makes sense, where we are happy. It's quiet, sane, comfortable, non-challenging and creatively inspiring. It all comes down to how we charge ourselves. Now I know that sounds really stupid. We are not mobile phone batteries needing to be plugged into a wall socket at the end of every day.

Or are we?

We do need charging, all of us. We have to charge up our brains and our bodies because introverts and extroverts not only lose their energy charge in different ways but they also charge themselves differently. Introverts lose energy rapidly, and I mean really rapidly, when they are in the presence of lots of people, especially when they are people the introverts don't know or don't particularly like. It's stressful to them. We are like a large light-bulb attached to a small battery. Loud noises, business or work pressure, crowded rooms or sidewalks, queues at bus-stops or restaurants, all these types of situations drain the energy from introverts like draining oil from the sump of a car. It just drops away leaving the introvert completely exhausted.

The extrovert, on the other hand, sucks energy from exactly the same situations. Busy places, clattering restaurants, high tension sports, combative work situations, competitive games, all stimulate and energise the extrovert.

An introvert needs to get away from such draining situations so that he or she can recharge in quiet solitude. The extrovert loses energy and becomes bored in such situations and seeks the stimuli of people, noise and excitement in order to recharge.

When alone with their thoughts, however wacky, introverts are at peace with themselves. This time alone has been described as being as beneficial to the introvert as sleeping or eating. It's not just something that introverts do because it's trendy, or an excuse to get away from people for a while. It lies at the central core of who we are. Aliens in a world of happy and noisy extroverts and ambiverts.

This is so profound that I've decided to call for a national day to be Kind to Reclusive Introverted Vegans — I'll call it K.R.I.V. Day. We could make it a national holiday and have parades of introverts dressed in shorts and muscle-shirts or pyjamas marching down the main streets of country towns.

Wouldn't that be fun!

On second thoughts, maybe not. No introvert would turn up!

Chapter Five

It's Rude to Exclude the Nude Dude

I live in my own little world. It's a pleasant place to be except when people come to penetrate my hard-earned seclusion with offers to find God through Jehovah or buy a Christmas cake because the profits go towards purchasing used Steven King books and turning them into spooky park-benches for theme parks. (Which has really happened by the way, although apparently they weren't all Steven King books and a few of mine might have been used too).

Let's face it, reclusive introverts are usually people who don't get along too well with other people and that may be because recluses have often lost faith in human nature and think it's rather a good idea to stay away from people generally. I have loads of wonderful vegan and reclusive followers on Twitter and a great number of them include in their profile that they are also misanthropists. Yet reclusive hermits are everywhere; they're like some kind of slightly invisible but beautifully motivated pestilence, and some of them certainly exhibit evidence that they border on the loony. Any kind of eccentricity is considered to be a little barmy, depending upon its form and severity. There are, for example, many hundreds of hermits living in Australia and Britain. Precise numbers are not known. It's not even possible to calculate approximate numbers because they are hermits, after all. They keep to themselves and often live in particularly isolated regions such as the wilds of Scotland; the mountains of Wales; council houses in Stepney; the Outer Hebrides; the Simpson Desert; as film extras at Broken Hill, or somewhere rather stinky within Manchester's sewage system. They are off the grid. They often support themselves without the need of much financial income, growing their own vegetables and making soap out of secondhand deep-fryer oil mixed with recycled coffee capsules scented with half-used urinal cake. They are ghosts, unseen and unnumbered.

I have long pondered what might be the collective noun for hermits. There are many nice collective nouns and a few not so pleasant. I've always felt that the collective noun, 'a murder of crows' was a bit unfair, as is 'an unkindness of ravens'. My wife once cared for a young crow that had been tossed out of its nest by its parents and it was a lovely, bright intelligent bird. It used to swallow small pebbles during the day and then spit them out at night. It sounded like someone happily playing marbles in our laundry. When I first saw the bird I was so startled I thought for a nanosecond that my fossilised pterodactyl from the Neolithic caves of Gower had somehow come to life because the bird's beak appeared to be about as large as the rest of its pink body which, at that time had been almost completely devoid of feathers.

Collective nouns are curious things, usually an accurate and colourful description of a gathering, but how should one describe a gathering of hermits? The plain fact is that no one ever need come up with a collective noun for hermits because they simply don't collect. A collective noun would be both superfluous and a complete waste of space and ink in the *Oxford English Dictionary*.

Actually I did a little research and discovered that there is a 'sort of' collective noun for hermits and it's, 'an observance of hermits'. I ask you, what kind of boring nutter came up with that one? I then learned from my intensive research (aka Duck Duck Go [which, by the way, unlike Google, does not track you like an escapee from Alcatraz]) that the 'observance' originally came from a description of hermits who would gather for religious 'observances'. Apparently it's in a 1702 dictionary (now probably out of print) but in reality it might not actually be a collective noun, just a general description of hermits at that time. In 1702 just about everyone on the planet was religiously insane and anything was possible. Someone else came up with the term, 'a group of hermits' but that's also stupendously boring. I'm yawning just thinking about it. However, if anyone did actually want to use a collective noun for people who never actually collect I would (humbly, of course) suggest: 'A whisper of hermits', (because we are all impossibly quiet); 'a crack of hermits' (for those hermits who insist on walking around with bare bums) or possibly, and slightly more derogatorily: 'A pong of hermits'. That one would probably suit the hermits living in the Manchester sewers.

In history there have been many slightly odd recluses who have become well known despite their abhorrence of publicity, including the triple-barrelled William John Cavendish-Scott-Bentinck, the rather unusual 5th Duke of Portland who, although he had ample opportunity to massacre the deer on his estates with a singular ecological recklessness, decided instead that he preferred to remain indoors for almost his entire life. The duke lived at Welbeck Abbey in North Nottinghamshire but his dislike of being seen resulted in his having about fifteen miles of deliciously damp, low and spooky underground tunnels constructed beneath his home. In that way he could move about without a single person ever seeing him although it probably played havoc with his lungs and bent knees. His private rooms at the abbey had two letterboxes, one for incoming mail and another for outgoing. The only person permitted actually to look at him was the duke's valet. The duke would not even allow his doctor to look at him, and all his estate workers received their orders in writing. If the duke ventured outdoors it was mainly at night and on those occasions he was preceded by a servant lady bearing a lantern who would have to walk at least thirty metres ahead of him. When he ventured out by day, which was an extremely rare occurrence, the duke wore two overcoats, a very tall hat, and a high collar and would carry an enormous umbrella, behind which he would hide if approached by anyone. He once sacked a worker just for wishing him good morning. The duke was not a vegan, by the way, in fact he was probably responsible for the deaths of more chickens than any single man in English history. He loved a barbecued hen and his instructions to his cooks were quite clear. Chickens were to be kept roasting on the spit every hour of every day so that he could tuck in whenever he felt the urge to rip off a leg or two. His food was brought to him in heated trucks which ran on rails laid throughout his underground tunnels. It was like a cross between Kentucky Fried Chicken and Mini British Rail.

I've always been fascinated by people who not only like to be alone, but live to be alone, and I've written about them quite a lot during my career. There is something very special about people who do not *want* to be special, and are comfortable in their own anonymity. They never wish to be in any way outstanding or unusal, yet the very fact that they *are* seclusionists make them instantly noticeable. It's a paradox with no apparent resolution and recluses have to struggle with that paradox on a daily basis. Reclusiveness has featured in many literary masterpieces including the famous short story titled: *The Three Hermits* by Leo Tolstoy. It's also rather telling that hemits are often portrayed in literature as both vegetarian and 'wise old men', which actually reinforces comments I make in the next chapter concerning how reclusive people are able to delve deeply within themselves to find the truths of who they really are and what their existance actually means.

More orthodox and mainstream religious recluses are also to be found in many parts of the world. There is actually a term for the religious recluse; they are known as the 'diocesan hermits' and are recognised by members of the Christian religion which is interesting because most Christians actually abhor religious seclusion in other religions such as Buddhism. Religious recluses abound, even today. They live all over the world but appear to congregate in India, for some reason. Perhaps it's the happy climate or possibly because a 'funny fag' in India is a lot cheaper than anywhere else in the world.

Some of these strange people go around without any clothes and I can't tell you how much I admire not only their calm nonchalance to nudity, (which can be a bit challenging at times), but also their whole ethos. These are the *Digambara* monks of the Jain sect who carry a *picci*, a broom made of naturally fallen peacock feathers with which they sweep insects away from their feet as they walk because they don't want to step on them. They do the same before sitting down because there would be nothing worse for a titchy little creature like an ant, for example, than being instantaneously crushed to death by a bum.

The monks wear no clothes. Clothing would kill the microbes on their bodies. Millions of microbes would be massacred. Saving the little lives of insects and microbes is a praiseworthy part of the sect's religion and very commendably they refuse to kill anything. They are the epitome of the conscientious vegetarian. Actually I adhere to the same principal and the few people who come to my home think I'm a bit bonkers when I ask them not to step on the ants on my garden path. I've even tweeted about it with a photo of the ants showing their appreciation by forming a love-heart on my windowsill. It's true, although you now think I'm probably as cracked as a chimney-pot. I should add that I'm never ever naked when sidestepping insects nor, thankfully, do I suffer from a painfully sunburned twinky.

Nobody really knows how many ants there are in the world but it's been estimated that the number is up around 10,000 trillion, give or take a few, because apart from the Jain monks, and myself, of course, people are stepping on them all the time. Interestingly, this number of ants, if you could gather them together and get them to stand still for a few moments on a set of digital bathroom scales, would actually weigh about the same as the total number of human beings on the entire world, which means we share our planet equally with ants. This is another reason not to step on the little buggers even when they are biting the living daylights out of your ankles.

If I were to admire any religion specifically, then Jainism would be one of them. (The other would be Buddhism). Jains are the rarest of people because their beliefs are fundamentally good for all humankind. For example, one of their core beliefs is that of *ahimsa*, or non violence. This means it's basically wrong to pick a fight in a supermarket aisle over a roll of toilet paper even if you are suffering from the amoebic trots. But it goes far beyond petty violence and into something quite pure and spiritually uplifting. Adopting Jainism and its principle of *ahimsa* means that one must completely abandon all forms of violence, not just physical but also violence such as hatred and bigotry in thought and also in speech. In other words, thinking nasty thoughts or abusing people who pinch your parking space are considered to be forms of violence and therefore totally against the principal of *ahimsa.*

Jainism's fundamental tenet towards violence is that all religious behaviour that does not include total non-violence is worthless. This is an essential truth which means that most religions are flawed by their cohesion to violent thoughts, behaviour and punishments. An eye for an eye and a tooth for a tooth, for example.

The Seven Deadly Sins of the medieval church were supposed to be punished with the kind of violence that has been carried out and perpetrated by religious tenets since time immemorial. Pride and vanity, for example, which is still prevalent just about everywhere, were to be punished by being tortured on a large stone wheel, although thankfully there are probably not too many of those around these days.

Envy, according to *ye olde* Christian law, drew a sentence of immersion in freezing water which would probably be all right on a hot day, especially in the Simpson Desert or Saudi Arabia. Gluttony was punished by being made to eat rats, toads and snakes, all of which would be pretty tedious, I should think, especially for the rats, toads and snakes. For the crime of lust the punishment was to be burnt alive and you'd probably need rather a lot of sunburn cream for that. Anger and wrath means that your arms and legs have to be chopped off so that you would look just like that wonderfully brave Black Knight in *Monty Python and the Holy Grail* who, after a stupendously ridiculous sword-fight, is left with only his bloodied trunk, both arms and legs having been dismembered by his opponent's sword. But even then, standing on his leg-stumps, he is calling to his adversary to, 'Come back you coward, ' or words to that general effect. Oh happy days! I'm not making any of this up, by the way (well, apart from the Monty Python bits). It's the real deal. Ye olde Bibliophiles of the Dark Age really believed this stuff.

Many religions preach non-violence but, when it comes down to it, how many armies go into battle believing that God is on their side. If there is any truth to the belief that Moses came down from the mountain with his magical ten commandments to heal the ills of humankind, then one of them, as we all know from our endless hours in Sunday school, is that, 'Thou shalt not kill'. Now God did not, apparently, specify on this very important point. He (or She) — (it's time the world had a serious talk about the acceptable use of God's pronouns) — did not say, for example, thou shalt not kill other men or women. The message from space (who's to say that it wasn't an alien intervention) just stated that one should not kill. Jains are not Christians and to them Moses is just an old fart who needs to borrow an electric razor, but they hold to the purest belief that thou should not kill *anything*, including animals and insects. I think that is far more noble than some wishy-washy commandment that allows mere mortals to decide what should or should not be killed, especially when they are a bit peckish and a slice of dead cow would smell good on the barbecue.

Jains are totally vegetarian. Any activity that does harm to animals is wrong so obviously killing animals is on that really big hit-list of things not to do. Jains will not even eat root vegetables such as potatoes, carrots, beets or onions because they believe that pulling the vegetables from the ground kills or harms the microbes attached to them and prevents the roots from seeding. Eating a potato, for example, prevents it from growing its seed and thus creating little son and daughter potatoes which will in turn seed. Isn't that nice? It almost makes me want to stop eating hot chips, but not quite.

Yet there's lots of really interesting stuff the Jains don't do. It's almost as if they are the purest forms of human life imaginable. They believe that one should only speak the truth and good words. They will not take anything unless it's given to them freely. They renounce all worldly goods and clear their path of all living things to the extent of four cubits.

Now you might ask what's a cubit? I didn't know either but it's also the measurement given by God to Noah when ordering the Ark to be built and that was, I think, 300 cubits by 50 cubits wide and 30 cubits high. I'd probably have to check with Russell Crow on those exact measurements because he should know having constructed one all by himself. A cubit is about eighteen inches, so Noah's Ark would actually have been a bit titchy to take all the animals in the world, two-by-two plus seven of every clean creature although I'm not entirely sure what God meant with that description because all animals have to poo at some time and God should have known that because he's the one who endowed them with bums in the first place.

Anyway, enough of all this heavy philosophising and didactic theorising. Let's get back to where we started on this subject and that was with recluses and hermits like me. Now, as we all know, hermits, who are often called 'solitudes', by the way (and I quite like that name), are generally regarded for their benign philosophies, sometimes their strange lifestyles and almost always their body odour. Yet the overall impression we get when someone says the word 'hermit' is one of gentleness, strangeness, long hair and smelly socks full of holes. Occasionally stolen shopping trolleys filled with plastic bags come into that equation as well. Apart from the socks it's actually quite a pleasant impression. However, not all hermits in history have been rewarded with such esteem, especially those driven by religious insanity.

Peter the Hermit was one of these. For those of you who have never heard of him, don't worry, he was a real knob-polisher if ever there was one. When Pope Urban II (no relation to Keith Urban, I should point out for legal reasons) decided in the late 11th century that he'd really had enough of all those Muslim chappies living in the holy city of Jerusalem, he decided to unleash his Crusading armies against the people of the 'Islamic faith', although his description of them was slightly more insulting than that.

Sadly for the poor old pope, the men in the various armies, and especially those who would have to fork out fortunes to pay them, took some convincing. Sending a vast army of men, arms, wagons, horses, mules, supplies and equipment all the way from western Europe to Palestine would be a huge and hilariously expensive operation. The pope wanted blood, so much was evident, the more blood the better. That was his way and the pope would have to be obeyed under threat of excommunication and a rather beastly rationing of holy wafers. Yet, the army leaders reasoned, it might be possible to delay for a while — a year or two — to see how things worked out. Perhaps the pope might have a good hair day and change his mind about unleashing the war to begin all wars. This thought, having invaded the minds of those who were to carry out the crusades, particularly those who would actually have to fork out about ten squillion euros to pay for it all, caused delays to be set into place immediately.

To be fair, it probably wasn't all deliberate obfuscation and postponement. Lots and lots of knights and squires couldn't wait to start butchering Muslims now that they had been given *carte blanche* to do so by the top guy in the Vatican whose ring everyone slobbered over with shameless sycophancy, but it all took an unconscionable amount of time, and time is a damned frustrating thing when your blood is up and there are lots of perfectly innocent Muslims to be slaughtered.

Peter the Hermit was frustrated. By God he was! Peter wanted blood more than anything. His kind of seclusion had bred nothing but religious fervency on a scale almost unparalleled in history. He could not wait for the knights and squires to have the requisite chastity belts made for their women. Oh no. That would have taken far too much time. For all Peter cared the randy damsels in their castles could shag themselves rotten while their knights were away happily pillaging and raping. Peter the Hermit couldn't care less. He would gather his own rat-tag army of zealots and arm them with pitchforks, knives, the odd sword or two, lances, and even one or two chastity belt rejects hastily formed into effective slingshots. Thus armed, more with religious fervour than real weaponry, Peter the Hermit set off, months in advance of the real Crusader army, to march east through Europe to launch a holy attack on the naughty Muslims of the holy city.

About two hours later the entire army completely ran out of food while supplies of sherbet lemons and gob-stoppers were getting perilously low. It was a complete disaster, largely because Peter the Hermit had a brain that resembled a golf-ball in both size and density. The men of Peter's imbecilic battalions began to starve, their women too, which was worse because while women are strong and can easily march on an empty stomach, it takes real courage, grit and determination to keep marching when the promise of a good shag remains as unlikely as a politician ever telling the truth.

Peter's nitwit army hunted and scavenged their way across Europe, killing farm animals like the Muslims they so desperately sought. They raped, buggered and pillaged because they had nothing else to do and it all helped to fill the otherwise slightly boring Sunday afternoons. When finally they arrived in the Holy Land to take up a Holy War against the enemies of the Holy Church they discovered to their complete astonishment and rancour that the men of Islam were not actually ready to offer themselves and their families up for slaughter, and Peter the Hermit's army of complete cretins was so thoroughly smashed, mangled, minced and mutilated that almost nothing was left of them but dry bones in the desert dust.

Peter the Hermit, thankfully, was one of them.

It was actually downright embarrassing. The whole of Peter the Hermit's madcap army had been so hopeless they could have gained useful employment with Rowan Atkinson as extras in *Black Adder*. At least they could have given us a bit of a laugh and earned a screen credit at the same time. One can almost see the High Council of Islamic Generals in Jerusalem sitting together over glasses of steaming mint tea, scratching their heads, smoking their bubbling hookahs and asking the patently obvious question: Were all Christian armies such completely useless muppets?

The answer, of course, was no.

The defeat of Peter the Hermit's casting agency rejects did not prevent Pope Urban II from continuing with his plans for genocide. He was completely enamoured with the idea. It was probably one of those really bright ideas you get while sitting on the bog. I've always found they seem to be the best.

In 1099 Jerusalem fell to the pope's Crusaders and for the following weeks the city was literally swamped in blood. It was said that Crusaders were slaughtering men, women and children at such a rate that the killers were literally up to their knees in blood and gore. The death toll has never been ascertained with any accuracy; it was a little before the invention of the electronic calculator, and Robin Hood hadn't yet returned home to let everyone have the true facts of the case before he set to his real task of robbing the rich to give to the poor and shagging Maid Marian rotten.

The Muslim world later estimated that around seventy thousand people had been butchered in Jerusalem. The Crusaders thought that figure was completely bonkers and, not wanting bad press at home, they stated that only around ten thousand had been killed (isn't that a relief?) and that as it was a religious war, fought in the name of God, the deaths were unimportant anyway. Jerusalem was back in the hands of the Christians. That was a jolly good thing, wasn't it? That was bloody shagadelic!

No one was actually saying anything about the Sixth Commandment, *Thou shalt not kill*, but then it didn't really matter because they claimed that all those who had been butchered were just infidels. The Sixth Commandment therefore did not apply. Null and void. A lot of old camel-poo. At least that's what the pope said and he should know because he was the pope, after all, and popes know absolutely everything because they contemplate for an impossibly long time while seated on the lav.

At least that's what Pope Pius II probably did before he sat down to write his highly erotic novel, *The Tale of Two Lovers*. That spicy story, as hot as a Scandinavian tub massage with real penises, was released in the 15th century and is therefore probably also now out of print. I think they made an X-rated film of it in Nevada somewhere starring a busty bird named Gertrude Boobstar and the lead male actor had a donger over two feet long, although I don't think it was quite that extensive in the pope's original version of events. Please, please, please, don't think I'm exaggerating here. The pope *really* did write a very naughty book. Someone should republish it. Mills and Boon might be interested, although I think I might have exaggerated the size of the donger — just slightly.

The important point to remember in all this is that while obscure religions such as the Jains appear to be completely potty, they are, at least, peaceful and full of love and without x-rated literature and money-shots, so the next time you see a naked chap brushing away ants with a peacock's bum-feather, whose penis isn't two feet long, it might be a jolly good idea to ask him in and offer a cup of herbal tea because it would be terribly rude to exclude the nude dude.

Chapter Six

The Deep Thought Centre & Other Uncanny Concepts

Noise is stress and noise is everywhere. For the recluse who is seeking quietude in order to be creative, noise is a barrier that has to be fought on almost a daily basis, depending upon the place where the creative thought processes are to be carried out, of course. Yet people hear noises differently. Ask anyone who wears a hearing aid. With modern hearing aids most extraneous noises can be squelched out, leaving only the sounds that are needed, like the voice of the person who is talking to you. Yet with older hearing aids, especially the horrible things that went by wires from the ears down to a box in the top pocket, noise-cancelling was not an option and all kinds of sounds just belted into the eardrums making almost deaf people totally deaf within a few short and horribly clangorous days.

I had a headmaster like that. He was so deaf he'd take the amplifier box out of his pocket and hold it up to my face like a 1950s microphone. Admittedly, it *was* the 1950s. It was really embarrassing. I always felt as if I were giving evidence at a Court of Petty Sessions or something. When I was talking to him I had an almost irresistible urge to stop actually voicing the words at all and just keep mouthing them so that he'd think there was something terribly wrong with his hearing aid and begin shaking it and thumping it with his fists so that he could hear me again. I never quite plucked up the courage to do that because had I done so I would have peed myself laughing and the game would have been up immediately. It wasn't just the prospective flood of hilarious leakage, of course. The headmaster was about ninety feet tall with really long arms so the swing and trajectory of his caning arm would have been devastatingly effective. I'd carefully calculated all that beforehand, naturally, which is something that reclusive little introverted twerps do because they tend to think rather a lot.

For recluses, noise comes as a huge wave. When I walk into a shopping-centre, for example, which is about once every ten years, the noise can sometimes smother me like a prickly blanket of discordant sound — in short, it's a really ugly and annoying cacophony. Yet to most people it's just the chatter of people, the rolling of shopping trolleys, the clink of glasses and cups in the coffee shops and the various tones and beats of music coming simultaneously from half a dozen shops. It's just shopping-centre background-buzz. Most people actually like it. Shopping makes them happy so these sounds are synonymous of that happiness.

Therefore, if noise is stress to introverts and recluses, then quietude is not just silence, it is a place, almost a physical place, where we need to be as often as possible. It's where we live. People often think, and comment aloud, that reclusive little squirts like myself are a really peculiar lot, uncommunicative, moody and anti-social, but only the anti-social part of that is true. I can't speak for all introverts, of course, but generally speaking we are not a moody lot; we just go into what I call the Deep Thought Centre (or DTC for short), and stay there, sometimes for quite a lot of our time. That doesn't mean that we are angry, sad, depressed or experiencing any other kind of negative emotion. Quite the opposite, in fact. In the DTC we are often engaged in intensely creative mental pursuits that can result in many forms of expression such as books, poetry, sculpture or art.

In my experience at least, such creative expression almost always requires a level of quietness and seclusion that is difficult to find in our modern world of motor-mowers, washing machines, irritating neighbours who are hammering, welding or grinding car panels all day, or Christian missionaries knocking on one's door because they're suffering under the completely bonkers delusion that we all need saving from ourselves. They're probably really nice people but have you ever noticed that they are also annoyingly clean? They knock on my door and although I never bother answering I occasionally peek out of the window at them and they are always so pinky-fresh-faced with shiny shampooed hair and eyes like electric eels and I can't help thinking that somehow they have been scrubbed by God and that God has used a really stiff scrubbing brush.

I have to admit that there is a slight element of regret that we as introverts are unable to socialise, mix and mingle like ordinary people, but it's only a very minor element of regret and quickly overcome. Contact and communication through personal interaction can be an effective stimulus for creative endeavour, but despite this, most introverts — certainly this particular introvert — would prefer to find the creative spark in the DTC. It's also here that, apparently, it becomes possible to see into the future.

'Stuff me! Now he's really gone off the rails,' I can hear you hollering.

Now I know this sounds freakishly outlandish, like Benny Hill saying he's giving up chasing girls, but hear me out on this one because for some really silly reason which I'll never be able to understand I have quite a bit of experience of this and frankly at times it scares the poo out of me so perhaps I should explain what happens.

Seclusion and introversion generally breed deep thinkers capable of looking into important matters and intelligently analysing them, but not all such hermits are gentle or capable of deep-seated thought processes. There have been seclusionists in history who adopt the lifestyle either to get closer to whatever god they serve or to enter some kind of ethereal meditative world where they claim to be able to see into the future. Now, I don't actually have any real problem with people seeing into the future. It would be really handy on Melbourne Cup Day, for example, or when the landlord is due to arrive to collect the last six months of back-rent. However, many people and most religions theorise that seeing the future is quite impossible, that the future does not exist yet as time so how can we see into it?

I'm certainly not going to begin deepening the overall crazy-factor of this book by delving into the various theories surrounding nihilism (that human life does not have meaning), existentialism (that humans are aware of their mortality and must make decisions about their lives), and the space-time continuum, (your guess is as good as mine). I'm really far too dense to do that anyway. I'll leave that to major geniuses like the late Stephen Hawking and even later John Lennon, God bless them. *But* (and I put that word in italics because it's a really big *but*) I personally have had some pretty profound experiences with life-and-death type premonitions and they have left me with a few major questions — the sort of questions that can only be answered satisfactorily, I believe, through deep thought and seclusion and as both John and Steve are now deceased it's a bit difficult to ask their opinion even if I had been able to find their email addresses because megastars, and even cooking show hosts, are pretty good at keeping them to themselves. (Although why anyone would actually want to email a cooking show host is quite beyond me).

My personal premonitions have sometimes left me scratching my head in confusion. They seem to be so real. You don't have to take my word for it, my wife will attest to the truth of what I'm about to tell you and I do have some written records such as diary entries etc. I have premonitions but they are neither frequent nor regular. Some seem crazy, and really are, but others usually come true within the space of a few days or up to about two weeks. I just happened to be looking through one of my old journals a few days ago when I found an entry for August 1986 in which I wrote that I had a feeling that there was going to be a major oil tanker accident in Sydney and that someone was going to die. About nine days after that prediction an oil tanker crashed in Sydney, burst into flames and two people were killed. That's all recorded in my journal. I only mention this precognitive incident because it was one of the earliest I experienced although there would be many more.

For some reason many of my predictions have had air accidents as their focus. I can't explain that other than to state that I have always been interested in flying and during my 30s undertook flying training to obtain a private pilot's licence. Incidentally, on my very first solo flight I made history by experiencing a genuine flap failure. Happily I managed to land the Cessna safely without joining the angels. (I had failed miserably to predict *that* one, by the way).

Now I know that lots of people think about the Kennedy family. The bloody demise of John F. in Dallas was one of the most iconic events of the 20th century. Therefore it will probably come as no surprise to learn that many people have had premonitions about the Kennedys. The assassination of John F was predicted by hordes of people, especially in the U.S., and to a lesser extent so was the killing of his brother, Robert.

I never really thought too much about the Kennedys. When John F. was president I was too busy learning how to kiss girls. Events in the Bay of Pigs hardly broke into my new-found concentration on the possibilities of female erotica in the form of high heels, hair ribbons and getting your trembling hand around a girl's shoulders while desperately attempting not to lose the plot of the latest Audie Murphy movie at the Odeon.

Yet in July 1999, long after my cinema-fumbling days, sad to say, were over, and at a time when I had not thought of the Kennedy family for many years, I suddenly dreamed that John F. Kennedy Jnr., the son of President Kennedy, would be killed in a plane crash, as would his wife. I didn't actually know at the time if John F, Jnr. was married. I only remembered him as a child with his father in the Oval Office and saluting at the funeral of the former president in front of a worldwide TV audience of millions.

My dream was very specific. John F. would be flying a light aircraft and it would crash into the sea. By now I was able to differentiate between what was apparently a dream and what was probably a premonition. Dreams came in a very *ad hoc* way and were never repeated. Some dreams were fuzzy and easily forgotten. However, the precognitive dreams were always more detailed, specific, clearer and were usually repeated several times throughout the night, playing over and over in my mind so that when I awoke in the morning they were still clear to me. On the morning of the Kennedy dream I immediately told my wife. By now she was becoming used to my dreams. She gave me that look which said: *Mmmm: another Kennedy disaster. That family is cursed.*

Less than a week later, on 16 July that year, to be precise, John F. Kennedy Jnr., was piloting a Piper Saratoga from Essex County Airport in New Jersey to Martha's Vineyard. On board were three people: Kennedy as pilot, his wife, Carolyn Bessette and sister-in-law, Lauren Bessette. Kennedy was not rated for instrument flying and could therefore fly only under what is known as VFR or visual flight rules. Conditions that day were difficult, obscuring landmarks and making the flight challenging. It was later ascertained by crash investigators that Kennedy had suffered what is known as spatial disorientation while flying over water and had lost control of the Piper. All three on board were killed. This was just one more in a fairly long line of dreams and sudden daytime flashes that appeared to be some kind of precognitive experience. I couldn't understand them and perhaps I didn't want to.

I began thinking a lot about premonitions and why they appeared to be coming to me. What did they mean? I'd seen a television documentary film on the prophesies of Nostradamus and while the film appeared to demonstrate that the ancient philosopher seemed to know what he was talking about, and that many of his premonitions had come true, in reality, when I looked into the case studies a little more deeply, I discovered that his prophesies had been written as rather obtuse quatrains in such a manner that they could easily be interpreted in any number of ways and that they could be prophesies of impending doom and disaster or just pleasant little poems he'd written after drinking too much cask-wine. My premonitions were far more specific and I definitely wasn't writing quatrains about them, and anyway, I'd given up cheap plonk because it gave me migraines that made the zombie 'flu seem like an itchy nose.

Further research revealed that lots of people in the world have premonitions, often very accurate ones, and that organisations had even been set up to harness the power of these premonitions in the hope that somehow, with considerable coordination, some impending disasters, for example, might be prevented. I wasn't too sure that such a concept was even remotely possible but it was evident to me personally that premonitions were real. Perhaps there was something special about spending a lot of time alone and letting one's mind drift aimlessly like the Kon-Tiki raft.

On the very night that the first Stealth bomber in history crashed, I dreamed about it and told my wife the following morning. That night it was on the news. The crash occurred on 23 February, 2008 when the *Spirit of Kansas* a U.S.A.F. B-2 Spirit Stealth heavy bomber took off from Anderson Air-force Base in Guam. Its flight was probably the shortest in Stealth bomber history because it crashed on the runaway minutes later.

The pilots survived, having ejected, although both were injured and subsequently hospitalised. The bomber crash had cost the American taxpayer US$1.4 billion which, when you think about it, is an awful lot of vegan KFC dinner specials.

On another night I dreamed that my brother-in-law's business, a panel-beating workshop, would be destroyed by fire. It was a particularly vivid and colourful dream that repeated over and over that night, and with some hesitation, because this was family, and personal, I told my wife the following morning. Six days later the brother-in-law's workshop burst into flames causing considerable damage including the destruction of two beautiful vintage Ford Model T cars, one of which had been lovingly restored.

The premonitions just kept coming. Not all were accurate, of course, but enough were so precise that they led me to start thinking about what it all meant. I predicted the crash of an aircraft somewhere in the African desert killing everyone on board. Two days later exactly that happened, the white aircraft wreck shown on the news worldwide was like a downed pelican on the desert sands. It made me feel a little wobbly that I'd seen it exactly in my dream and the last thing I need is more wobbles.

Then I dreamed that a fighter aircraft of some kind would dive to the ground killing a lot of people and that the accident would happen in England and very near the sea. In my dream I saw that despite the fact that the plane would be completely destroyed, its pilot would miraculously survive. A day or two later exactly that happened. On 22 August, 2015, an ex-military vintage Hawker Hunter T7 crashed during an air display at Shorenam, fairly close to the beach, killing eleven people on the ground and seriously injuring sixteen others. The pilot, a highly experienced flyer, survived by ejecting from the aircraft. He was badly injured and remained in hospital until the following month. When that news bulletin came on TV my wife and I looked at each other incredulously. How could I have seen that precise event two days before it occurred? In the super-quiet and ordinary world in which we lived none of this was making any sense.

Then I went through a period during which I received no recognisable premonitions until one night in February 2022. The time was almost ten o'clock and I was walking up the passageway to bed. The house was in almost complete darkness with faint illumination coming from just a couple of small night-lights. Then suddenly a face flashed before my eyes. I recognised it immediately. It was the British actor Anna Karen, made famous through her role as 'Olive' in the 1970s sitcom *On the Buses*. The image was so powerful that it literally stopped me in my tracks. I stood there for half a minute, wondering why Anna's face had suddenly flashed before me. There was no apparent reason. I had not thought about *On the Buses* for years and it had been decades since I had watched the program. Yet here she was, in full colour, looking at me through the darkness. Then the image faded and was gone. I went to bed that night, pondered for a while, wondering why I had thought about Anna so unexpectedly, then fell asleep.

The following morning I was seated in a lounge chair when my wife, Lensie, who was reading the news on her mobile phone, looked up and said: 'You'll never guess who died?'

'Don't tell me,' I replied. 'It's Olive from *On the Buses*'.

I'd had another of my premonitions!

One of the things to come out of all this was for me to begin questioning why I was having these premonitions. I'm just an ordinary person, a bit weird at times, I know, and not a lot of people understand what's going on inside my radish-fuelled brain, but something was evidently happening. There was something buzzing away in there and it was tuned to a strange frequency. Was it the fact that I like to be alone so much, lost in my own thought processes, silent, thinking deeply about many issues, researching for my work as a writer, historian and novelist? Did this kind of deep thinking process open up some kind of portal into the future? I really didn't know although I gave it considerable thought. What I do know is that I saw these things before they happened which means one of two things. Everything is preordained to happen and is therefore predictable in some way, even though it might only be through some esoteric means such as precognitive dreams, or: time actually flows in *both* directions. In Einstein's Theory of Relativity, time is distorted by motion and gravity so there really is no restriction on time flowing both backward and forward. Is there even a 'backward' and 'forward' in time or does it all just swirl about like one of those multi-flavoured Mr Whippy ice-creams? All this, of course, is way beyond my limited understanding of the Space Time Continuum, but if geniuses like Einstein believed that it's possible for time to flow backwards, I'm going to go along with that concept and flow with it because I'm definitely seeing things in the future and they are flowing back and unconscionably bumping into me.

There is a third hypothesis, of course, and that is the possibility that I'm as bonkers as Peter the Hermit.

I'm not claiming to have super powers or anything like it. Some people say that I'm psychic but I believe that we are all capable of precognitive experiences. It's just a matter, I believe, of reflection, quietude, and a willingness to allow ourselves to be as divorced as possible from our physical realities. In short, to be alone.

If for a single moment they can be taken seriously, astrologers have predicted that the 'Age of Aquarius' will bring about the expansion of consciousness and that many people will experience mental enlightenment well in advance of the rest of humanity and be recognised as leaders — precognition being a possible part of that little fantasy. I'm not saying that a plonker from Wales comes into that category, but this mystical Age of Aquarius is said to hold much promise for the future.

No one really knows when the Age of Aquarius actually began. Theories abound and some hold to the belief that it goes back in time to about 1433, which would make it rather a lengthy period of promised enlightenment, especially when the world at that time still had to get through some of its darkest periods including the rather bloody Middle Ages, witch-hunts, the Crusades, Vlad the Impaler, the Black Death and Donald Trump on his caddy's day off.

By the way, I once read that Vlad the Impaler, who had a penchant for pushing long poles up people's bums and then planting them in the ground like runner-beans, was actually related to our late Queen Elizabeth. Perhaps she should have bribed somebody to have the bugger deleted from the family tree, although I have to admit that going back that far it's probably a very tenuous relationship.

I have to be truthful here. I had no knowledge whatever of the Age of Aquarius until I heard the song on my car-radio and even then I didn't know what it meant or, in fact, what the lyrics of the song really were. You know what those 1960s car-radios were like. There was usually more static than a Chinese nylon shirt, and with all the clunking engine noise, rattling, roaring and gasping from my clapped-out 1964 Triumph Herald — especially when the clutch-plate was in the process of noisily committing suicide — it was really difficult to hear the words correctly. I thought they were singing. 'This is the dawning of the age of a hairy arse … the age of a hairy arse … '. You know the lyrics so I expect you will understand my confusion. I also had to question why a hairy arse would need its own Age.

It's now been decades (hairy-arsed decades in fact) since I had my first premonition and while a great many of them have apparently not come true, a sufficient number of them actually having taken place has made me think that something really interesting is going on and I wish I could have some kind of premonition about what the Dickens that might be. I know it's somewhat esoteric but it's probably not as weird as seeing ghosts, for example, or talking to dead people like my lovely Auntie Beatrice, God bless her. If there is any relation between being alone, existing rather a lot in a quiet, contemplative state, and being able somehow to see into the future, I have never been able to correlate it with any precision. However, I do know that when I have premonitions that come true, then it is usually when I am not under work pressure or under the stress of meeting a publisher's deadline, for example, or preparing for an important book launch or media interview. Premonitions can come colourfully, sometimes almost explosively in dreams, but they usually appear when I am calm, relaxed and tranquil. From this I can only theorise that the dreams come to me because my mind is open and unstressed and there are, perhaps, elements in that contemplative state that open up possibilities of the mind we have yet to understand.

Chapter Seven

All the Things You Wanted to Know About Reclusive Vegans
(but were too terrified to ask)

Samual Taylor Coleridge loved his fruit but would only eat it while it was still attached to a tree. How warped is that? The ancient Incas, who sadly did not have the luxury of Google watches, measured time by how long it took to boil a potato. Therefore the universe in their time would have been about five hundred billion trillion potato-boils old. (Or possibly older if they were Dutch Creams which take a little longer to boil especially if they haven't been peeled).

You see what I'm getting at. Fruit and vegetables are not just fruit and vegetables. They have a really important place in the universe.

Life as a vegan is bloody confusing and it's even more confusing when one is an introverted vegan recluse. We live in a world that is full of questions. We wonder, for example, why it is that so many people like to place a small cemetery on their dinner table every night. I'm not being melodramatic, really. Most people would not even understand why such a thought would pop into anyone's head, but for me and others like me it's a question we often ask ourselves. It's especially confusing for us when we know that a significant percentage of the world's population is educated and intelligent, so why is it that these sparky-bright people, many of whom hold intellectual jobs such as university professors or similar, have been unable to fathom out that dead things on pretty plates, even when accompanied by instant gravy and bake-at-home rolls, do not necessarily make an edible meal and they certainly don't make an ethical one.

We are weird; vegans are completely bonkers, and if you believe some of the leading journals and political figures of the world, especially a number of really red-faced Australian and American political figures with pregnancy bag stomachs, then vegan introverted recluses are evil incarnates contaminating our otherwise nice clean and healthy society. What could be more stupid than eating lettuce and carrot-sticks all your life? It might be all right for rabbits or tortoises but for normal people, going vegan would be really silly, like trying to build the Brooklyn Bridge out of Lego blocks.

I should mention, by the way, that just today, while doing some research at the Internet Archive, I noticed that someone has actually made a horror movie featuring nothing but Lego blocks. I know that horror movies are supposed to be horrifying but just that concept alone gives me the serious willies. Perhaps a certain former U.S. president should have attempted to build his Mexican wall in Lego. At least it would have been colourful!

Vegan craziness is not all one-sided, of course. There are two sides to this looking-glass and vegans are well known for shaking their heads in wonder at the confusing proclivities of some members of the carnivore community. Vegans have real trouble trying to understand, for example, why anyone, even if they are Scottish and psychologically certified as being perfectly non-bonkers, would want to eat haggis. In Veganland this is one of life's more baffling enigmas. It's a complete mystery to most people why the Scots would ceremoniously pipe-in a tray of animal offal consisting of a sheep's heart, lungs and liver all nicely stuffed into a sheep's stomach that has recently been ripped from some unfortunate animal. It turns my tummy just to think about it. Yet the Jocks, God bless their colourful little hoses (that's 'socks' to all you non-Jocks out there) take it one step further and serve the mess with a plate of turnip. Now although I'm a vegan I'm not too keen on turnip but even *that* humble root deserves better than that. It might also be interesting to mention that while the Scots love their haggis it has actually been banned completely in the U.S.A. since the 1970s. This is quite surprising given that Americans love to hunt just about everything that walks the earth and when successful usually consume their 'kills' down to its moles, warts, testicles and lower bowels where all the shit lives, so it's a little puzzling that they would actually ban a perfectly good belly-bag of sheep's lung.

I once attended a Caledonian dinner, trying to do the right thing for my newly acquired father-in-law who was of Jock descent and loved his Highland flings. I had recently married about the most beautiful young lady on the entire planet and was trying desperately to fit into the family unit — part of which, sadly, was attending a dinner where haggis would be served and the Highland pipes would be wailing — to my ears at least — like cats recently castrated without an anaesthetic. Yet I did my duty and went along, not knowing what to expect because even the thought of attending such a function had never before entered my tiny Welsh brain — even for a fragment of a second. I should add that I did not wear a kilt or sporran, or hoses, largely because my knees are too white and sporrans remind me quite terrifyingly of external pubic clusters. Being a self-conscious super-sensitive type of chap I wasn't quite ready to take up *that* particular challenge and couldn't possibly imagine what I would have looked like while wobbling around a Scottish hall in a wobbly sporran with a thicker than normal set of representative pubic hairs on public display, especially when they had been made of dead rabbit fur!

I was also at a loss as to what I would have done, while wearing a kilt, should I have needed to wee during the evening which would have been a natural occurrence as there was a fair amount of drinking involved. I never really figured that out until years later when I attended a Scottish field-day and when I went to the loo there were three Scottish gentlemen standing at the urinal, each enjoying a well deserved pee because the McEwans beer had been flowing well that day. I was quite astonished to discover that the kilts had been pulled up in front, the man-knickers (which, by the way, are underpants *not* fitted with Y-fronts) placed into the 'drain position' (tucked beneath the bollocks) and the sporrans had been roughly thrust to one side where they resembled rather hairy bum-bags. At least in that position they didn't get wet, which is fortunate because piss-wet sporrans smell a bit like mouldy dog's balls. This also proved to me without a shadow of doubt that Scotsmen actually *do* wear man-knickers beneath their kilts so almost without knowing it I had solved one of the greatest mysteries of the age.

Anyway, to return to my night of the Caledonia ball. When the haggis was finally piped-in with all its amazing Highland ceremony I was expecting to see something *really* spectacular on the plate, something almost noble, in fact. However, when I leaned over and looked more closely I was completely astounded to discover that the much-vaunted haggis looked like a lump of dead turkey-stuffing with an uncanny resemblance to a fur-ball coughed up by a camel. It was really good that all the people present in the hall were Christians because they needed a miracle to make this lump of dromedary-upchuck go around two hundred hungry Jocks, all of whom, for some unfathomable reason, were desperately fingering their sporrans as they waited for a quick taster. It's entirely possible, of course, that the sporrans had unaccountably been infested by fleas. Vegans, naturally, never have to worry about Scottish haggis, at least not until the Linda McCartney company comes up with a soy variety.

However, I shall move on from the mysteries of the Highlands to examine the burning philosophical questions surrounding really strange vegans. These are, of course, where did vegans come from and why do they all look like born-again aliens with shiny bright skins and bums to die for?

Well, vegetarianism has been around for millennia but in the western world it is a fairly modern phenomenon. I only use that term because it is unusual in the west for anyone not to eat dead animals so I guess it is some kind of phenomenon. We have been eating animals since we first came into being when we lived in caves and hunted wild creatures for food. Why should we now change?

There is a fairly serious school of thought that people only become vegans because they are the first people served their lunches on long distance airline flights. For some obscure reason anyone pre-ordering a vegan meal on these flights receives a little plastic tray with a plastic knife and fork a whole hour before anyone else on the flight is served. This is great if you are a vegan, and hungry, but often leads to envious and hostile looks from other economy-class passengers as you tuck smugly into your baked potato with Mexican beans and broccoli, all nicely overcooked, squishy and microwave-reheated to absolute imperfection. Yet I am here to disavow completely that this is the reason why so many people are today becoming vegans or vegetarians. It has absolutely nothing to do with airline food, even when they were actually serving food on aircraft before the infestation of the planet by some sucker-headed microscopic bug with the rather odd ability to reduce the size of men's penises. (That's just a fun fact you can Google). The reasons for our growing vegan population of today actually go far back to a period that even predates the Wright brothers — neither of whom, by the way, was vegan.

In this brief outline I'm not going to travel back into ancient times to talk about all the religious vegetarians in history, mainly because that would be so boring it would be like watching looped repeats of *The Lone Ranger*.

However, Mayans and Aztec children are reported to have been vegetarian until the age of about six years. After that it didn't matter any more because their parents could not exactly promote a gentle loving lifestyle or raise their kids to have compassion and sound social values when they continued to tear the living hearts out of their enemies during rather noisy sacrificial ceremonies. All in the name of jolly good fun, of course.

Benjamin Franklin was a vegetarian when he was just sixteen years of age but we can probably assume that this was just a wee bit of teenage rebellion as he later returned to steak and chips with the kind of carnivorous gusto reserved only for bum-eating forest trolls. Franklin did have a redeeming feature, however. In later life he was the person who is said to have introduced tofu to the United States although I'm not entirely sure how that would have gone down with the beaver-hatted brigade like Davy Crockett. I'm fully aware that many people, especially those in the Wild West of 21st century America, will have cursed Franklin for having introduced tofu to American tables as there are people in the world who believe that tofu tastes almost exactly like a bowl of boiled Gestapo knuckledusters.

The Choctaw Native North Americans were almost totally vegetarians. I love these guys. Their shelters were made of wood, mud and bark rather than animal skins popularised by Hollywood and Kevin Costner doing the Salsa with a wolf. Their principal food was not bison but corn, pumpkin, beans, wild fruit, nuts and seeds. (God that's making me hungry). Even their clothing was animal-free and they refused on principle to wear birds' feathers in their headdresses.

It comes as no surprise that these peaceful, spiritual, gentle people would later be forcibly removed from their homes (by carnivore soldiers) and set upon what became known as the 'Trail of Tears' to Oklahoma, then considered to be a barren wasteland suitable only for 'Injuns' (and presumable vegans). Many died en route. There was sound reason for naming the trail.

The Apache, however, were the complete opposite, and while they may have been a 'spiritual' people they were also responsible for killing tens of thousands of bison and selling their fur and tongues to traders for a mere bottle of whisky. Combined with white hunters, the mass slaughter of bison was one of the greatest wildlife tragedies in the history of the planet and almost led to the extinction of the species. It's happening today in Australia as trees are cleared for housing development and squillions of creatures are wiped out, joining the millions of kangaroos shot and killed in an atrocious, government-approved annual cull that goes on for months.

For years after the bison slaughter, Native North American tribes prayed to their deities and danced the hugely illegal Ghost Dance, hoping for a return of the bison. They never came, of course. They had gone for good, like cigarette advertising, although that would not have worried the Choctaws too much. Tobacco smoking was both a treasured pastime and a ceremonial event and they didn't need any Foxtel advertising to tell them that it was great, sexy and attracted women like dung-beetles to mustang poo. A white man was always welcome in the Choctaw camp because it meant that the peace-pipe could be dragged out and passed around and everyone could have a jolly good puff.

Leonardo da Vinci was also a vegetarian. Painting the Sistine Chapel roof, he'd be popping olives and slurping cheap Italian plonk, although how he did that while dangling upside-down at fifty feet is another of God's little miracles that was probably organised by the pope.

In 1847 the Vegetarian Society was founded in England, largely coming about through the influence of a man with the rather unfortunate name of William Cowherd, a reverend who had founded the Bible Christian Church in 1809. Members of the society were dismally afflicted with the reverend's genealogical misfortune and largely became known as Cowherdites which, as vegetarians, is *exactly* the opposite of what they would have liked to have been called. Even Tofuites would have been better. I'm not making this up just for a laugh, by the way. It's all absolutely true.

It really surprised me to learn that during the Victorian era no fewer than twenty-six vegetarian cookbooks were published. Fourteen of these were written by women who were actually at the forefront of promoting cruelty-free food. Queen Victoria was not one of them, of course. Vicky was probably the complete opposite of a vegetarian. She ate tens of thousands of calories per day, most of which had been unwillingly donated by the animal world. That's probably why she ended up looking like one of those enormous blimps her favourite cousins in Germany would later build to bomb the crap out of London during the First World War.

In 1870 a vegetarian restaurant opened in Manchester which would have been little short of miraculous. Another followed in London, apparently opening its doors in 1880, just in time to enjoy the patronage of people like Jack the Ripper — although it's probably unlikely that Jack was vegan.

And then came Mahatma Gandhi who arrived in London in the 1940s seeking to establish independence for India. The British, most of whom had never seen an Indian, let alone Gandhi, had even toyed with the idea of stringing him up as a traitor. That would have been a jolly good wheeze, eh what! And then this frail little '*dhobi wallah*', as he was cuttingly referred to in posh English upper circles, had suddenly stepped off the number 76 bus at the Strand wearing nothing but a pair of worn sandals and a grubby bed-sheet with some peculiar stains on it. People were literally rubbing their eyes in astonishment. There was also considerable press speculation about whether or not he was wearing any man-knickers and would he be asked to meet the queen.

It came as no surprise to the British public to learn that this rather 'scrofulous little bounder' with round glasses and a gentle smile was actually a vegetarian. Kids turned to their mothers and asked, 'What's a vegetablebum Mum?' The mothers didn't know either but it sounded damned foreign, just what you would expect from someone from Bombay or Cawnpaw or wherever the skinny little four-eyed runt had come from. The major advantage of Gandhi's visit came when bureaucrats in Whitehall were later dreaming up ways to save vast amounts of money on the newly minted National Health Scheme. They thought of Gandhi and his cheap little wire-framed glasses that had probably been cobbled together from a wire coat-hanger in some *punkah-wallah's* garden-shed and suddenly a thought-bubble exploded above their tiny heads. That was *exactly* the design they needed for National Health glasses: cheap, ugly and completely unwearable. Unless you were John Lennon, of course who instantly turned them from being hideously hilarious to legendarily iconic.

George Bernard Shaw was one of the most outspoken activists for vegetarianism and I expect he would have been really annoyed to find that he was dead when the first aptly named Cranks vegetarian restaurant opened in London in 1961. Several more Cranks restaurants opened in later years and it comes as no surprise that they were thus named because even at that time of liberated thought, knicker-throwing and *Jumpin' Jack Flash* being a *Gas-Gas-Gas*, it was still considered to have been completely bonkers even to think about going into a restaurant and actually paying for food that was not meat. After all, you could pick up potato peelings in restaurant garbage bins any day of the week so why pay for them?

I remember many years ago I had been commissioned to write a history of a small city called Maryborough in Queensland and while working on the research for that project I came upon a short news article in a microfilm of a Victorian era newspaper called the *Maryborough Chronicle*. The story was actually about one of the town's councillors who had just arrived at the city hall to attend some kind of gala function, and at the front door of the hall he had been met by a journalist from the newspaper. They chatted for a while, the journalist no doubt licking the stub of his pencil and scribbling notes about the ceremony that was about to take place and also the grand ball and dinner that would follow. It was quite an occasion. It was almost as if Queen Victoria had suddenly arrived in town (without Albert, of course because he had kicked the royal bucket in 1861) and members of the press were completely in awe. There were to be fireworks afterwards. As the conversation drew to a close the journalist casually remarked (no doubt with a touch of envy because it promised to be a significant banquet), 'Have a pleasant dinner, Councillor. I think I can smell roast beef and Yorkshire pudding.'

Well the councillor, somewhat rounded in the tummy and suitably bewhiskered, as was the fashion at that time for prosperous townsmen, quickly responded. 'Dinner my boy! Good God man, I've already had my dinner. Before coming here this evening I dined sumptuously on three bananas.'

I particularly remember that news report and the councillor's use of the word 'sumptuously'. It all sounded so thrillingly brave to me.

The councillor, it transpired, to the complete amazement of the entire town, the colony of Queensland and probably all Australia was actually admitting that he was a vegetarian!

Stuff-a Duck!

Australia didn't just take pause. It stopped in shock. A town councillor had actually stated that he did not eat meat. It was sacrilegious. Even Jesus had eaten dead things! God probably did too, for all anyone knew. Who was this jumped-up pen-pushing tosser who was candidly admitting that he no longer supported the cattle industry, or the pig industry, or fowls, or sheep, or any kind of industry apart, perhaps, from banana growers. It was a crying shame. Something would have to be done. Ring the church bells really loudly. Light the warning fires along the clifftops. Gather the mobs and light paraffin torches so that everyone can look suitably evil as they dash around town and country lanes late at night, baying for blood and hunting down every living vegetarian in sight.

Being a vegetarian in the late 1890s was probably not quite such a highly strung activity as my imagination may suggest, but the fact remains: the councillor had admitted to refusing to eat meat. Tongues were certainly wagging. However, as far as I'm concerned, for someone holding public office at that time, it was a Vegan Victoria Cross moment.

Vegans and vegetarians were a rarity then and although things have improved we still remain at the fringe of society. In fact we may never have been called vegans at all. The term is, by world evolutionary standards, fairly recent. Veganism remained almost unknown until after the Second World War. I was born in 1949 and if someone had asked me as a child what a vegan was I would only have been able to guess. Was it someone who came from Las Vegas? Was there a planet somewhere in the Milky Way named Vegan and, if so, were the residents Vegans? And, if so, that begged another question. Should the Milky Way actually be renamed the Tofu Way? It was all very confusing.

Just about everyone was completely ignorant of the term, vegan. Up until the 1940s, in fact, there was no such word in existence. People who shunned meat, eggs and dairy from their diet and refused on principal to wear leather products, wool or other animal derivatives were then known only as lunatic asylum inmates. I'm exaggerating again but you get my drift. Actually, even though vegans existed they did not know what to call themselves; there was no umbrella under which to hide. No tribe to join. They were a nameless, faceless, group of lunatics who did not even group, largely because a lot of them were recluses like me. They were just individuals struggling to understand why they were so different in a world that shunned them. Gay people were often bashed when they were snogging on park benches. Unnamed vegans were probably not treated quite so violently, largely because they did not gather in public spaces to kiss each other, but they were subjected to significant ridicule nonetheless.

At first, adherents to the practice of dairy-free and egg-free vegetarianism came up with the name of 'dairybans', but that was about as potent as a eunuch's reproductive organ. It also did not tell the full story in a single word which, as any marketing and public relations guru will tell you, was obviously the desired outcome. Other titles bandied about included 'vitans' or 'benevores', somehow suggesting vitality and physical benefits from not being carnivorous, but these proposed titles were also marketing disasters and therefore quickly abandoned. It was a difficult decision to make. What does one call oneself when one does not eat animals or use animal products? Had I been on the committee I might have suggested the name of 'quickducks' — a cunningly clever double entendre intended to bring to light the plight of ducks at that time when they were so popular on many dinner tables and had to move really quickly to avoid that particular fate, but also because adherents to a non-animal diet would constantly have been ducking beneath tables to escape the verbal and physical abuse being dished out by animal farmers, abattoir workers and rather irate eiderdown salesmen.

In the end, a small committee which included the pioneering animal rights campaigner, Donald Watson, decided that those who disavowed all kinds of animal products would henceforth be known as vegans. There! We had a name. We were like a football team, working and pulling together for a better cause. Crikey, a team! We could even have had hot and hairy showers together. Wouldn't that have been fun? The only problem with this concept is that most of the newly branded vegans were, like me, introverts and recluses with an aversion to hot, hairy, communal showers and there were so few of us we could hardly make up a cricket team. With such a minuscule clan of social misfits it was almost impossible to begin the vegan revolution. That's why it's taken so long for us to come out of the shadows.

Veganism is a kind of transcendence, although that sounds boringly superior and condescending when it's not meant to be.

It's just so difficult to describe what goes on in the vegan's brain. We are a strange bunch. I guess you could call us modern day Hobbits but rarely do we have hair growing between our toes nor do we disappear when we put on our wedding rings. If we did we would wear them all the time.

At least I would!

The difference between vegans and those who eat the dead is that we have more concerns about our fellow creatures. We think more about their welfare, happiness, health and care. I'm not overstating this but it is similar to the concern most people have for their children. It is a deep love of all animal life that is intensified rather heartrendingly because animals, unlike most children, are treated so badly everywhere in the world, killed in their millions every day for food or fun, for their fur, their testicles, skin, blood, for experiments, for their tusks, penises, bladders, horns, or just out of sheer maliciousness. It's almost impossible to believe that a large number of Chinese chappies still think that snorting powered rhino horn will give them an erection you could bounce marbles off. I mean, really! This is the 21st century, guys! Get real. Go to the chemist and buy a packet of little blue pills. And then, of course, there's the whole new development of animal body parts being harvested for human organ transplants — an entirely different ethical issue we will have to address fully in the very near future.

Animals have few defences against human malignancy. They are easy prey to our hunger for death. Veganism is just one person's personal journey into a strange world where the emphatic core to one's existence is to attempt to do as little damage as possible to all animals. I call it strange because once the journey has been undertaken, life changes completely. Nothing is ever the same again. Non-vegan friends and even family melt away as if they are ice-blocks taken out of a refrigerator during a Mumbai summer. They don't understand the basic ethic of veganism and think that people who suddenly become vegans are afflicted with some incurably contagious disease and if anyone catches it their bums might drop off.

But here are some really weird facts about vegans. Firstly, we are human. I know it's hard to believe but that's true. Speculative aliens maybe, but born on Earth with a sufficient amount of human DNA to qualify for participation in the government pension scheme, but only if we are over sixty-seven years of age with a plethora of suitable wrinkles, and are the proud owners of knees that have the rather annoying habit of locking up suddenly like a Robbin Island cell-block.

Secondly, vegans, generally, are rather bright. I'm not saying that because I'm a vegan. Even my maths teacher at Clevedon College, God bless him, would testify, if he's still somewhat improbably alive, that I was the dullest of his trigonometry students, largely because his nose was so huge that it transfixed me and I rarely heard a word he said. It was so enormous that when he turned to the blackboard he caused a wind that in turn caused a weather pattern of its own making that in turn caused a cyclone that later destroyed the entire city of Darwin half a planet away. It was truly awesome. The nose, I mean, not the weather or the destruction of Darwin. It caused a butterfly effect. They even made a movie about it. The butterfly effect that is, not my teacher's nose.

Some people have claimed online that those who bring up their darling little rubber-stamp-kids as vegans are being cruel to them — that children who lack a meat diet are slower, less interested and undernourished. All I can intelligently add to that widespread belief is, 'pish, tosh and gibberish'.

Kids brought up on a vegan diet are generally healthier, not only as children but also in later life. Studies have demonstrated that they are also smarter. A British study has shown that intelligent kids are far more likely to become vegetarians or vegans and the higher the I.Q. the higher are the chances that they will adopt a meat-free diet as adults.

Vegans are also, generally speaking, hugely aware of the many ways they are assisting to ensure the protection of our environment and to plan for the future needs of a rapidly burgeoning world population.

For example, the massively expensive and influential sales and marketing efforts of meat producing enterprises rarely mention the devastation caused to the land through intensive cattle raising or the inequality of land usage between crops grown for human consumption and land used to graze cattle. Precise data is difficult to come by, but researchers have demonstrated that on one hectare of fertile land only about 187 kilograms of beef can be raised while up to 220,000 potatoes may be grown on the same size of land. If accurate, this is damning evidence that we are wasting the world's resources when in the future we will need to feed billions more people. Apparently these would mainly be call-centre workers who appear to be multiplying at an alarming rate.

Twenty vegetarians could live off the one hectare of land that would support only one carnivore. If every American, for example, reduced his or her meat intake by just ten per cent, then about twelve million tonnes of grain would be saved in feeding cattle. This could then be used to feed up to sixty million people which means that we would end hunger among call centre workers which would be a jolly good thing I should think! Cattle flatulence has been calculated to cause as much as thirty-five percent of the world's greenhouse gasses. My God! Are we really going to murder our ozone layer with cow farts?

The well known, hugely amusing and much loved Ronald McDonald (there have actually been dozens of 'Ronalds' over the years) later became a vegetarian. It's possible that Ronnie's smell had something to do with his dramatic change of culinary intake. Research has demonstrated that men who avoid red meat have a more pleasant body odour and are more attractive to the opposite sex. Fortunately it works for women too so two vegans bonking like bunnies will smell really pleasant. People who are vegetarians have better sex lives than carnivores and this is all down to certain plant-based hormone levels. Perhaps I should email this to the plonkers in China who still persist in eating tiger's testicles and powdered penises to get their rocks off. How embarrassing must that be? You get home after a hard day's work at the office and the wife asks you what you had for lunch and if you're the honest type you have to admit that you ate a tiger's dick!

I wonder how that would make you smell.

And while we are on the really fascinating subject of body aromas it's well known that vegan farts don't smell. Actually that's a complete fabrication perpetrated solely by me but it's a beautiful lie and I love telling the story. I had a friend and colleague who worked with me at one of the television stations where I was ungainfully employed during the early 1980s making television commercials and documentaries. I'd recently become a vegetarian which was a bit strange even for the '80s but most of the people working at the station were creatives and the concept of vegetarianism wasn't too far-fetched for them, even in those days. My colleague, however, was intrigued and wanted to know what the principal benefit might be for becoming a vegetarian. With a straight face I told him that since I had taken the non-cruelty pledge the principal benefit for me was that my farts no longer had an offensive smell. Well, that stopped him in his tracks, literally. He turned in the corridor and looked at me completely askance. 'Really?' he queried, astonished.

I just nodded confirmation, like a sage dispensing age-old wisdom. After that the word got around the station and people would come to me and ask what my farts actually smelt like. I'd invent all kinds of imaginative aromas. Wild chamomile. Vanilla essence. Ageing teddybears that had been left in the rain and then dried with a hair-dryer. Fresh toast with Vegemite. Dried cloves. A new car's glove compartment. Fig jam spread on rye bread. I was having fun.

Years later I was with the same colleague in a car at the historic Nanango goldfields. The car was being driven by a member of the local council and I was there to interview him and write a story on the history of the goldfields. I was using a small tape recorder which I'd inadvertently left running when I got out of the car to open a farm-gate. Days later when I listened to the recording while writing the story I came to the part when I had left the car. The recording was clear. As soon as I had walked away from the vehicle and out of earshot the driver had said. 'Nice chap. Seems to know his history.'

My colleague had responded. 'Yes, a nice chap. He's vegetarian you know. Their farts don't stink!'

Even today vegans are treated as if they ritually perform human sacrifices around druid stones at the summer equinox. It's almost as if we worship the devil or perform witchcraft, casting spells with dried toads, nettles and Chinese baby formula. If this were the Middle Ages all vegans would be rounded up and burned at the stake, or stretched horribly on the racks of the Catholic Inquisition which would have had the rather disconcerting effect of making you six inches taller while simultaneously popping out all your fillings and sending them ricocheting around the torture chamber like machine-gun bullets.

In fact there has never been an age when vegans or introverted recluses have been accepted into society as normal people.

I actually don't know why reclusive vegan introverts like me are still regarded as being from Tolkien's Middle Earth. More and more people are becoming vegetarian and vegan. There are more than two million of us now in Australia alone. Germany for example, a nation which has a history of hunting, shooting, killing, maiming, and making really nasty sausages from smoked blood and farmyard scrapings, is now embracing the vegetarian ethos with considerable gusto. It's a hopeful sign that the world is changing for the better and that animals can have something to look forward to. Some fairly recent statistics demonstrate that about twelve per cent of German women and three per cent of German men are now vegetarian, which is progress, of sorts, but clearly many German men are still clinging to their really big blood sausages in a way that almost suggests something masochistically self-fulfilling.

Travelling east, the situation for vegans becomes a little more difficult as we move deeper into the heart of traditional Catholic territory. Da Vinci might have embraced a cruelty-free lifestyle but it would certainly not have been approved by the Church. In Poland, for example, a deeply Catholic country where traditional animal foods remain a staple of everyday life, becoming a vegan is still regarded as an action for which you should be excommunicated. Well, I'm probably exaggerating a little there but only slightly. There *are* vegetarians in Poland but they have to suffer a kind of Middle Ages oppression. Newspapers refuse to take advertising for meat-free events and if you go into a Polish restaurant and ask for a tofu curry it's likely that you will be served with turkey curry instead.

Catholics, historically, have never been too keen on vegetarians especially vegetarians who also believe in reincarnation. What an abomination that would be! The Catharists in France were persecuted and murdered *en masse* at the behest of the pope during the eleventh and twelfth centuries, principally because they were vegetarians who apparently reincarnated at the drop of a hat. Exact numbers are not known but it's possible that up to 200,000 men, women and children were slaughtered for their beliefs, 20,000 in one day alone. Many were burned alive in huge bonfires lit especially for the occasion. It was like a mad Guy Fawkes night with live Guys. Yet it's little wonder the Church went after the Cathars with such grisly determination. Not only did Cathars refute God's right to take the lives of animals for food, but they also refused to believe in baby christening, the Last Supper and 'transubstantiation' — the concept of miraculously changing the body of Christ into Communion bread or of his blood suddenly becoming claret. I mean really! I know it's all a bit far-fetched, but what did the Cathars *think* was going to happen to them?

Even today, living the life of a vegan recluse is like stumbling onto a *Monty Python* movie set. I keep looking around for Brian being harassed by crowds of Christian followers demanding to know if he really is the Saviour flavour of the month, until Brian becomes really pissed off and tells them that he *is* the Saviour and would they now all fuck off. That's his terminology, by the way, not mine.

Speaking about *Monty Python* scenarios reminds me to mention that I had once been asked to present some kind of prize to an abattoir that functioned at a small town in Queensland. I mean really, Charlie Chaplin could have made a silent movie about this and everyone would have been toppling off their cinema seats laughing. When I was told by my boss that I had to present the prize, it was a bit like that moment in the *Life of Brian* when a Roman centurian is introduced and his name is Biggus Dickus. Everybody was snickering but poor old Biggus Dickus couldn't understand why. That was me when told I had to present the award. It was my task to make this presentation because I was working for the television station that broadcast into the area and the station had sponsored the prize. I drove up to the abattoir with considerable trepidation. The prize was some kind of rod-shaped thing that rose into the air at one end, I can't recall exactly, but I think it was supposed to represent, in three dimensional form, a steady rise in production and sales. It actually reminded me a golden dildo mounted on a small wooden base, and so the correlation to Centurian Biggus Dickus was complete. It was covered with a glass dome that was probably plastic or something equally as crass. I'm fairly sure the prize was not actually real gold but just cheap gilt, the kind you buy in a trophy shop along with amateur hockey awards and swimming shields for nine-year-olds.

As I slammed the car door, golden dick in hand, the general manager rushed out, face flushed either with excitement or an over-abundance of cholesterol-induced blood pressure, and grasped my one free hand in his meaty paw. 'Come and look around the works,' he gasped, eyes wide with orgasmic excitement while he rapaciously eyed my golden donger. This was a big day in the history of the meat-works. They had a dinner planned in my honour. It wasn't every day that some weedy little chap arrives on your blood-soaked doorstep with a big gilt thingy in hand. What an occasion!

I didn't have much of a chance to answer: the golden dick was suddenly snatched away and I was left standing in the cowshit-encrusted dust, forgotten, at least for the moment, as the G.M. disappeared once more into the beating heart of the death camp to show everyone the wonderful trophy that would now take pride of place in the boardroom. It would sit there in the centre of the enormous boardroom table like some monstrous golden erection, testament to the virility of meat. The vision of it was quite stupefying.

It was at that moment I saw a slim chance of escape. While the sounds of the cattle crying as they were being killed with stun-guns poured out from the doors of the factory, I hopped back into my little Ford escort panel van and beetled away into the steamy afternoon, hoping that I would soon be lost in the hot Australian dust before I was found to be missing from the presentation ceremony and luncheon that had been planned for months. It was a bloody narrow escape and it's not often that you can say that literally.

I bet there wasn't any tofu on the luncheon menu either.

Recluses usually have a lot of time to think. Alone in our own little world we contemplate our navels perhaps a little too much. Generally speaking we are irritatingly well read. That's probably because we spend such a lot of time alone, but it also means that we have rather a lot of time to philosophise. Listening to the philosophies of lone vegan hermits is perhaps a strange thing to do. I mean, what could anyone learn from a socially awkward vegan geek with embarrassingly narrow shoulders and a predilection for Puccini's arias?

Recluses delve into themselves, sometimes not liking what they see but at least they're able to be honest about who they are and their personal values. I've always found that it is really easy to become lost in the labyrinth of who we are. We are not easy creatures to understand and everyone is different which makes the task far more complex as we often judge ourselves by the values and actions of others.

Ethical vegans look into themselves and find a joy in their existence and way of life that flows directly from their compassion towards animals. They are *connected* to the animal world in a way that non-vegans have great difficulty in understanding because we in the western world are conditioned from birth by what I call the Great Disconnect.

Most people are connected to animals only in a way that develops a means by which the animals may serve them. Santa Claus is a typical example. I have absolutely nothing against Father Christmas, at least not much. I sat on his knee once and asked for an air-rifle but what I got was a pair of striped pyjamas, a gold-coloured dressing gown that looked like a posh smoking jacket for tall people, and a stocking containing oranges and walnuts which I successfully peeled and cracked respectively with my penknife while also succeeding in cutting my thumb to the bone which was frightfully irritating.

But Father Christmas is a typical example of the Great Disconnect. He might love Rudolf and all the other reindeer in his sleigh-team but has absolutely no hesitation in harnessing them up every year so that he can dash around the world delivering hideous dressing gowns to idiotic little boys called Anthony.

Most ethical vegans reject all forms of animal exploitation and also their unfortunate status as a commodity. I know that sounds radical right now. We 'own' animals and we should have the right to treat them within the laws and use them as 'God' intended, as the old saying goes. If we follow that line of reasoning then we have to step back in time to the days of the African slaves when they were being kidnapped from their villages, placed in irons, transported on board hideous slaving ships, sold on the open market, still in chains, then worked as nothing better than farm animals, whipped when it was thought necessary and imprisoned on plantations for their entire lives and the lives of their children and grandchildren. And what is really depressing about all this is that everything we did to the slaves was not only legal, but for years — decades — it was also considered by the vast majority of the white population to be morally right and proper and was what 'God' intended. There are some people in the Deep South who still believe that today. I saw a report of a lynching just two days ago and the rise of white supremacy in the United Klans of America is terrifying.

Compare that to the plight of animals today, especially farm animals. They are not kidnapped, although some are taken from the wild such as emus, ostriches, crocodiles, dolphins and salmon. They are placed into farms where they often have to work hard to earn their keep, particularly horses, donkeys, mules, dairy cows, dolphins, camels and even elephants. Those who do not have to work are stock animals used either to breed more of their species or raised for their meat. Many of these stock animals are placed aboard ships where they are so densely packed that uncountable numbers die during transit. They wallow in their own urine and excrement just like the men, women and children captives on the slaving ships. When they reach their destinations they are often prodded ashore by force and led to their deaths in third-world killing factories where the word 'humane' has yet to be invented. Some are killed by sledgehammer blows, others have their throats cut. Some are being cut up while still alive. In the 'good old days' escaping slaves were caught, whipped, tortured and sometimes lynched or beaten to death. It is patently obvious from these comparisons that the lives the slaves of yesteryear and the short lives of animals today are linked in a terrible abrogation of ethics and morality.

I am an animals rights advocate but I'm not here to preach about animal rights. I only draw these comparisons to demonstrate how the world generally perceives animals as commodities rather than as sentient beings in their own right. Animals have feelings and emotions; they love, fear, feel happiness, joy, sadness, distress, depression and emotional pain. They cry. And actually we all know this — at least those of us who have dogs or cats as companions. Yet in places like South Korea, for example, there are actually dog-meat farms, the animals being kept in stinking cages, sometimes for months at a time, before being sold alive to be butchered for food. These dogs include Poodles, Huskies, Beagles, Golden Retrievers, Pomeranians and Boston Terriers. Dogs are highly intelligent and sensitive non-human beings. They show us great love and give us unending comradeship and loyalty. Why on earth would we kill them with a meat cleaver? I recently saw a horrific photograph posted by one of my Twitter followers of two dogs being barbecued on a flaming grill. They were not skinned or butchered. They were being cooked whole, Their tongues were still hanging out!

Happily some of these dogs are rescued before reaching that terrible point. One recent case involved the rescue of a large number of dogs by the Humane Society International, a wonderful organisation that helps to promote the human-animal bond. The South Korean dog-farm owner was offered a price for the animals and then convinced that he would be better off growing cabbages instead. All the dogs rescued were ultimately given the veterinary care they required and sent to caring homes in America. I wish we could do the same for the so-called wet markets.

We have a very real difficulty in understanding such cruelty and no matter how much we talk about the treatment of animals it seems to me that it is almost impossible for most people to understand it on the same level as vegans. That's because the Great Disconnect begins when we are born and it only dissolves over time for *some* of us. For the majority of the population the Great Disconnect remains for their entire lives which is terribly sad because it also means that animals are the ones who will continue to suffer for it.

Stories about domestic violence or family violence as it is sometimes known are in all the newspapers on radio and on television. We all know that we should not abuse our children or spouses. People who do that either need psychiatric assistance or are just plain evil. Right?

Yet there is very little difference between family violence and animal violence apart from the quite obvious fact that family violence is universally condemned while animal violence is universally condoned — despite the fact that family violence results in death in only a relatively small number of cases while animal violence results in death in almost all cases. Over fifty-six million farm animals are killed every day and that does not include fish or other sea creatures, the slaughter of which is so enormous that they are counted in tons, rather than individually. Every second of every day more than three thousand animals are killed in abattoirs around the world, a figure that is increasing dramatically, and by 2050, unless we have a wave of ethical, environmental and technological change, (which is coming, as outlined in the conclusion to this book) that number will probably have doubled. Yet these numbers mean almost nothing to most people. They are just a statistic, about as boring as the next tennis club election for president and there is actually nothing on this entire planet as yawningly boring as that.

This is all a part of the Great Disconnect or what has been officially termed 'cognitive dissonance'.

Put simply, the Great Disconnect is this. We are brought into this world by parents who, usually, have eaten meat all their lives and are unable to see any reason not to eat meat or to give meat to their children. That's the way it's always been and that's how it's going to remain. We come into this world drinking our mother's milk which is fine. It would be better if it were flavoured like Italian-made vegan Magnums but that's not really important. We then move on to baby-food and this is usually comprised of tubes, jars or tins of indeterminate mush. It's often made from a pastiche of pumpkin, rice, milk, cereals, corn and some obscure kind of meat, fish or other animal-sourced protein. It's probably likely that if babies were to be given a choice, they'd stick rigidly to the booby-food rather than move on to baby-food and that would be quite understandable, of course, although it's fairly improbable that babies will be able to express that preference anytime soon. It's a progression, naturally, and we all have to accept it, although there are cases of internal revolt and I am a typical example.

Finally we grow a little and move out of baby-food onto slightly more substantial meals but these generally consist of something that once had fur or skin on it. I vividly remember my first gravy dinner, having progressed successfully through nipple university to baby-foods. I was still only about three inches tall but recall that I was seated in a baby-chair in front of a coal fire in the living room of our modest terraced house. My mother brought me a bowl of food which, as I recall, was comprised of some mashed potato, little bits of meat cut into tiny squares so that they would fit into my tiny mouth and a puddle of gravy about the size of a village duck-pond. I just looked at the food completely dumbfounded. I was a recovering boobmilkatarian. What was I supposed to do with *this*? It didn't even look like food. Food was either white milky stuff that should, but did not, taste of vegan Magnums, or squishy mush of an indeterminate nature that could be sucked and swallowed almost without any effort on my behalf. With considerable reluctance I picked up my little spoon, had a quick taste, and upended the entire meal on my head.

God that felt good!

I did eat meat as a child and also as a young adult, as I have outlined elsewhere in this book, but it was always with some reluctance, forced upon me by the general social malaise of the Great Disconnect.

From birth we are educated to treat animals as food or commodities. It is burned into our psyche. We learn that meat is an important part of our wellbeing. We need it to grow and flourish. We see it everywhere: in the shops, on television, on pub counters and in restaurants. There are bill posters the size of small nations up on the sides of buildings. They promote the health benefits and the delicious taste of meat. Meat advertising is on the sides of city buses and in the tunnels of the London Underground. If meat producers could afford it, and if environmental protection agencies would allow it, meat producers would have every major river in every major city dyed a pleasant shade of red as a big advertising campaign for beef, lamb or pork. Morning TV shows would scramble to cover the events and suddenly a million rump steaks would fly out of the butchers' windows as if they had wings. That's the power of gimmicky advertising, although one has to ask the obvious question: why would anyone actually want to eat a cow's bum?

We have competitions for the best sausages or meat pies, and the world pie-eating championship is held in Manchester each year. In 1998 a man stuffed eleven pies into his mouth and ate every crumb within the space of just thirty minutes, setting a new and completely ridiculous world record, although why anyone would want to do that unless they were gastronomically suicidal rather evades me. In 2005 another man ate seven meat pies in just three minutes but I bet you anything he was belching like buggery for months. Interestingly, under extreme pressure from the many cruelty-free organisations, the competition was opened to vegetarians in 2006 when a vegan version of the meat pie was permitted to be consumed in lieu of the traditional pie.

Which reminds me to mention the now iconic stinging-nettle-eating world championships, a hilariously awful vegan bonanza designed deliberately to make one's tonsils feel like they have been napalmed. The championships are held annually in Marshwood, Dorset, and came about in the late 1980s when two farmers were arguing over the lengths of the nettles in their respective fields. One of the farmers, finally frustrated with the seeming impossibility of winning the argument, stated that he would eat any nettle in the other farmer's field if it proved to be longer than his. I have to say that he must have been a particularly brave guy. Since that agonising moment the championship has been won by a number of people with pain thresholds better than James Bond — some eating up to eighty feet of nettles in one sitting.

I think vegan pie-eating might be a tad less toxic.

Meat fills the supermarket shelves and freezers. Butcher's shops are adorned with dead creatures and death is so close you can actually smell the blood as you walk past. We even see meat *ad nauseum* on TV cooking shows that seem to have proliferated in recent years to such an extent that it's quite possible the world has been taken over by food zombies with brains the size of Spanish olives. Proof of that statement is the fact that not too long ago I was astonished to see a tub of bacon-flavoured ice-cream in a supermarket fridge.

How completely stuffed-up is that?

Eat more meat, we are told. I realise that business is business and they all require growth, but that growth means even more destruction of animal life. Humans today, in western civilisations at least, do not need to eat more food. In fact they should think about reducing their calorific consumption in order to improve or maintain their wellbeing. Americans, for example, have been reported as being the plumpest people in Earth, and Australians are not far behind. Meat is so deeply entrenched in our lives that we need to go a lot farther than generational change for us to realise that we no longer live in the Stone Age. We need evolutionary change.

We see the disconnection from animals every day. It is everywhere. We walk past butcher's shops, see the sides of meat covered with blood and somehow fail to connect that with the death of the animal. Surveys have been carried out in schools which demonstrate that some children, especially those in the cities, have no knowledge of what meat actually is. They think it's just a manufactured product that tastes nice when cooked with onions. We could feed them pork-flavoured cardboard and they wouldn't know the difference. I can't tell you how many times I've gone into a restaurant and ordered a vegan meal only to be served with something that had been deceased for some time. A vegan pizza I ordered in Manila came back smothered with ham because, according to the chef, ham was definitely not meat and therefore I couldn't get a refund. I ended up giving the pizza to a starving waif although I had to struggle with the ethics of that too.

Many people in the hospitality industry have absolutely no idea what vegan means. My wife and I were once staying in a hotel at Oban, on the west coast of Scotland, and we informed the owner during the evening that we would like a nice vegan breakfast in the sun-room the following morning. When the owner arrived with the tray of steaming food he presented it with a happy, proud-faced flourish, '*Voila* ... smoked kippers!'

Fuck me!

Oops!

Fish, apparently, is a vegetable, as is bacon. Ask any greasy-spoon chef. For those who prepare the food in cafes with plastic tablecloths, meat is specifically confined to beef, lamb and pork but everything else including veal, fish, eggs chicken, haggis and ham are, apparently, mutated vegetables. They have been scientifically modified, their DNA has been altered in such a cunning fashion that they are now fully fledged garden greens.

Only Baldrick could have thought of that one because he always has a cunning plan.

Actually, I'm quite sure there is a chain of grimly awful hotels in Britain and possibly elsewhere in today's new third world and for some unfathomable reason my wife and I seem to have stayed in all of them, and all the owners or managers appear to have a lot of fun dealing with vegans. I swear I'm going to write a book about the hotels I've stayed in over the years. It's time the terrifying truth was revealed.

My wife and I once stayed in a rather dejected looking Cromwellian period hotel in Somerset which had an alarming lean to the right, a bit like the tower at Pisa but not so tall and not so round and not leaning quite so much if you'll pardon the appalling triple negative. The hotel had advertised rooms with a private ensuite, and being a stickler for privacy and an aversion to other people's toilet smells I booked a room immediately. Yet when I attempted to find the promised private loo I discovered that it was mysteriously absent. However, after much searching and sliding around on a floor that had an alarming incline of about 1"-in-1", I finally found it cleverly hidden *inside* the built-in wardrobe. I'm not exaggerating. The plumber who had installed it must have been some kind of evil genius. One side of the wardrobe was where you hung your shirts and trousers and the other side was where you crapped! A miniature toilet-roll holder had been glued to the inside of the wardrobe which held a roll of the imaginatively named ShitBegone toilet paper. I can actually *see* your rolling eyes now. You think I'm pulling your leg! I'm not. It's a real brand name and the brilliant idea of a man named Jed Ela who formed a business to manufacture and sell his new conservationist bog-roll which was promoted as being soft on the bum while also being totally recycled. I have to say, as a conservationist, that the manufacture and distribution of Shitbegone was a wonderful idea and although it now seems to be unavailable it once had loads of customers and supporters because it was possible to buy huge boxes of ShitBegone rolls that would last an entire year. They even came with a ShitBegone mug. How excellent was that?

So there I was in our tiny hotel room which slid down convincingly to a toilet cleverly masquerading as a wardrobe. I was so astonished I forgot that I needed to pee. I sat on the end of the bed and just looked at it like a tourist. There is, however, one positive thing I can say about my imaginative wardrobe ensuite. The entire edifice was at least convenient. You could pick lint off your suit while also attending to other business.

I must have been bonkers, I know, but many years ago I agreed to move to a small country town in Queensland. Unfortunately our house was quite close to an abattoir and while I thought I might have been able to ignore that fact, the reverse was actually the case. My wife and I would lie in bed at night and listen as the cattle were unloaded from the trucks and prodded with electric rods through the doors to the killing floor. Then would come the smell of the process. It reeked of death and hung over the entire area for hours. It seemed that we were the only people in the neighbourhood who were appalled at this. Everyone else thought it was perfectly okay. Another example of disconnection with the reality of death.

Movies and television both assist in promoting the Great Disconnect. Remember the scene of the naked little girl in Vietnam running away from an American attack on a village where napalm had been used? The child was badly burned and the image of her screaming at the camera lives on in our collective consciousness, even today. (The girl and photographer were reunited for the first time in 2022). Another scene from the same war was of a South Vietnamese officer about to shoot a north Vietnamese soldier in the head. Both scenes were flashed around the world, even in the days prior to the introduction of social media, and created a shit-storm for the Americans, helping enormously in the public campaign to bring the war to an end. Yet when another scene from a movie about the same war was released worldwide in cinemas, it received little or no criticism because the victim in this instance had been an animal. It appeared in a movie showing a buffalo being hacked to death by villagers. It wasn't computer-generated imagery as you would see today. It was real and very bloody, and the sight of that animal being killed, weltering in its own blood, has haunted me forever. However, the only people it affected were those like me. It did not stop any wars. It did not prevent more cruelty to animals. It was just a scene in a film designed to make money for the producers. We were disconnected.

Of course there is an even deeper aspect to this cognitive dissonance which can, at times, take us into an entirely different dimension. We see it most often when people of two completely different ideologies are brought together in opposition. That's when the 'apathy' of the disconnection can become so deep that violence may result. One sees this, for example, outside abattoirs where vegans are protesting or giving water to pigs or sheep that have been shut into transport trucks for many days — often in terrible heat — without food or water. Carnist people who are completely disconnected can sometimes feel threatened when vegans protest animal deaths, even when a fragment of kindness is being offered to an animal that is scheduled to be killed very soon. It's a bit like a double-disconnect, heading down into the darkness from apathy into anger. However, it's my firm belief that no matter the situation, neither violence nor anger are the way forward, but peace, love and compassion very definitely are.

As you may guess from all this tripe (that *was* a double entendre, by the way), my love for animals knows no bounds and I will do anything I can to protect them and raise awareness in others that they are all beautiful creatures that deserve to live their own little lives in peace, without violence being constantly inflicted upon them. They have their lives, we have our lives, and life is precious to all of us — non-human and humans.

I loath the killing or harming of animals in any form and I am especially against the hunting and killing of animals for sport. Did you know that live pigeon shooting was an Olympic sport in 1900? I think you will agree that it's a crazy old world. The next thing you know they'll be giving gold medals for polar bear hunting in the winter Olympics. Wouldn't that be fun!

I recently read that there is considerable human interest in the history of using duck decoys. Now if any of you have seen a duck up close, or have had one for a companion, you will know two things about ducks. Firstly, they are super intelligent, and secondly, they produce about three tons of squishy green poo every ten seconds which is wonderful for growing tomatoes and parsley but quite annoying when walking romantically barefoot through the grass because it's rather difficult to get out from between your toes — especially if they're a bit hairy.

I'm not sure why we need to reflect back on the somewhat grotesque history of killing ducks, especially when one learns that during the heyday of duck killing, and even these days probably, big brave men (and I use that description hilariously) would bring out weapons literally the size of cannons to blast hundreds of ducks from the sky in just a few minutes. It was like World War One but without the barbed wire. These cannons were mounted on punts and had barrels up to twelve feet in length. The hunters even used specially designed shotguns that could fire six barrels simultaneously at the touch of a single trigger. Dead ducks were raining from the sky like confetti at an Italian wedding.

The use of decoys to lure unsuspecting ducks into their sights was also ingenious. One decoy was shaped conveniently like a coffin with rather erotic sexy duck replicas perched on top. It had to be mating season, of course, or the whole crazy idea would never have worked. The concept apparently was to attract live ducks to really slutty plastic ducks with the false promise of a jolly good duck-fuck. (Gosh, there I go being slightly rude again).

When the randy ducks arrived all bright eyed and ready to perform, waving their little ducky erections like mad, a rather sinister duck-hunter hidden inside the coffin would suddenly slam open the lid and blast joyously away with his multi-barrelled shotgun while being showered with blood, gore, beaks, feathers and shredded duck-dick.

Another decoy the hunters were prone to employ actually looked like a duck sitting on the water with its bum in the air. What purpose that served has actually escaped me but perhaps the duck hunters just like looking at bare duck bums.

Life is too short to contaminate it by inflicting pain and suffering on others, especially animals who are incapable of protecting themselves against our avarice and cruelty. I always have a wonderful feeling of freedom from any kind of guilt by consuming only cruelty-free foods, most of which are also organic, so that not only am I minimising the chemical pollution of my body, I'm also doing my small part in working towards a world that uses less chemical pollutants. I know it's a kind of pipe-dream, and I'm not evangelising, but wouldn't it be marvellous to go back to an organic, meat-free world where everything was grown by the sweat of our brows aided by generous dollops of good old-fashioned poo? That would be the bees knees.

(Bees really do have knees, by the way. I checked).

Chapter Eight

The Weird Lives of Aliens Who Live Among Us

The world is made up of extroverts, ambiverts and introverts. All the psychological experts espouse this theory so I guess they must be right because, generally speaking, they are a brainy lot. What makes us who we are is down to nature and life's experiences and we can't help ourselves too much although we can attempt to hide our true selves in what I call the Distortion Personality Performance. Doesn't that sound amazingly spiffing? I expect real psychologists with framed certificates on their awe-inspiring interior-designer walls have some other impressively cool name for it.

In short we can all be actors on the stage of life and we all have the capacity to become what we are not — at least for a while, but the persona we portray during our Distortion Personality Performance has nothing to do with the real us. It's just an act. Introverts can act as extroverts just to achieve a satisfactory outcome. A successful book launch for example. An extrovert can act as an introvert for the same reason: trying to bonk a really yummy introverted young lady, for example. That sometimes works too. Yet in my experience in life it appears to be more difficult for extroverts to pretend to be introverts than vice versa. I'm not entirely sure why that is the case but quite obviously a good bonk is worth at least three book launches, however successful they might have been.

Pretty much all introverts are forced to have split personalities. That's not to say that they are candidates for the Memphis Mental Institute, it just demonstrates that in a world where social and business protocols are constantly requiring us to throw ourselves into the rapid stream of life, introverts have little option if they want to survive financially but to put on their *other* face and pretend for a while that they wouldn't prefer to be curling up like a kitten in front of a fire in some remote log cabin in the mountains.

On the other hand, the thrill of the chase, the uncertainty, the risk-taking, are all part of the extrovert's fundamental and rather unsettling persona which is why most of them end up with broken legs on the ski slopes of St. Moritz while the classic introvert is still in the dressing room of the ski-lodge attempting to fathom out how the stupid ski-clamps work and is it all worth the damned effort anyway!

It may surprise you to learn that introverts make rather good military leaders. It certainly surprised me. Ukraine's Volodymyr Zelenskyy is a typical example. Despite the fact that prior to becoming president of Ukraine he worked as a stand-up comedian, Zelenskyy has been described (in the publication *The Atlantic* of 3 December, 2019) as an introvert who listens carefully and thinks even more carefully before taking any kind of action. That's so typical of an introverted personality. And we have now seen how effective Zelenskyy has been as a military leader since the mind-numbingly stupid Russian invasion of Ukraine.

I know this concept is something of a contradiction in terms but in reality not all introverts are conscientious objectors and a military life might seem appealing to them. The days have now long gone when military commanders had to be colourful, brash, larger-than-life figures capable of inspiring their men to take on almost suicidal tasks such as storming the beaches at Normandy in the face of astonishingly destructive opposition. These days such extravagant waste of life could never be condoned by any modern Western power because those who had ordered such folly would be absolutely slaughtered on Twitter. The use of force has changed dramatically and military commanders needed to lead those forces have also changed. Now the top dogs in the military rarely seek the limelight as did leaders in the past. Patton, (with his controversial theory of reincarnation); Montgomery, (for whom my dad once cooked bully-beef stew at a camp in the desert); Rommel, the ill-fated German general who ended up on the wrong side of a poisoned challis, and even General Haig, the British commander on the Western Front who cleverly allowed twenty thousand of his men to be butchered in a single day in 1916. If that slaughter happened today it would lead to revolution in the streets (except in Russia, of course,) but by that time in the 'Great War' the conflict had already been so brutal that all those deaths hardly seemed to matter. They were just a rather ugly statistic with crosses over them.

Much worse was to come on the Somme although the soldiers in the rat-infested trenches had no way of knowing that because they were kept largely in ignorance of the real horror and fed a load of religious and patriotic platitudes. In those far off and particularly brutal days a commander with a big personality and huge personal presence was necessary to convince the poor sods under their command that what they were doing was right, just and necessary and that God was on their side. It would be a good way to die, despite the fact that God appeared to have been on every side and yet the doomed soldiers were still cut down like wheat in a summer field. Commanders like Haig were famous, and heroes, even if they *were* responsible for more deaths than Genghis Khan, Putin and Covid 19 combined. I wish there had been social media back in the days of the 'Great War'. The men would have taken one long look over the trenches and told everyone via Twitter to get stuffed with knobs on!

However, these days the big military moguls are hardly known to us. Many are introverts who never seek publicity. They command men who do not need to be pumped up with fervent, moral-building team-spirited speeches that have the rather annoying and now quite deadly habit of spraying saliva everywhere. Wars are fought remotely, from the quiet seclusion of highly secret locations where the weapons are technology, stealth and really cool video games. The days of the military extroverts with penises *in extremis* are largely over. It's a really strange phenomenon that yesterday's beefy, violent, whisky-drinking soldiers have suddenly morphed into introverted caffiene-sucking computer geeks with acne and permanently untidy bedrooms. It was one of those keypad finger-twitchers, for example, who, in March 2022, exposed the entire Russian espionage network in Europe consisting of over six hundred spies. That one act alone probably did more damage to Russia than a hundred James Bonds.

Introverts and extroverts are like pieces on a chessboard and just as complex. It's a well known fact that extroverts are the crash-test dummies of the world. They're the ones who can't stop talking at dinner parties (mainly about themselves), and you end up getting a really good view of semi-masticated Beef Wellington while also being sprayed liberally with hazardous particles of soggy pastry.

Extroverts just can't help themselves, they have to be the first to do everything such as driving their newly rebuilt 1964 Ford Mustang at 128.5 miles per hour in a desperate attempt to earn the not entirely inappropriate crash-test dummy nomenclature they evidently merit.

Loud, brash, colourful and noisy, that's the typical extrovert, the constant centre of attention and inevitably the one person in the room destined not only to succeed spectacularly but also the one most likely to end up spectacularly broke, leaving behind a pile of broken hearts, empty wallets and an unpaid bar-tab amounting to $264.

Extroverts are quick on their feet, fast thinkers, impulsive, and love to eat hilariously hot food really quickly which is a trait almost certain to lead in later life to rather annoying clusters of stomach ulcers with the burn capacity of a Boeing inboard engine.

Without the excitement of fast cars, fast talking and fast women, the typical extrovert simply couldn't function. To the extrovert, bright colours, stress, adrenalin and even danger are all essential elements of life. Extroverts often appear to be unwilling to accept personal responsibility for the consequences of their actions. They live for the day. They are the suntanned beach-volleyball players who don't mind in the least that their skin-cancer possibility levels are now reaching the dizzying heights of serious probability or that their little blue budgy-smugglers are doing a really good job of demonstrating to the world that at least a little forethought should have gone into the habitual practice of scoffing six sugar buns with their morning tea for the past twenty years. In other words, great rolls of well-tanned, over extroverted, but alarmingly wobbly cellulite appear to cause not the slightest embarrassment when one is conscious only of being in the face of almost everyone on the beach all at the same time.

I've known many extroverts and, of course, they can be really nice people capable of doing the right thing. An extrovert might hand a hundred dollar bill to a homeless person but it would probably come with the proviso that the gift must somehow be acknowledged, perhaps publicly, whereas the introvert would probably hand over fifty dollars (they are rarely as well-heeled as extroverts) and then disappear anonymously into the gathering gloom before anyone could have even the remotest chance of recognising them. They quite like gratitude and acknowledgement but don't like being the centre of attention.

The world assumes, or at least there is a general perception, that extroverts are usually the really successful people whom everyone admires and attempts to emulate. The forceful, overly colourful chappie from Texas or Silver Springs, wearing a $900 Stetson and with a face the colour of rapidly impending apoplexy is bound to be more successful, happier, sexier, richer, plumper, shagged out and constantly energised than a little Welsh twit from the coal valleys with a face the colour of parsnip soup.

High-octane energy, Colgate teeth, and cheekbones like Sitting Bull are apparently mandatory elements of success in the 21st century, so where does that leave skinny little introverted aliens with the energy of a used Duracell, teeth the colour of John Wayne's coffee and cheekbones like Quasimodo?

The answer, of course, is that it doesn't really matter.

High-octane activity and all the other dubious attributes of extroversion are simply elements that are necessary for the average extrovert to gain happiness through being 'out there', a part of the scene that takes the world by the scruff of the neck and shakes it rather violently until something really good drops out. Money for example.

Introverts don't need to expend all that colourful energy to find happiness and money. Generally speaking money is relatively unimportant to introverts as long as there is enough to pay the bills and prevent the ribs from showing too much which can sometimes be a bit tricky when wearing somewhat threadbare t-shirts from the op-shop.

Extroverts are only happy when they are the centre of attention, preferably with flashing coloured lights, really loud music and ten thousand adoring fans some of whom are so excited they are colourfully peeing themselves or having secretive orgasms in their too-tight jeans. These types of extroverts are in a class of their own. T.V. evangelists come readily to mind and you can almost see the money falling out of the pockets of their 'hypnodazed' followers. (As you can see, I'm inventing some really riveting new words for the *Oxford English Dictionary* to think about including in next year's edition, thus making me universally famous — although in a quiet, introspective way, of course).

Introverts on the other hand are those people who are happier buying that old railway station, closed since the 1960s due to economic depression, putting lots of potted plants along the platforms, some of which might be ever so slightly illegal, and quietly writing a book about dwarf pygmies in Central Brazil. It's highly likely that no one will ever actually read the book, even if it is by some miracle published, but that doesn't matter. What matters is that the introvert is in a perfect place and is happy, or even over-happy if he's harvesting his funny pot-plants slightly too often.

Introverts are like tortoises, they not only hide whenever possible but they also move almost in slow-motion. I am always dawdling. Everything introverts do is deliberate, planned, well thought out, quiet, reflective and calm. Yet despite our introversion and apparent disinterest in everything that is going on around us, we are not necessarily as divorced from reality as many would believe. In fact introverts are probably more perspicacious than many extroverts because we hide, observe, study, analyse, think critically, act strategically and consider carefully. We don't talk much because we are more prone to believe that we are better able to express ourselves in writing. We also prefer listening rather than talking.

Extroverts dash off dozens of seemingly ill-considered and often really silly tweets while an introvert will calmly write a 100,000 words thesis or book on exactly the same subject. It doesn't matter that the extrovert's tweet may be more widely read, or that it's just 280 characters of well compressed folderol, what's important is that the introvert's more considered output consists of words that have been well chosen, wise, true, accurate and gives everyone a good old guffaw now and then. Actually that's exactly what happened with this book. It started out with a few stupid sentences pencilled on a paper napkin while seated almost invisibly under a shopping-centre potted plant, and ended up being more than a hundred thousand words of brilliantly written poodle-poo.

Life's a funny old thing isn't it?

I am a reclusive introvert because that suits the way I like to live, and I think it likely that many other people who live as I do are particularly self-conscious and not very fond at all of having other people look at them. It makes me even more self-conscious and, as I explained in an earlier chapter, I begin to wobble. At least it feels to me that I'm wobbling although people tell me that they can discern not even the slightest little stagger in my gait. It's all in my brain, I'm told, but it's nonetheless real. I deliberately walk where fewer people will watch me. If a street is in shadow that's where I'll be. I always wobble a bit in doctors' waiting rooms, for example. Have you noticed that the moment you push open the door and step into a waiting room about six dozen pairs of curious but lacklustre eyes swivel up from the pages of well-thumbed magazines on home improvements or gardening or fishing in the Great Lakes, most of which have recently been thoroughly disinfected with Glen 20 and smell like hospital wards? Actually these days the magazines have largely disappeared from those waiting room coffee-tables to be replaced with bottles of hand-sanitiser and wet-wipes. My question is why wasn't that done before we all started dropping like flies?

As you enter the waiting room everyone looks at you balefully, as if you are about to jump the queue. There is something malevolent about doctors' waiting rooms; everyone has been there for so long that they worry someone will come in with an agonising sporting injury, dripping spectacular quantities of blood, badly staining the new carpet, and will have to be rushed into the doctor's surgery ahead of everyone else despite the fact that you have been waiting to see the medico since before sparrow-fart while being unconscionably confronted by a large colourful sign which advertises non-surgical treatment for vaginal atrophy and also vaginal steaming — if you have one of those doctors who like to think they are 'alternative'. I actually didn't know what vaginal steaming is so I checked and now wish I hadn't.

So you wait and wait to see your doctor and then wait some more until your bum needs to be massaged surreptitiously because it has gone to sleep on the hard chair. I always find that rather interesting. People rarely fall asleep on waiting room chairs simply because they are about as comfortable as a Mumbai fakir's nail-bed, but for some unfathomable reason bums have absolutely no trouble falling asleep on them.

Finally, your name is called and with everyone watching and wondering what kind of sickening ailment you might be suffering from you get up from the Gestapo-manufactured chair and follow a nurse into the doctor's surgery trying really hard not to rub your bum while doing so because that would be totally embarrassing with everyone watching.

For me that's when the wobble starts, especially if I have to walk past all those other patients who are only *pretending* to play with their phones. I know they are only pretending because out of the corner of my eyes I see them look up as I pass, their heads swivelling to watch me as I wobble towards the surgery. I have amazing side-vision. I literally can see in almost all directions like a rock lizard. Nothing escapes me, if my eyes would only swivel a little more I swear I would be able to walk backwards for five miles without stumbling over anything. Perhaps that's why I'm so conscious of everyone watching me. I have 330 degree chameleon vision.

No doubt clever psychologists will have a name for my habitual wobble. It's probably called something really scientific ending with 'drome' like 'self-inhabiting instability syndrome'. In fact it's just because I do not like people watching me.

I once flew to the Philippines to conduct some historical research and remained in my seat during the entire eight-hour flight even though it was becoming increasingly necessary for me to pee rather noisily into one of those vastly interesting airline suction toilets which is always a terrifying experience because if you stand too close or actually sit on the stainless-steel seat there is every possibility that your willy might accidentally be vacuumed down the loo. The thought of that is so disconcerting that I never pee down vacuum loos. That's what those really huge disposable coffee cups are for.

During my flight to Manila I remained in my seat for the entire journey because I didn't want to get up and wobble the length of the aircraft fuselage while being gawped at by three hundred other passengers who no doubt would be wondering if I was going for a number 1 or a number 2 and would my willy survive the sudden life-threatening suction. It's completely bonkers, I know, but extreme self-consciousness is a central element to reclusiveness and at times it can be a bit debilitating especially on the bladder and more especially when passengers are passing ten dollar notes around at five-to-two on your willy.

I once had to chair a meeting of a history committee where I was expected to discuss a book I was writing. The meeting was scheduled to take place in the boardroom of some local government council offices. Beforehand I carefully reconnoitered the room and set my chair directly in front of a large set of glass doors so that the light would come from behind me and I would be just a silhouette against the glare. It wasn't an accident, I did it deliberately to become virtually invisible, and it worked. I was both the centre of attention and also the most invisible person in the room. I also turned down the air conditioning really low so that everyone would be freezing and would therefore want to leave quickly thus shortening the meeting as much as possible.

It's all part of a day in the life of an introverted reclusive alien.

And then, of course, there are sports. Hyper-extroversion is possibly the reason why I loath sports so much because those who are on the upper fringes of macro-activity and who are simply unable to sit still for even a nanosecond because the fire-ants in their britches are, apparently, biting like the devil, use their hyped-up state of readiness to attempt to inflict exactly the same frame of mind on others who might prefer to remain slightly less intoxicated with themselves. We see it a lot in sports locker rooms before the big matches where the coach is so emotionally unstable there is every reason to believe that he might be having some kind of apoplectic fit, or at least the *casu marzu* cheese sandwich he had for breakfast is giving him quite ghastly gas because he keeps thumping himself on the chest making his face go redder every second. By the way, I'll be writing more about *casu marzu* cheese a little later in this chapter and that's a story you really won't want to miss. I guarantee you'll be discussing it in the office tomorrow, or on Zoom, and there will be a lot of pasty faces looking decidedly sickly.

Beefing up the team before an important game is the same technique of pumped-up mass hysteria that hugely successful 'life-coaches' use in their uproariously expensive and massively attended seminars to sell their stories of success through super confidence and smiles with the gleaming whiteness of Zsa Zsa Gabor's impressive set of gnashers. They intoxicate the crowds with their own stratospheric enthusiasm and ego. The message is so strong, so carefully crafted and presented with such pumped up razzle-dazzle that it's almost impossible not to get caught up in the illusion. People are ready to do anything. They even have public orgasms — literally — and it has nothing to do with tight corduroys or knickers made from deliciously irritating Brazilian bamboo fibre.

Being super positive or even super negative and pumped up to capacity at mass confidence-boosting public rallies is hormonal. Trump uses that all the time. People come to believe they can do *anything* and will believe *anything*. In that state of mind they will swim the English Channel, run for president or walk on a bed of hot coals. Yet it doesn't mean that they are suddenly ready to be the hugely successful billionaires they dream of becoming. It just means that, for a while at least, their minds have been kidnapped by some red-faced business 'guru' in a really expensive pair of super-tight designer jeans with deliberately ragged knees. I've never really been able to understand why people will pay $400 for jeans that have been deliberately worn out at the knees before you even put them on. I bet you anything that only extroverts and people with really nice knees buy them.

An introvert could never be suborned in this crassly commercial way. We are fiercely independent and the thought of being even slightly influenced by some super hyped-up extrovert advocating that we should all drink tequila with worms and then run around with cactus bushes protruding from our bottoms would be completely out of the question — even if we did have a slight fondness for Mexican drinks with a tendency to send you completely blind and rob you of erections for the next ten years.

Neil Armstrong was an introvert. Why do you think he went to the moon? He wanted to be alone, of course. Buzz Aldrin's mother's maiden name was Moon so that clearly explains why he wanted to go. Yet being on the moon would never have been what Armstrong sought. There could be no seclusion when being watched by hundreds of millions of people on shaky black and white 1960s TV screens. Introversion was as dead as the witches of Salem at that point. Life would never be dull, boring or private again for any of those first lunar astronauts.

Yet what do introverts do when they become bored out of their brains? Well, that's easy. If you believe a lot of people in the world who are emphatically not introverts then the answer is that reclusive introverts, especially those who are also veganalien, don't actually have any brains so there is an element of mutual exclusivity in the question. It's not really worth asking. It wastes everyone's time which could be better spent focusing on the poker game or mindlessly watching so-called 'reality' programs or endless repeats of American sitcoms

But introverts are rarely bored and some really do have brains. They daydream — often about Kylie Minogue, apparently — or compose really appalling poetry or write songs or books that never seem to sell enough copies to justify the publishers actually bothering to post any royalty cheques.

All kinds of things amuse or occupy veganaliens. How to get the groceries without actually going to the shops. How to mow the lawn without being seen by neighbours. That could be done at night, of course, but neighbours would probably become a little irate at the sound of a really cheap mower revving its pathetically inadequate two-stroke motor at top speed when it's almost midnight. Additionally, in certain circumstances, for those living in Queensland, for example, the death toll among cane-toads would be enormous because the ugly little buggers come out only at night and, generally speaking, mowers do not have the luxury of brakes or headlights.

Introverts like to watch people, to see what makes them tick, and this is especially true of writer introverts. They do this from behind the security of dark glasses — the darker the better. My sunglasses are so dark I usually need a white stick to see my way around. People stop me on the street and give me donations for the blind. As I walk past I hear them whisper to each other, 'Ah poor old bugger. Blind as an earthworm. Why is he wearing a camouflage shirt do you think?'

Our examination of the human race, generally, is usually quite fascinating. Sometimes we are critical of what or who we see and there are certain classes of Earthlings who really capture our attention. Mall-cop lookalikes in social security offices, for example, are usually guys placed there deliberately to intimidate white-haired pensioners. They almost always have pot-bellies and have to stand on the edges of their feet because their beer-fuelled man-pregnancies are so enormous they are giving them bunions.

We introverts watch and think. Sometimes our judgements are good and sometimes not quite so good. Middle-aged men with earrings usually come in for some eyebrow-raising.

Youthful shop assistants can also be interesting people to watch. They almost always look bored. They are so bored you can see their thumbs twitching to start sending text messages again. It's like a terminal case of spontaneous tremors. And they will do anything possible to avoid serving customers including the impressive feat of emulating reclusive introverts and becoming almost invisible. When you do have the modest good fortune to capture their attention for a fleeting moment or two they puff themselves up considerably as if to demonstrate that they weren't actually hiding or pretending to be invisible after all. They then proceed to answer all your questions with a degree of fluency and knowledge that can't fail to impress. It's only later — much later — that you discover, usually when the warranty has run out just two days previously, that everything you had been told had either been complete shite or had blatantly been plagiarised from a Denis-the-Menace comic.

I quite like studying people who are experimenting with vegan food for the first time. Not that they are planning on taking up veganism anytime soon, but usually because they have either been backed into a corner and are unable to extricate themselves from what they perceive to be a completely embarrassing situation, or possibly they have been taken out to lunch by their granddaughter, who very much is a vegan, and they are therefore too embarrassed to order ribs with all the fried-onion trimmings. I've seen it quite often.

Sometimes people don't even know how to pronounce 'vegetarian'. My wife and I were once at a coffee-shop in Southport, many years before Covid unconscionably crashed into the planet, of course, when some old chap wandered in and browsed the glass-cabinet where all the food was displayed and then, with a wavering finger (because he wasn't too sure whether or not he was making a fatal mistake), said, 'I'll have one of them vegeeeetarun things'.

People are endlessly entertaining and actually I use many of these types of situations in my novels because sometimes I literally can't believe what I'm seeing. In another restaurant, also many years ago, my wife and I watched a man eating great slices of pizza. Between slices he'd take a bit of a break and stuff a handful of green jelly and a handful of hot chips into his mouth at the same time. It was like some kind of mashed-up sorbet from hell.

Lollipop people are also good subjects for close examination and analysis. They are the men and women, dressed in bright orange, retina-destroying high visibility traffic-vests who stand at either end of dusty roadworks with an enormous lollipop sign in their hands with the words STOP on one side and SLOW on the other. Really, someone should write a book about these quite heroic people. Firstly, they stand out in the open roads where no one else would dare to venture, with about thirty thousand cars *pretending* to go slow as they race though the roadworks, or come screeching to a halt just as the sign has turned to STOP. I've seen drivers try to race them like they race traffic lights. The sign might say STOP but many people literally read STOP as secret code for GO EVEN FASTER I DARE YOU. Lollipop people have to scatter in all directions. They are like brightly coloured bowling pins.

Introverts could never be lollipop people because the job calls for too much visual exposure. In short, it would be impossible to be invisible while wearing an orange shirt with the words 'Sydney City Council' emblazoned on it in letters ten feet tall. Additionally the lettering is usually printed in some kind of reverse-secret ink, previously unknown to humankind, which has the astonishing ability to shine in the sunlight as if it has been pooped on by a glowworm. It all adds to the 'hi-vis' effect. I suspect the reverse-secret ink was one of the intergalactic secrets brought to earth by the spaceship that allegedly crashed at Roswell, New Mexico, in 1947. For some time, people in the region were running madly around looking for escaped aliens while the newspapers were having a joy-filled field-day publishing all the 'verifiable' witness statements when nobody had actually seen anything apart from a scared bunny or two and a group of really weird people who were having sex while almost completely, but not quite, wrapped in the relatively new invention of aluminium foil because that's about as kinky as it gets — at least in the 1940s. Incidentally, the bits that weren't wrapped in foil were the bits that were in use at the time.

You see what I mean though. Nothing is ever boring about people so it's difficult to understand why recluses like myself want to distance ourselves from the very people we like to observe so carefully. No doubt ordinary people would like to observe introverts just as closely. Introverts could be fascinating people to watch and learn from, or at least they might be able to provide some amusement. However, studying introverts is almost impossible because hardly anyone ever sees them, which is why our knowledge of introverted reclusive aliens is so sparse. We are like one of those rare tribes hidden in the steamy Brazilian jungles. Everyone knows they are out there somewhere as they leave footprints in the mud, but no one can ever be sure what they look like because they have never had any contact with the rest of the world. The only real evidence of their existence appears to be the smelly little scats they like to strew haphazardly around the jungle like little organic landmines.

Introverts could never be soapbox orators on street corners nor could they be pavement artists because everyone would be stopping to watch them. Being the captain of a cruise ship would be completely out of the question because that would mean they would have to socialise with passengers at the captain's table with over-fed over-rich, over-garrulous, over-dressed American women from Florida wearing fake diamonds because the *real* diamonds were still safety tucked away in a deposit box at Trump's *Mar-a-Lago* resort where ridiculously expensive bling is, hilariously, still in fashion.

Similarly, introverts could never perform as 'human statues' in Trafalgar Square because lots of people would be looking at them, and if they stayed there long enough they would be covered in so much pigeon guano they'd look like an oversized candle that had been dripping for too long.

Neither could an introvert donate his or her remains to a body-farm because that would mean lying dead out in the open where absolutely *everyone* would be able to look at them, and when you have worms in your eyes it's not a particularly attractive sight. Similarly, introverts would not have a webcam installed in their coffins so that people above ground could watch them slowly decompose. Now I know that sounds completely loony but I assure you that I once met a chap who intends to do exactly that when he eventually pops his clogs.

Obviously he's not an introvert!

Body-farms and coffin webcams being completely out of the question for the average recently deceased veganalien introvert, what else could imaginatively be possible when one does not like being looked at all the time? As it happens there is another alternative although this too, while having the rather morbid attraction of rendering the subject completely immortal, also has the drawback of attracting keenly speculative eyes. It's called the memorial diamond and has absolutely nothing to do with the fake diamonds adorning the necks of Florida heiresses while cruising the Caribbean.

Technology is such a wonderful thing. It's brought us car-reversing cameras and mobile phones with directions on how to find the closest burger drive-in, and that's frightfully important as everyone knows. Now it's also given the world memorial diamonds so that not only will we be remembered forever but our remains will be the centre of attention wherever we go. However, it's likely that there will not be a great demand for memorial diamonds among the reclusive introverted community.

For those of you who are still completely baffled by this concept I shall try to explain why your great-great-great-great granddaughter might just be wearing your penis on her finger in about two hundred years time (assuming that you have a penis, of course).

Diamonds take billions of years to form so it's easy to understand why they are so rare. Or are they? In fact there are enough diamonds in the world to give everyone on the planet a cupful and if they weren't so commercially restricted through market manipulation they would be as cheap as a monster veggie-burger with chips and coke. Actually it's now possible to make diamonds out of peanut butter which could be a reason to buy shares in a Queensland peanut farm. I'm not exaggerating. The peanut butter diamond is a reality and it's coming to a jewellery store near you quite soon.

Memorial diamonds are real diamonds that have been manufactured from the carbon deposits left over after a body (or possibly a jar of peanut butter) has been cremated. They are man-made but nonetheless real diamonds, not the cheap cubic zirconias you can buy in any jewellery store for four dollars. The process of manufacturing your diamond is complex and takes about nine months, slightly less than the normal three billion years it takes to make a natural diamond but the result is a pure diamond which can be exquisitely cut to standard specifications. They now come in clear, yellow, red, blue, green and probably super-crunchy varieties.

To have your loved ones turned into a diamond you simply take the urn of ashes along to one of the companies making the gems and leave it with them until the process has been completed. Just a small portion of the ashes is needed and the remainder will be handed back to the family. Up to fifty, one-caret gems can be produced from a single human body so if you have enough money you could wear your entire late and lamented husband around your neck. Wouldn't that be fun? Alternatively, you could have a single diamond made that would put the Great Star of Africa to shame. Of course you would have to kidnap somebody really important or infamous and get away with a major ransom to pay for it all. However, a modest single carat would set you back around $20,000.

Diamonds can also be made from human hair. One company in America has made three diamonds from Beethoven's hair, one of which was auctioned on eBay and sold for over $202,000.

Pets can become diamonds too. Cats make a really small gemstones but goldfish diamonds would be so small they would be the size of pinheads. The best diamonds would come from elephants because they would be so huge you could never lose them. In fact you could use them as coffee-tables.

Frankly, I'm not entirely sure that I would want to become a diamond. Apart from the fact that everyone would be looking at me, and I mean really intensely, I'd always have this weird feeling of being Marcel Marceau, trapped forever on the inside of the diamond and desperately searching for a way out.

The next best thing to becoming a diamond at the point of one's earthly demise would simply to be cremated and then have the ashes put out with the rubbish on a Wednesday morning. It would be quite practical as recluses have no friends or acquaintances so would be spared the embarrassment of having a funeral attended by only the undertaker and two skinny blokes with big spades. Of course it would be really important when putting the ashes into the rubbish bin that they were not accidentally placed into the recycling container as that could mean you might have to experience the ignominy of an earthly reincarnation as an ink-jet cartridge and that would be a bit too weird.

But my preferred method of disposing of my 'earthly shell' is now 'terramation'. What the heck is that? I hear you ask. Well, actually it's really quite simple. Terramation is the process (becoming increasingly popular in the U.S.) of having one's body placed inside a steel container, rather like a very large square coffin, and allowing it to decompose like compost. It is, in fact, composting. This process transforms bodies into nutrient-rich garden soil much like the soil one buys at the local garden centre to put into pot-plants. It's actually quite a gentle process and takes about sixty days. The steel containers where the bodies decompose are heated to just the right temperature and a constant flow of warm air is added so that the decomposition takes place reasonably rapidly. Relatives can visit during the process and add additional composting materials such as flowers or leaves, (or possibly vegan food scraps or rejected book manuscripts) all of which helps with the process. I think it would be jolly nice to end up in a flower pot in the corner of a room with a lovely green aspidistra growing out of my little Welsh bum.

Camouflage absolutely complete!

~~~~~~

There will probably be quite a lot of unanswered questions in this little chapter. I am a recluse and an introvert, as you all now know. I rarely have anything to do with people so it's quite possible that minimalist social interaction plays its part in my lack of understanding them. That said, it is simply because I'm an introvert and also a writer who needs to study human behaviour for my work that it's possible I might be even more perspicacious about human behavioral patterns than many of my contemporaries. In short, wherever I go, I'm looking, closely, always observing, and at times making notes about what people are doing and how they are reacting to any kind of external influences. It's enormous fun and not only entertaining but also highly educational. If anyone wants to write, whether it be short stories, novels, creative non-fiction, essays or poetry, then the place to start is in the quiet, unobtrusive study of human beings in their normal habitat and to do that one has to be virtually invisible.

Over the years I've come to understand a lot about humans but there is also a great deal I will never understand. Why Americans voted Donald Trump to be president, for example. That's a good one, although it's probably a question that, in a way, answers
~~~~~~

itself when one discovers with some alarm that the education system in the U.S. is so poor that forty-six per cent of Americans are unable to read the labels on their prescription medicines. Evidently then, there are some major gaps in their overall knowledge which might affect their judgement when it comes to electing political leaders.

I don't think anyone in this solar system was more astonished than I when Trump became 'leader' of the free world — which is actually a stupefying oxymoron. When you have a U.S. president who has the love, support and adoration of the Klu Klux Klan, and when his supporters are moronically chanting Civil War slogans while wearing a dozen six-guns and Mexican bullet bandoliers, you pretty much know that the world is completely stuffed and real freedom no longer exists. It's immensely interesting that we appear to have reached a point in the Earth's development that has apparently whooshed us through a black hole without us even noticing the wind rushing through our hair. We have, apparently, travelled back two hundred years in time and somehow regressed to the 'good old days' of the cotton plantations and slave-blocks. It's a bit like being trapped inside a really silly Dr Who script but without the rather important benefits of a sonic screwdriver, but it proves my point, in an idiotic kind of way, that time can travel in both directions.

Yes, the world remains a bit of a mystery to me and I have many questions about what the devil is going on. Other questions I'd like to have answered include the obvious: why do the Balinese eat deep-fried crispy dragonflies? What did dragonflies do to deserve that kind of fate? Why are tax departments and social services agencies around the world staffed by people who, judging from their universally blank expressions, have radically overdosed on really cheap Botox? (Botox, by the way, is made from botulinum poison, half a pound of which would be sufficient to turn the entire world into a post-apocalyptic desert. I bet you never knew *that* the last time you went in for an eye-bag touch-up).

Why did Andy Warhole wear only green underpants? (It's true). Why do Asians eat four million cats a year? Why are crickets and worms being massacred in their trillions to make protein bars for brain-challenged people who love to eat insects? Is there really a registered and *bone fide* 'Masturbate for Peace Club' or did some wanker forget to take down the website after the 1st of April? Why do Ecuadorians insist on eating sloths when they are about the cutest animals on earth? Why do Peruvians eat more than sixty million guinea pigs every year? Don't they know that they make great pets and if you brush your teeth with their poo it's an amazing aphrodisiac that actually makes your penis grow by an inch every year. (I just made up that last part by the way so please don't throw out your Viagra or penis pumps just yet).

Recluses stay away from people generally but there are certain individuals who come in for special evasion measures. Men wearing excessive amounts of bling in the form of rings, bracelets, earrings or 'danglers', especially heavy gold chains around their necks with large St. Christopher medallions. The name, 'Christopher' means Christ-bearer, by the way, because he was reported in the Biblical press as having carried little Jesus across a river. Actually the bling-kings wearing these danglers probably don't realise that St. Christopher was never formally canonised because he became a 'saint' long before popes were invented, so the St. Christopher 'feast day' was dropped by the Church during the 1960s. I have to ask does that make the tinkling little medallions any less efficacious as protection charms?

People wearing tee-shirts with 'Honk if you're Horny' are usually also avoided by seclusionists. They are obviously attention seekers with chronic erectile dysfunction. I'm also always wary of men with size fourteen feet who insist on wearing skinny jeans. Don't they realise that it just makes them look uncannily like Bigfoot?

Covid precautions apart, public gatherings are also to be avoided and more especially if it's one of those gatherings where you are expected to be happy, laughing, joking, having fun and being the archetypal friendly neighbour type. Parties would be the typical example of these types of gatherings. They are filled with laughing people, colourful balloons, sparkling wines, happy faces and ribald stories. The average recluse just loathes gatherings like these. They drain us like bathwater going down a plughole, but sadly no one can see how stressful they are to us. People think that as we are at a party with lots of booze, noise, balloons and beautiful people we should be enjoying ourselves, so if we are not enjoying the moment there must be something tragically wrong with us.

The other point I should make about parties is that they generally come with a strange phantasmagoria of foodstuffs which sometimes should be labelled: *Muy peligroso* which is actually Spanish for, '*Oh shit — Duck*,' or … well — you get the point.

At the few parties I ever attended I would always, without variation, stand in the corner eating a handful of peanuts from my pocket, principally because I like to be alone or I've been a little distrustful of what's on offer in the culinary line. People who prepare home-cooked dishes and then bring them to parties with a couple of bottles of $5 Lambrusco don't even think about cross-contaminating haggis leftovers, for example, with a bowl of steamed broccoli, which can be quite disconcerting for a vegan. The other reason, of course, is *casu marzu* cheese. I did warn you earlier that this story would soon be coming up and now might be a good time to duck for cover.

The story of *casu marzu* cheese really amplifies the point that as far as most people are concerned I don't have a clue what is actually going on in their brains! My principal question when initially confronted with *casu marzu* cheese was what brainiac came up with the entire concept in the first place and why didn't their wives hand them over to the Roman Catholic Church for an exorcism ceremony involving lots of green vomit?

Hands up everyone who has ever heard of *casu marzu* cheese. If you have heard of it well done. If you have ever eaten it you have to be applauded for your bravery. If you have never heard of it and you have a slightly weak constitution then perhaps you should stop reading right now.

I can only recommend to any party-goers out there in Earthling-land that it would be wise, when approaching the food trestle at any function where the origin of the cuisine is somewhat in question, to examine the cheeses carefully before consumption. If one is caught unexpectedly by *casu marzu* then the party may well be prematurely shortened by the sudden appearance of significant volumes of Earthling up-chuck followed quickly by a convoy of ambulances with flashing blue lights. *Casu marzu* cheese is a demonic enterprise guaranteed to turn normally healthy internal organs into potted fish-paste, cause incurable piles and make one's lower bowels run like the River Ganges during a malodorously muddy monsoon. I might be exaggerating this slightly but if ever I actually ate *casu marzu* I'm reasonably sure that all the above would happen to me.

I'm only mentioning all this because happily I came upon the *casu marzu* delight only once in my life and naturally it was during a party. It was one of only a few I ever attended and the party was in a posh London flat full of posh people I'd met at a posh opera. They evidently had far too much money, drove E-type Jags and brand new MGBs so that probably explains everything, especially the fact that I was as poor as a Presbyterian dumpling and totally out of place because my car was a clapped out, slightly dying-of-rust, 1964 Triumph Herald in desperate need of a new clutch-plate.

For those of you who might meet the monster *casu* at your next party of opera *aficionados* I should probably explain that *casu marzu* cheese is rather easily recognisable so it would be difficult to consume by accident, although it's now apparently illegal to sell it in most parts of the world so you're probably pretty safe. Sitting in the middle of the cucumber sandwiches, the little sausages on sticks and the oysters wrapped in bacon rind, *casu marzu* stands alone because it looks uncannily like a large dollop of whitewashed camel poo into which some very sick person has been digging little holes like miniature graves and that tiny zombie-like creatures are now crawling out of those same little graves. And for once in my life I'm *not* being over-descriptive.

To explain this a little better I should go back a thousand years to the moment when *casu marzu* was first invented. No one actually knows who first came up with the *casu marzu* concept but I'll bet you anything it was a bored Sardinian husband, back from fighting in the Crusades or something, and having told all his stories of killing everyone in sight and sacking a few desert castles he had now become completely bored and, taking a stone jug of *grappa* and a slab of cheese, had gone to sit outside in the sun where he had promptly fallen asleep, having drunk far too much homemade plonk. When he had awakened a few hours later the sun was going down and his slab of cheese had literally taken on a new incarnation. It had become *casu marzu.*

Casu marzu cheese is actually made from sheeps' milk. How one actually milks a sheep is a mystery I never want to explore in any detail but evidently it would require a really short milking stool — but that almost goes without saying.

Casu marzu begins its long, complex and terrifying life as a simple *pecorino* cheese which would be okay if it stayed that way, I guess, but the really spooky part comes next. Once the cheese is made it's taken outside in the sun and the top of the rind is split open to allow it to air. While the cheese is thus gasping like a lungfish in fresh oxygen it's invaded by hordes of heavily pregnant cheese flies, which, of course, have a Latin title because all evil things must be academically recognised, noted, analysed and placed into a museum so that children can look at them in awe and not have a clue how to pronounce their names. The cheese fly is officially known as the *Piophila casai,* although it probably doesn't know that and I expect some of them are actually named Berty or Gertrude or even Madonna. Its sole aim in life at this point is to land safely on the surface of the broken cheese, always a difficult manoeuvre when one's tummy is swollen with child, and lay its eggs — all five hundred of them. That's not an exaggeration by the way. No wonder they have swollen tums. Every fly that lands will lay about five hundred little eggies and God knows how many flies will stop for a nap and a quick egg-squirt on the cheese during the course of a single dozy afternoon. It staggers the imagination and, realistically, makes you want to gag a bit. Soon after this creative event the eggs hatch and an equal number of maggots (give or take) begin to eat the cheese in a really disgusting manner. By the time the cheese is ready to be eaten it usually has thousands of maggots on and in it. It's especially disgusting because as the maggots eat they literally excrete, so one is left with a cheese that is writhing with thousands of maggots swimming in a soft soup of their own cheesy poo.

Cripes! Doesn't that make you hungry!

The *casu marzu* maggots are actually rather good athletes. They can jump to a height of about six inches which is pretty good when one considers that they are only about the size of tadpole excrement. Some people find all this jumping about a little disconcerting and for those who like to eat their *casu marzu* live, they generally hold one hand over the bread as it, and the cheese, are being placed into their mouths. This prevents a few hundred maggots from jumping into their eyes and temporarily blinding them. It's true. Honestly. Now you know why I'm a vegan!

Being vegan, of course, solves a lot of those problems but not always. I was once doing a national magazine story for an island resort when I ordered broccoli soup as a starter, believing that it was vegan. Sadly the chef (and I use that description with a kind of tragic comedy) decided to place the leftover scraps from the ham-bone into the soup and to blend it like mad so that crazy little vegans would never know there were the remains of a deceased creature in it. Sadly, the ham had been on the *al fresco* table for what must have been a month and was as rotten as a poisoned dingo. The result of all this culinary hilarity was two days of imperfectly aimed projectile vomiting, stomach cramps that felt like the Gestapo had finally managed to catch up with me, and a dose of the runs so violent I thought my entire head was about to be sucked screaming out of my bum.

And that would definitely not have been a good look!

Chapter Nine

A Whisper of Hermits

Working for some years as a national magazine features writer, it was necessary for me to meet people and deal with everyday life. It was sometimes difficult and always made me somewhat uncomfortable but I enjoyed meeting ancient recluses and hermits because although they too preferred to be alone, they generally tolerated my presence possibly because my marking scent was exactly the same as theirs. When they realised that I was also an introvert they would often open up and tell me stories they probably would not have told to a living soul. This is actually so true and profound that it has become a defining aspect of my career. People have told me the innermost secrets of their lives — secrets they had never breathed to anyone, including their families. It has been one of the more extraordinary aspects of my life as a writer and historian and I have always felt humbled that people have trusted me sufficiently to confide in me and to tell me personal details they have kept in the darkness for years.

One old man lived on a small farm in outback Queensland. I didn't need to know that he lived in a cabin in the middle of nowhere to realise that he was an introvert. At the time I met him he was in his late nineties. His eyes had faded to that opaque translucence that comes only with great age, but they were gentle eyes in a long, slim, sunburnt face that had seen many years of hard manual work in the bush with an over-abundance of blistering heat. He'd been a farmer all his life and when I saw the country he'd farmed it was easy to understand why his face looked so weathered. The droughts, the floods, the wild animals, the savage storms, had all carved their character into his features, but nothing had changed his love of the world or of people generally, although he kept everyone at a distance. He lived the life of an almost total recluse, helped along by some neighbours who would bring him food occasionally. He never married. As we got to know each other better he leaned over one day and whispered, 'You know, Tony, I've never been with a woman.'

I'm not entirely sure what expression was on my face at that time. Incredulity, perhaps astonishment. He nodded sagely, a solemn kind of confidential confirmation of the truth of his quiet statement. A whole life without the comfort or company of a woman. He was saddened by it, I could see, and at his age he would live for a few more years at best. Seclusion is a beautiful place to be, but sometimes it comes with a terrible emotional and physical cost.

I'd like to tell you about a few of the recluses I have met over the years, people who had wonderful stories and who wanted to share their experiences with the rest of the world. I especially like telling their stories to radio audiences. I've written and narrated over five hundred programs, mainly for ABC Radio, and I'm always extremely comfortable in doing so, largely, I think, because I'm just a voice. I can't be seen. Radio-land is actually the perfect place for invisible people, especially if they have a story to tell.

I really like talking to people who are very old and reclusive because they are generally full of wisdom and I am able to learn from them. I also like to talk to people who are close to death. Now that might sound strange. In fact, I admit that it is a bit weird. Yet people who know for certain that death is just around the corner appear to me to be the wisest people in the world. Not only that, but they are usually the most honest. I've met and interviewed quite a lot of people who were just at the end of this world and the beginning of the next. Old soldiers from the First World War or pioneers of Australia's colonial days who could still remember when Queen Victoria was on the throne and the cat-o'nine-tails was being used. I've also spent a lot of my life researching the lives of recluses. One of my favourites was Ian Fairweather, an ancient veteran of the First World War and later world-famous artist who lived as a complete hermit in a Polynesian hut on Bribie Island. Ian once managed to sail himself to the Dutch East Indies on nothing more than a raft comprised of old fuel tanks and a ragged sail. Upon his arrival Ian was arrested and regarded by the authorities as a spy. His solitary life was so colourful and unusual that I included a detailed biography of him in one of my earlier books.

~~~~~~

Another wonderful person I met in order to write about her extraordinary life was an elderly lady named Nell Bowley who lived alone on top of a mountain.

Nell was eighty-eight years of age when I visited her. She lived in a mist-enshrouded eerie on top of Spring Creek Mountain near Killarney, Queensland, and at that age was still trapping or shooting dingoes for the government scalp bounty — not something that, as a vegan animal rights campaigner, I would necessarily approve. However, she was an interesting woman nonetheless who lived an astonishing life in her little mountain retreat surrounded mostly by ducks and clouds.

I recall driving up the mountain on the day that I was to meet her for the first time. It was raining and the track was a morass of mud. I had to stop at a nearby caravan park to seek directions. Possums were looking down at me from the trees, their eyes accusing because apparently I had not come bearing gifts of bananas or carrot cake. (My wife and I remedied that shortcoming sometime later and fed them about a crate of bananas).
~~~~~~

A few kilometres later I turned off the road, opened an annoyingly springy and complex barbed-wire gate which took me half an hour in the rain to figure out, and drove finally onto Nell's mountain holding. I sat in my gravy-coloured utility, the windscreen wipers working furiously, and looked at the gravy-coloured track ahead. It appeared that I was melting into the scenery once again. Almost invisible.

The track was running in rivers of brown rain and had an inclination similar to that of the Great Pyramid of Giza. Even in a four-wheel-drive I wasn't sure that I would ever make it to the top of the mountain. Should anything happen to me, should I slip off the track and slide down the muddy slopes into a lake that looked from a distance like toffee, I would be gone forever. In ten thousand years they would fish my petrified corpse out of the lake and put me on display like Otzi — the skinny little treacle-coloured relic that had been dragged out of the ice in Italy in 1991 after being there for more than five thousand years. I really didn't want that happening to me, largely because I don't like people looking at me, as you all know, and Otzi is now a tourist attraction at the South Tyrol Museum of Archaeology in Bolzano, Italy, and one of the most poked, prodded, analysed and looked at people in the history of the ancient world.

Resolutely, and with not a little apprehension, I put the Subaru into gear and crawled forward, grinding up that hill as if I were being winched up by some invisible chain. When I arrived eventually at the lip of the precipice, my nerves stretched tighter than Tiny Tim's ukulele, the top of the mountain suddenly levelled off to a grassy plateau in the centre of which was a tumbledown, paint-flaked wooden cottage. It looked like someone slightly demented had constructed an oversized chicken-coop complete with rotting window-frames and a rusting stovepipe, like a broken top-hat, bent at an almost impossible angle. I sat there for a few minutes as the rain began to ease slightly. I got out of the vehicle, grabbed my notepad and camera and walked to the door.

Chickens, ducks and geese were clucking and honking like feathery guard-dogs. In the distance, through the rain, I could see a bunch of wallabies gently enjoying a breakfast of sodden grass. They looked up at me as if I were an alien. How perspicacious of them!

I knocked on the door and waited.

No answer.

I knocked again. Each time I knocked, the ducks and geese squawked, quacked and flapped loudly. If anyone was about, surely they would hear all this racket.

No answer.

Maybe Nell was away doing what she apparently did best — executing dingoes! Either that or maybe she had died in her sleep and was lying in bed slowly rotting. It was hard to say. I checked the closed windows to see if flies were clustering. Not a blowie in sight. You may think I'm exaggerating but I'm not. I really did that, despite the rain. I think I'd been watching too many of those British pathology shows or murder mysteries. Flies always cluster at windows in those. They're like Alfred Hitchcock's *The Birds* — only smaller and much more irritating — especially when they do an annoying little poopy on your avocado sandwich.

I waited for a few moments — knocked again. There was still no answer. I decided that rather than standing here getting soaked I might as well have a jolly good look around. Maybe Nell was boiling her clothes out the back. That's the way they washed in the old days. Light up the old clothes-boiler, throw in a handful of soda with some home-made animal soap and boil away like mad until everything was either clean or at least tender.

I walked around the cottage. It appeared to be quite deserted. Held high on rotting stumps, the building had seen better days — rather a lot of them in fact. Rain was pouring through rusting holes in the gutters, and the ground around the wooden stumps which held up the house was like a muddy lake. Green-frogs were croaking in the rainwater tank and pot-plants. I circumnavigated the entire cottage without any sign of the gun-slinging gran but when I arrived back at the front door it swung open suddenly, scaring the poo out of me and there was Nell, a shock of white hair above a face that could only be described as having been sculpted by searing suns, hard work, long years, gunpowder residue and dry-as-dust bush humour.

'You'll be the writer-man I'm expecting,' she greeted me with a twinkle. We went inside and I entered a world that few people ever get to see. Once again I was time-travelling.

We passed through the enclosed verandah. The bare wooden walls without any pretence of paint, were decorated with dingo skins and rusting nails. A wooden frame was resting against one of the walls. That was where the skins were cured.

Apart from the verandah, the cottage was principally composed of a small dark kitchen that looked as if it had been designed with the 1860s in mind. I expect there must have been a bedroom somewhere but if so it remained hidden in mysteriously dark recesses smelling slightly of soot and foot-oil. The kitchen was the central room. This was where Nell lived and worked, where she cooked, ate, tanned skins and, as far as I knew, loaded her own buckshot like Annie Oakley.

We sat at the kitchen table on rickety wooden chairs that had a tendency to wobble rather alarmingly. The table itself was liberally sprinkled with china bowls and plastic ice-cream tubs containing a morass of cheesy goat's milk. The milk had evidently been there for a while because a skin had formed on top and about a dozen flies were now attempting to extricate their wings from the porridgy mess. It was a bit like watching synchronised swimming for tiny little drunks.

Nell Bowley seated at her kitchen table in her mountain-top home.
— Tony & Lensie Matthews collection.

The other items of interest on the table included chipped enamel bowls of goose eggs. I'd never set eyes on a goose egg before and was surprised to see how large they were compared to chickens' eggs. 'I eats 'em every day for me breakfast,' Nell cackled, seeing my look of interest. 'Goose eggs. Boil 'em, scramble 'em, fry 'em, eats 'em raw, turn 'em into custard or porridge. It's all good stuff. That's why I've lived so long.' She breathed deeply, sniffing like a drugs-dog. 'That and mountain air,' she admitted with a gappy-toothed smile.

Nell Bowley on her 88th birthday.
— Tony & Lensie Matthews collection.

Nell was one of those really colourful characters who belonged uniquely to old Australia. The Australia into which Nell was born on 15 September, 1900, had been one so vastly different from the Australia of today. The country may have moved on but Nell had remained steadfastly fixed in the era of bullock teams, chuffing steam-engines, Model T Fords and expansively bearded bushrangers with cumbersome but rather deadly six-shooters. Apart from her much-loved goose eggs, Nell also loved eating goats. The vegan in me wanted to weep. A good old goat stew for breakfast in the morning was the best way to start the day, she told me as she began to stir more luckless flies into a pot of stew she was cooking on the wood-stove. Nell turned to me suddenly as if she had badly been neglecting her manners. 'You eaten yet young writer-feller? There's plenty here.'

As gently as I could I told her that I was vegan. She scrutinised me carefully for a few moments as if I were a species from a portion of the universe that wasn't even visible through the Webb Space Telescope.

'Some milk then?' she brightened.

I looked at the bowls of goat's milk on the table. One or two of the flies had now unhappily given up the ghost and their feeble little corpses were floating bum-up as if they were sunbathing without swimming trunks. I told Nell that I'd already had a cuppa in town. I'm not sure that she understood what a vegan actually is.

Rain was hammering on the roof as Nell ladled out a tin-dish of steaming stew and sat at the table, spooning meat and carrots at an amazing rate into a cave-like mouth. For a few moments she was unable to talk without subjecting me to scenes of unimaginable oral horror so I kept the questions to a minimum for the time being and took the opportunity to look more carefully around the room. I would really have preferred her to talk without half a goat in her mouth because my constitution was not actually up to it.

The walls were all locally sawn timber, the colour of the wood darkened with age. The nails holding the planks in place were bent and red with rust. On a dresser that looked as if it belonged in a Welsh farmhouse was an array of framed photographs, each with images of unsmiling, straight-laced pioneers who, by the style of dress, clearly belonged to a time when young men could still get away with wearing boater hats without being bashed. One man, dressed in a Crimea-shirt and moleskin trousers was standing beside a bullock team, whip in hand. He was looking uncertainly at the camera as if he'd never seen one before — which was more than plausible. Nell noticed my interest. 'My dad, Daniel James' she said, swallowing hard to get rid of some of the meat. 'He was a bullock driver in the old days, before becoming a dairyman. Hauled logs from the forest down to the sawmills in Killarney.' She shovelled in another load of corpse and continued chewing like a ruminant.

Then the phone rang. Nell dropped her spoon with a clatter, wiped goat-grease-gravy from her grey moustache and rushed to the verandah to answer it.

'That was a friend,' she beamed a few minutes later, returning to her stew. 'It's me eighty-eighth birthday today and that's the eighteenth phone call I've had this morning.' Her antique eyes were sparkling in the same sad way that very old jewellery does.

I wished her happy birthday.

Leaning against a corner of the room, close to the old black stove, stood an even older 410 shotgun. Nell finished her breakfast and brought the weapon closer for my inspection. 'Made in 1910,' she said proudly, 'and never let me down.' Nell handled the shotgun with loving care. Clearly, they were old friends. Its wooden stock was softly burnished with use. 'I once shot seventy-four dingoes within the space of just two years, she said, her eyes going back, remembering fondly. 'There was a plague of them on the property. They was killing all me chooks and lots of calves. Something had to be done.'

She told me that her father had originally purchased the farm way back at the time when Victoria had been Queen of Australia and the *Titanic* hadn't even been constructed. As a young girl she had helped around the property, hand-milking up to one hundred cows every day, but had attended school for only a few years. Having once 'gone bush' without her father's permission, her shoes had been confiscated to try to control her roaming. It made no difference. Nell went barefoot everywhere, even in the depths of bitter mountain winters when the frost on the grass was like snow. Nell would thaw her feet in the sun or stand beneath a stream of warm cow's urine. 'That worked every time', she told me.

Nell had been married twice but both husbands were now long in their graves. She gave me the impression that she could outlive another two. There was something about her that appeared to be resilient to the ravages of time. She was like a walking fossil. Preserved but somehow ageless.

Nell Bowley was a true recluse. When I left her that day, my utility sliding almost uncontrollably down the mountain on a track of pure mud, my mind was filled with the theory that old Australia still lived out there. It had not yet passed irretrievably into time. It was still a part of us and I hoped that Nell would live for many more years — that she would keep the old days alive for as long as she possibly could.

She did.

Nell died peacefully in 2009, just one month short of her 109th birthday.

There was something about being with recluses like Nell Bowley that was special. I was never actually able to put my finger on what it was, exactly, although I think I felt a certain kinship, especially with recluses who were intensely creative. Lots of people are like that: ask Steve Wozniak, the co-founder of Apple. He was a loner in every sense of the word and it was his inherent reclusiveness that brought the personal computer to the world.

~~~~~~

Other recluses I have found both colourful and fascinating include Frank and Percy Biddle, who didn't actually invent anything, and probably weren't all that creative, but were two of the most intensely interesting and reclusive people I have ever met.
~~~~~~

Our paths collided during the early 1980s at a time when I was involved in making a series of historical television documentaries titled: *This Dawning Land*. The director and I were searching for locations where we could film a number of recreation scenes depicting the discovery of gold at a place called Gympie, a couple of hours north of Brisbane. The location had to be wild, unspoiled bushland with a natural creek or river running through it, exactly the place that one would expect to find a couple of really reclusive hermits.

I'd never heard of the Biddle brothers and neither had the director, Doug Fraser, but his mother knew them. She used to visit the Biddles at times and thought they were a fascinating pair. She knew that we were looking for a wild place to film the scenes and recommended Frank and Percy's old sugarcane farm to us.

One day Doug and I went to the property to meet with the Biddles and to scout the area to see if it was suitable. It was a memorable day. Their farm, set on the banks of the Mary River near the little village of Tiaro, was in rather a wild state and so the countryside looked as it would have done during the colony's formative years.

Frank and Percy, brothers in their eighties, had lived on the property all their lives. The dilapidated farmhouse was situated high on the banks of the river out of reach of the floodwaters that roared through the region on almost an annual basis. The house was an extraordinary affair. It had been constructed sometime at the turn of the century and if it had ever seen a lick of paint any such vestiges of aesthetics had long since disappeared. The weatherboard home was now falling into ruins, its planks sun-dried and rotten. A rickety set of steps led up to the front and side verandahs which had to be negotiated with considerable caution as the woodwork was old and cracked. The house had been raised about twelve feet off the ground to keep it above floodwater level and as the steps were rotten I was very conscious that it would have been perfectly possible to fall through and end up on the ground with about a million splinters in my unmentionables.

Frank and Percy met us at the side verandah. Both were as lean as whippets. They were dressed for comfort in drab grey-green working shirts and trousers. Their hands, arms and faces had been browned by long years under a subtropical sun to the texture of old walnuts.

Frank Biddle on the cluttered verandah of his river-bank home.
— Tony & Lensie Matthews collection.

On the verandah was an ancient spring-bed without a mattress. This was cluttered with a wild assortment of oddities including an old 12 gauge shotgun without a stock, broken packing cases, rusting chains, boxes of nails, rolls of old string and rusting engine valves. A dog was lying beneath the bed, snoring, its head resting on a sun-bleached kangaroo bone.

Frank and Percy welcomed us to their home and showed us inside. The kitchen was like something from Dickens' *Old Curiosity Shop*. There was a large wooden table to one side of the room and this was festooned with food scraps, old baked-bean tins, some of them rusting, a breadboard, pint-sized mugs with chipped enamel, bent nails, a tub of melting butter and a crockery pot of creamy milk badly curdled and crusted with age. There was a lump of cheese, hard as granite, cracked at the edges and going mouldy. A bowl of raw sugar was swarming with large black ants.

Looking around the room I saw the devastation of the years. I was, I discovered with great joy, time-travelling once again. There were rows of out-of-date electrical appliances including three refrigerators. The first was an ancient kerosene model rusting around the seals; this had evidently been replaced many years later by a round-shouldered 'Snow Queen', now also rusting and standing useless in one corner. A more modern refrigerator, which must have been a quarter of a century old, was rattling, popping and groaning away, attempting, not too successfully, I suspect, to keep abreast of the stifling heat in the room. The temperature must have been about 38 degrees Celsius although I'm not sure what that would be in Olde English.

Similarly there were three or four cookers in the kitchen, beginning with an ancient wood-stove through to something slightly more modern that probably dated back to the fifties. The wooden walls of the room were unpainted and unlined. The wooden floor was uncovered and in places planks had come away to reveal the floor-joists beneath. Where the joists could be seen these were smothered with Redback spiders' webs and egg-sacks. All around the room, resting on exposed wooden wall-frames, were rusting tins containing an assortment of goods from tangled fishing lines and welding rods to old nails, washers, screws and paintbrushes that had been left to harden like multicoloured fossils.

Frank Biddle
— Tony & Lensie Matthews collection.

Frank and Percy were about to have their lunch when Doug and I arrived and they invited us to join them. On the table, somewhere amid the clutter, was a large loaf of bread that appeared to have been at least a fortnight old, and an enormous joint of boiled beef looking as though a grey corpse had been especially dug up just for the occasion. Doug and I declined the Biddles' kind offer of lunch and so they went ahead in preparing their food. Frank took the bread and using an old ivory-handled carving knife with a serrated edge began to cut slices of bread that were almost an inch thick. The bread was brick-stale and while Frank was cutting, the knife was making a sound like a crosscut saw going through ironbark. I thought for a moment he would have to stop to sharpen the knife but he just kept sawing resolutely until the slices fell away with a mild clunk.

While Percy was boiling a kettle on the electric stove, Frank turned his attention to the corpse on the table. Using the bread-knife he cut two thick slices of beef. These he placed between the board-like bread slices and set one on the table for his brother. They did not bother with such niceties as dainty plates or cool pats of butter. The brew of mud-black tea being made, and two heaped spoons of homegrown unrefined sugar complete with ants having been added, the brothers sat down at the table and looked enquiringly at Doug and I as they began to eat. It was an absolute marvel to watch them worrying, sucking and gnawing on those oversized sandwiches with nothing more resilient than receding gums and a few blackened teeth that should have been pulled about a century ago.

Doug and I, seated beneath an enormous ormolu clock, watched silently, quite astonished. All that could be heard was the tick-tock-tick of the clock, the rusting galvanised iron roof of the building cracking in the intense heat, and the brothers' wetly masticating — almost exactly like someone cleaning out a blocked u-bend with one of those rather annoying, hand-held rubber suction-pumps. I noticed that as he chomped with his remaining teeth, Frank's foot was tapping in time on the floor. There was evidently some kind of rhythmic unison associated with the food and his feet, although for the life of me I couldn't see what it was.

'Nice place you've got here,' I remarked for something to say, perspiration running into my eyes and blinding me temporarily.

Percy looked at me, one eyebrow raised. 'We'll show you around after we've finished eating,' he said, mouth filled with a wet cement of meat and bread.

Later, as promised, we received the tour of the building. All the other rooms looked almost identical to the kitchen, a rare and delicious collection of neglect amid the ruins of a careless bachelorhood. With the exception, that is, of one room — the lounge. Here we discovered priceless antiques dating from the time when Frank and Percy's parents had owned the property. It had then been a successful sugarcane plantation with South Sea Islands labourers working in the fields. In the centre of the lounge-room was a dusty green-velvet 'love-seat'. I could almost imagine Frank and Percy's young mother and father sitting there during the colonial evenings, hands intertwined, while being served iced teas with little sugar-cakes on silver trays. This was sugarcane country and although life could be hard, at times, it could also be colourfully 'colonial'.

The room had not been entered or touched for more years than either Frank or Percy could remember. Festoons of dust-heavy spiders' webs were draped like grey mosquito nets from the ceilings; rotting velvet curtains hung in tattered shreds and mice had gnawed holes in the skirting boards. The Axminster carpet was so full of moth-holes that the bare floorboards could clearly be seen and these floorboards were, in turn, so full of wood-lice holes that they looked as if some mad person had escaped from a wood-drilling asylum. It was a room full of memories but the memories too were full of holes.

The old sanitary cart.
— Tony & Lensie Matthews collection.

Frank & Percy's home was littered with the detritus of generations.
— Tony & Lensie Matthews collection.

Outside the derelict home, and beneath it, was a clutter of ancient furniture and farm equipment, including a former sanitary cart, used in years long gone to transport the contents of the nearby villagers' poo-pans to the local rubbish dump. The unfortunate man who had driven the cart was always so pongy he apparently had rather a lot of trouble getting a girlfriend but that would have been quite understandable under the circumstances.

There was also a heavy brass ship's bell. This had belonged to the steamer *Karrakatta*, sunk after striking an uncharted rock in Western Australian waters in March 1901.

During the heyday of Frank and Percy's sugar plantation the bell had been used to summon workers from the canefields. With considerable difficulty but also absolutely determined to show off the bell's efficacy, Frank held it between his bandy legs, a few inches off the ground, and shook it violently so that it would ring for us. It gonged so powerfully that for a moment I thought Frank had become unimaginably possessed by Pacific island demons. He staggered around, the bell still in his hands, shaking and jumping like a cardiac-arrest patient undergoing electric-shock resuscitation. Even his *head* was vibrating like a tuning fork! I was actually quite worried for a while.

Frank Biddle with the bell of the steamer, *Karrakatta*.
— Tony & Lensie Matthews collection.

On the rear verandah of the house a water-tap was perched over a chipped white enamelled bowl. 'We get our drinking water from the rainwater tanks,' Frank informed us while Percy ruminated nearby, sucking shreds of boiled cow from one of his teeth. 'But this here,' Frank continued, 'is the water from the river. We use it for washing.'

Doug knelt and turned on the tap. Water rushed into the bowl.

'We had some people up here last week from the D.P.I.,' (Department of Primary Industries) Frank said.

Doug dipped his cupped hands into the bowl, and took a long, cool, satisfying drink.

'They said it was full of cholera!' Frank ended, shrugging.

Doug spluttered and coughed and we were quite concerned about him for a while, although, fortunately, he did not die because he was both a friend and brilliant director and we needed him to direct the new documentary.

Later, Doug and I walked together down to the river. It was slow and sluggish and had plenty of sandy banks. Just what we were looking for. In one small section of the river, close to the house, a cow had fallen into the water and drowned. Its bloated carcass, stinking hideously, was being eaten by black eels that rose up around the corpse to look at us with baleful eyes. It was a bit like a scene from *Apocalypse Now*.

Frank and Percy are now long gone to that hermitage in the sky populated, no doubt, by other recluses, each living in secluded little rooms filled only with rusting refrigerators and the furniture of memories.

~~~~~~

For some reason I've met quite a few reclusive people in my years as a writer and one of the first people I ever interviewed professionally was an old gold miner. His name was 'Harry' — although I'm unable to give his real name as his family may still be around and would probably not want to know anything of what I am about to tell you.

Harry was a short, immensely tidy, rather emaciated gentleman in his mid-seventies, dressed in a pristine white shirt and grey trousers. He liked to smile a lot. I met him for the first time in the back-garden of his brother's house where he lived alone in a tiny, 1950s style caravan made of rotting plywood. It had no wheels. The caravan was parked as far from the house as possible and stood half hidden in the shadow of a tree. It was covered in leaves, bird-poo and other garden detritus.

Harry had a bright, intelligent, birdlike face with twinkling eyes. Had I not known better I could have been fooled into thinking that he was a garden gnome. He was missing the floppy pointed hat, of course, and the colourful stripy socks that apparently are mandatory dress-code for garden gnomes, but apart from that the similarity was remarkable, especially as he was only about five feet tall with a rosy face.
~~~~~~

His little caravan had seen better times. It had probably been travelling on the long, harsh and lonely Australian roads in the days following the Second World War when people were beginning to think that it was time to start enjoying themselves rather than working night-shifts in bullet factories or throwing themselves at the guns of some really quite unpleasant Japanese chappies. The caravan was about the size of a large dog kennel, rounded at both ends and painted the kind of white that quickly fades to the colour of rancid cream. It was decorated with multitudinous blobs of mildew. With its covering of leaves and sparrow-poop, and in the deep shadow of the tree, it was almost completely invisible.

Yet Harry himself was snappy enough, which was surprising for a hermit. He wasn't your standard recluse and could often be seen around town, although always alone, I never once saw him with anyone else, unless someone had grabbed him in the street for a chat, and his solitary life at the bottom of an overgrown garden was a fair indication that he wanted to be left to his own devices.

He had a secret, you see.

Harry had agreed to my interviewing him but with a little reluctance. He didn't know me from a bar of lilac-scented Lifebuoy soap but shook my hand warmly, quietly, with just a word or two of greeting. He knew that I wanted to talk about his days on the goldfields when he had been both a prospector and miner. He was one of the last breed of gold miners and there were not too many of them left now.

What neither of us could possibly have guessed at that moment was the fact that Harry was about to surprise even himself by confessing to me something he had never breathed to another living soul.

Together we sat in the caravan as he told me of his life as a gold-digger and also of the years he had spent in the British

Merchant Navy during the Second World War. He still had his officer's uniform hanging in a small plywood cupboard that was only large enough to hold a few hair-brushes and some long-johns. Creaking with age, Harry got up from the little table where we were seated in the tiny caravan and hobbled to the miniature wardrobe. He opened the door with almost a theatrical sense of ceremony. There, hanging in a plastic cover, was the very uniform he had worn while serving as first mate in the navy all those years ago. The uniform was immaculate and looked as if it had just come from the tailor's shop. The dark-blue serge was clean and pressed, the buttons and gold insignia of rank shining brightly as if Harry polished them every night — which he probably did.

He smiled at me, almost lost in his own memories, closed the door and came back to the table. He'd served on the convoys in the North Atlantic during the war. A lot of his mates had been killed. He could remember them as clearly as if the convoy crossings had occurred just a week earlier. I knew a lot about that period. I'd done the research and had spoken to quite a few other men who had suffered the same experiences.

After we'd been talking about the convoys for a while, Harry looked at me carefully for a few moments, chewing his lips a bit, evidently trying to make up his mind.

'I'm probably going to die soon,' he confided eventually, looking quickly through the window of the caravan to ensure that no one was listening, 'and I want to tell you something. It's something I have to get off my chest and for some reason I feel I can trust you. You seem to know what it was all about out there. At sea, on the convoys. Can you keep a secret?'

I hadn't told Harry that although I had never served on the convoys during the war, being far too young, I had spent nine years at sea on warships including over two years on a destroyer that *had* been on convoy duty during the war years. It was even possible that my old ship had once been used to protect one of

Harry's convoys. Unlikely, I know, given the massive scale of the war, but it was a nice thought. I could empathise with him completely but he could not know that; it was just something I never talked about at that time.

Yet I also wasn't here to keep secrets. What I wanted was a good story that I could publish and keeping secrets didn't exactly mesh with that ambition. However, the look on Harry's face was deadly serious and I realised that what he was about to tell me would be interesting. I nodded thoughtfully and told him that whatever he said would remain between the two of us.

Harry looked again through the window, evidently making a final decision, then he leaned closer, lowering his voice to almost a whisper. 'We murdered a man!'

I was startled at this, but Harry quickly went on to explain: 'It was on the convoys, crossing the Atlantic. Those days, terrible! Nazi submarines were sinking tankers and merchant shipping in the convoys and thousands of sailors just like me were being sent to their doom. A lot of them were good friends of mine. The tankers were the worst. Full of high-octane fuel they went up like a roman candle when a torpedo hit them. The crews were incinerated in minutes. One day we picked up a German submariner in a raft. His U-boat had been sunk by a corvette or destroyer or something. We gave him short-shift though. We hated those bloody Germans so we just knocked him on the head with an engineer's hammer and when he was dead we bunged him into the furnace of the boiler.' He leaned even closer. 'We had to get rid of the evidence, see!' he whispered.

A cold chill swept through me. Never before had anyone confessed murder to me. For a few moments I didn't know what to say. My years of reading and research had given me a very real knowledge of the events surrounding the war in the Atlantic during which tens of thousands of British and American seamen had been killed by German submarines. It had been a particularly brutal and relentless war and the Germans had themselves been murderers. But this was different. This was cold blood and deep anger. This was revenge.

Harry was looking at me carefully, his eyes almost begging understanding.

I nodded to him. 'I think I know what you went through.'

Harry knew that I was writing an article about his gold-mining days but asked me to promise that I would never write about the murder — at least not while he was alive. I solemnly made the promise and since that time have never written about it until now.

Harry seemed to relax after that. He'd told his story for the first time since the war and now it was off his chest for good. He turned on the air-conditioning. It was one of those old 1960s models which sounded as if a Massey Ferguson tractor had suddenly driven into the room. My hearing was now completely paralysed and even my earlobes were shaking. Harry was talking, I knew that because his lips were moving but I couldn't hear a word he was saying. Harry held up an old china mug without a handle. From his raised eyebrows I decoded that he was asking if I wanted a cup of tea. I was a bit sceptical about the mug at first. It looked as if it hadn't been washed since Convoy IX-23 had left New York for Liverpool, but I nodded enthusiastically and Harry went to the little gas-stove to put on the kettle.

As the kettle came to a boil, Harry sat opposite me and began ruminating with his gums while he thought about what he wanted to tell me of his gold-mining adventures alone in the bush. I had a number of questions prepared for him but suddenly all these seemed superfluous as he leaned forward to turn off the air-conditioner and launched into a colourful description of the years he had spent alone in what seemed to me to have been the deep recesses of hell attempting, not too successfully, to wrest fragmentary slivers of raw gold from the rock and soil in which he had toiled. It was a story of hardship, seclusion, ridicule and disappointment. Even before he could really get into telling the tale, the whistle on the kettle started to shriek and Harry hopped up like the little garden gnome he was and made the tea.

That was an excellent afternoon, the tea was surprisingly good because Harry had brewed a few mugs of it during his days in the bush and knew what he was doing. He even rinsed out the mug for me, which was rather good of him seeing as it was his only mug. After I'd had my tea, Harry had his but didn't bother rinsing the mug again. That would have been just a waste of water.

The one thing Harry didn't talk about was people. He'd spent so much time alone that he really didn't have any stories to tell about them. He didn't understand them. People were as alien to him as reclusive vegans are to the general population of the planet. But he could talk about digging for gold and had all the stories. He told me of the dangerous depths to which he would have to descend in his never-ending search for the elusive metal. Crouching in small, dark, narrow mines, up to his bum in freezing water with only a hurricane lantern for light, he had hammered away at rock and soil, ever seeking that one vein of gold that forever eluded him. He told of snakes and spiders that could kill in minutes, or even seconds, and they were all down there in the depths of the earth with him. It was creepy.

I mean really. It was making my willy shrink.

People thought Harry was bonkers, of course, but that's a fairly common opinion of hermits who spend a lot of time alone and especially those who are digging for their own El Dorado forty or fifty feet closer to the centre of the earth. Harry was considered harmless but slightly loopy. The old gold diggings he was working had been excavated almost a hundred years earlier and no one believed there was much gold left in them. Those colonial gold-diggers had really known how to dig for gold and when they had abandoned the goldfield a horde of little Chinese chappies, probably ancestors of those who insist on eating tiger's dicks, had moved in to hoover out anything that remained. Harry found this to be true. When I asked him if he had any gold in his possession he gave me a long, careful look. After all, he'd only just met me and for all he knew I could have been Ronald Biggs. Yet he jumped up eagerly enough, went to his little cupboard and rummaged around among a load of old shoes and tattered cardboard boxes. Finally, after a few minutes, he stood triumphantly and looked at me with a gleam in his antique eyes. I hesitate to say that it was a golden gleam but in fact that is exactly what it was. Then he held his fist before my nose and as if he were a magician revealing the world's cleverest illusion, he opened his hand and there in the palm was a clear plastic phial — the kind that constipation pills come in — and I could see that it held about two ounces of gold in tiny specks and grains the size of sand.

It wasn't exactly Lasseter's Reef.

I parted from Harry that afternoon. He stood outside his Tinkertoy caravan waving goodbye with one hand, the precious tube of gold-dust still clutched in the other. He was a loner and loved to stay away from people but he had told me of his gold adventures and also cleansed his soul of the murder he and his shipmates had committed all those years ago. It was his final act of contrition.

I saw him a few times after that but within a couple of years he had passed on, floating up to that little goldmine in the sky. He was a lovely old hermit, a kind soul, who had finally found redemption. God knows what became of his gold. There may have been just enough to pay for his funeral.

Chapter Ten

The Hall Pass

Just when I thought I was coming close to finishing this book and would soon be able to shoot it off to my brilliant publisher, along came some bloody great virus that threatened to wipe out most of humanity leaving only moronic American 'free-dumb' fighters with automatic weapons in charge of the entire planet.

Americans are a funny lot. There were loads of people responsibly social-distancing while ten million gun-toting Trump supporters were frenziedly attempting to squeeze themselves into a backyard pool or, even more fun, completely topple the newly elected government of Joe Biden. Yet people were frightened. As the virus grew in strength, when Captain T was still in the Witless House, one priest, properly attired in mask, face-shield and rubber gloves, actually blessed his congregation with Holy Water by standing well back and happily squirting everyone with a water pistol.

It was really quite clever when you think about it!

Okay, I know, I have to be careful here because this is a sensitive subject. Millions of people have died since Covid 19 was released upon an unsuspecting planet and the world will never be the same again. A lot of people have suffered, some have starved, people will be grieving for generations but when it all boils down to the basic facts it's just what I've been talking about throughout this entire book. We have to stop abusing and brutalising animals and the planet generally because if we don't then this is what happens and it's going to continue happening until we are all fossilised.

Let's face it, despite Trump's assertions that this whole pandemic was a Chinese conspiracy to wipe out the western world and create a massive chain of steamed-dumpling fast-food outlets, no one really knows how it all started. It's actually going to be almost impossible to find the source. In late June 2020 by which time 484,000 deaths had been officially recorded, Spanish virologists discovered traces of the virus in sewage samples taken in March the previous year — long before the disease had been identified in China. Researchers at the Oxford Centre for Evidence-based Medicine (CEBM) were convinced that Wuhan was not actually the source of the outbreak and that it occurred 'naturally', that it was a dormant virus located in many parts of the world just waiting to be activated by the right environmental conditions. The Spanish flu of 1919-20 was a similar outbreak and that virus had killed untold millions. The question of the origin of the Covid virus is still up in the air and will probably remain so for a long time — possibly forever.

Yet the atrocious wet markets at Wuhan were an easy target and pretty much everyone blames them. Animals are kept in appalling conditions and then slaughtered in even worse conditions. Live frogs, for example, are piled on top of each other in plastic bags right next to the masses of bodies of those frogs that have just been killed with butcher's knives and meat cleavers. Chickens, ducks, geese and wild birds, many with open wounds or sores, are tightly bound together and are able to watch as other birds are killed brutally right next to them. Chunks of wild animal meat are held high and hawked to passers-by, the hawkers' hands covered in the blood and gore of the creatures they have just killed. The floors run with blood, urine and faeces, not all of it, apparently non-human. Rats, frogs and snakes are beheaded. Snakes are often skinned alive and their gall bladders ripped from their living bodies. Flies swarm everywhere. Pigs are killed with knives or hammers. Fish are dragged from tanks and gutted alive. Beavers, porcupines, monkeys, baby crocodiles, turtles, bear's gall bladders, tiger's cocks, absolutely *nothing* is off the menu in the wet markets.

Because of the conditions in which they are kept, the animals have often contracted diseases and these are transferred to humans during handling and especially as they are being killed. In any case, despite the obvious risks of human contamination, what blithering idiot would actually *want* to eat fried-bat soup or roast hedgehog? Why are the Chinese, Indonesians, Thais and Taiwanese eating domestic cats and dogs, snakes, pangolins and truly beautiful civets? Isn't there already enough meat in the world to drown us in gore and guts? What astonishes me in all this is that the people who are eating these lovely creatures don't even realise that they are being *totally totally* creepy.

The World Health Organisation actually gave its blessing to the reopening of the wet markets, right in the middle of the Covid crisis. Why they did so is beyond reason. Former Beatle Paul McCartney jumped in to state that wet markets were medieval and that reopening them would be the equivalent of letting off biological atomic bombs. Yet why are we only blaming the Asians? There are similar wet markets in God Bless America. New York is riddled with them so it's no wonder that the Big Apple was infected to its core (pun intended). To be fair, there have been calls to close them down but there are jump-up slaughterhouses all over the city, and streets are often littered with body parts, faeces and blood, sometimes within a few metres of schools and other similar institutions. It's like having a continuous St. Valentine's Day Massacre on back street corners and I should know because I had an uncle who was a henchman for Bugs Moran although I don't think he ever carried one of those iconically violent violin cases.

Here are a few really terrifying facts. If we don't change our human habits you and everyone else in the world, especially the free-dumb fighters of America, are going to die at some time in the future of some horrible disease that makes your cock, if you have one, turn bright purple and drop off with a clang. Most people are unaware that there are 1.7 million viruses out there that can infect humans and almost every one of those viruses also exist in mammals and birds — exactly the kind of creatures that are being brutally butchered in wet markets.

Nature will eventually choose very carefully from this vast library of viruses to reveal what is now known only as 'Disease X', and it is this disease that will make Covid 19 look like a mild case of rather burpy indigestion. As a vegan, of course, and an animal rights advocate, I loath and detest what is happening in the wet markets and can only hope that the whole of China, and other countries in both the East and West, will find some sense and compassion and put an end to this truly disgusting trade internationally.

Scientists are now, not for the first time, I should add, strongly advocating massive changes to the way we farm animals and there has been a very strong warning that if we don't change our attitudes we are heading for catastrophic disaster. A virus that could easily develop in a mass chicken farm, for example could wipe out half the world's population. That means around four billion dead and massive social unrest that would probably kill millions more. This is exactly what is happening in America as I write these words, and millions of chickens are now in the process of being culled because of massive outbreaks of a particularly dangerous form of bird flu which has already crossed over to humans. The more animals are jammed together under highly stressful and unhygienic conditions, the greater the risk of a deadly disease forming. Some scientists are saying that we are spinning a roulette wheel every day, and one day, very possibly in the very near future, like tomorrow, perhaps, the little bouncing ball on that wheel is going to stop on Black Death.

Human beings are responsible for the introduction of Covid 19. If we don't stop our mismanagement of the planet and our unrelenting torture of animals we are heading for the most deadly pandemic ever known on earth. And you don't even have to believe me on this. This grim news was published on the website IBPES which is an international platform led by scientists who report on world policy through science. The reports outline that all the recent pandemics the world has experienced have come about as a direct result of human activity and our ridiculous fascination with a global economic system that embraces growth at any cost. Rampant deforestation, mining that is out of control in many countries, uncontrolled agriculture and industrial activity, intensive animal farming, chemically-drenched agriculture and massive infrastructure development are playing havoc with the planet. Add to that the perfect storm of animal destruction, both domestic and wild, with all the chaos and disease these issues cause, and we are heading into Viral Doomsday and everyone had better begin digging really deep bug-proof shelters and stocking up on loo-paper. I can absolutely guarantee that the nuclear bunker beneath the White House has already had an entire ballroom cleaned out and stacked with a million rolls of ShitBegone!

They are probably going to need some air-freshener with that too!

There are upsides, of course. In many instances during this more recent outbreak, people have come together for the benefit of all and that is both noble and heartening, and many people have literally and courageously sacrificed their lives in order to help others. Covid 19 has done its best to destroy civilisation and the world, but despite its widespread destruction and loss of life, and despite gross governmental incompetence, especially in Trump's America, the U.K. and Brazil, it failed because of the resolute kindness and ingenuity and the willingness of people to be stubbornly brave even in the face of the greatest dangers.

Covid or the 'Rona' as it has also become known, has brought out issues that were always there, lurking in the background, and has demonstrated that in addition to being brave, noble, stoic and resolute, we can also be pathetically silly and selfish and are quite prepared to thump each other rather badly in supermarket aisles over a roll of toilet-paper, or for wearing a mask or not wearing a mask. I mean, really! Not long ago my wife was verbally abused by a young man outside a shopping-centre because she was protecting herself and those around her by wearing a mask.

There are also, apparently, young people out there who want old people like me to die not only so they don't have to pay them pensions but because if every old person in the world joined the turf club there would be much more bog-paper to go around. It makes perfect sense. We could stop bashing each other as we headed to the checkouts with our shopping trolleys loaded with Supa-Soft. It would be like a win-win situation. Of course the young people who are advocating the mass extermination of pensioners are conveniently forgetting that it was the pensioners, before they actually became pensioners, who paid for their education including all the convenient buses that took them to their schools, paid for their medical bills, raised them in hopefully good fashion, sent them to university and subsidised or even completely paid all their tuition fees or provided them with low interest loans which apparently are never repaid. Pre-pensioners also paid for this later generation's job-seeker allowances while they looked for work or subsidised their apprenticeship training or paid for their gap year when they travelled the world and got stoned in every continent and shagged out in Rome. Having done all that, the pensioners then had to try to come to terms with a really unpleasant world pandemic while pretty much every young person on the planet wanted them dead. It's a sobering realisation that everything in the world can change in a heartbeat as Trump discovered when he boasted that he would have 60,000 bums on seats at Tulsa and had 6000 instead — then went on to lose the election. Poor lamb!

Of course, there have been countless tragedies but there were also a few positives during this whole catastrophe. One of the positives has been, initially at least, the dramatic decrease in the crime rate almost right around the world. It's not that we became suddenly honest, or non-violent — that would be completely contrary to human nature, it's just that the opportunity to commit crimes had been significantly reduced. Chicago, for example, one of the most violent cities on earth, saw drug arrests plummet massively, principally, it seems, because people no longer had the ready cash to visit their local drug-dealer's corner-store and the poor old dealers were going broke. Gosh isn't that sad! But it wasn't only drugs. Robberies, murders and rapes were also at rock-bottom levels and not just in America. In El Salvador, for example, where, a few years ago the murder rate was up around six hundred per day, the number dropped to just two per day which was beyond astonishing and proves that there were at least some silver linings to the Covid outbreak even if it's just this little bug's capacity to quench our almost unending thirst for bloodshed.

Those most affected by our new-found penchant for non-criminal activity were, of course, the detectives and officers of the police forces and, initially at least, the morticians. Murders were down eighty-four per cent in Peru and funeral directors were literally falling asleep on benches waiting for new clients, although they soon came alive when the Covid bodies began to arrive in their thousands. Burglaries were down everywhere too. With the lock-down in place in most regions of the world, far fewer homes were being illegally entered as the residents were almost always home.

That's not to say that all crime had stopped, of course. In fact, given human nature, such criminal restraint could never hope to last forever. I did see one classic case of two youths who held up a convenience store. Naturally they didn't want to be recognised and also at the same time wanted to protect themselves from the virus, so, being the geniuses they evidently were, they cleverly cut a watermelon in half, ate all the fruity pink flesh, and, while spitting out the pips, cut eye-holes and placed the half-melons onto their heads while they carried out the holdup. They looked exactly like two aliens with green heads, although the melon juice running down their shirts and the trail of well-used pips rather tended to give them away. I'm not joking. This really happened.

Yes, it's been a shocking period and we have witnessed things we would never have seen in ordinary times. Mass burials in communal graves in New York, for example. The aerial images of all those cheap pine coffins lined up in endless rows while bulldozers poured soil over the top of them. People were looking out of their apartment windows in New York and seeing, to their complete astonishment, rows of portable refrigerated morgues being set up. None of this was making sense. A robot was gliding around the city's parks asking people if they had fevers or if they felt unwell. It was like something from an Isaac Asimov novel. Actually the little robot was pretty cute and people wanted to take it home and give it names like 'Andy' or 'Droidy', but others were freaked by the encounter and thought that the robot was creepy — well, until they heard it singing Beatles songs, of course, or dancing, which it was also perfectly capable of doing.

Meanwhile, Trump was astonishingly advising all his royal loyal subjects to drink a glass or two of disinfectant in the morning so they wouldn't also end up being shovelled into the communal pit at New York. These type of events tend to change you forever, especially when people actually began drinking disinfectant and *el presidente*, seated in his white palace behind a barrier of Secret Service officers spraying Glen 20, says, 'Well I was just being sarcastic.' Not long afterwards three people in New Mexico died after drinking hand-gel and another was permanently blinded after drinking methyl alcohol.

But this chapter is not really about Covid 19, or Trump, it's about us, the introverts and hermits who found that we were being ordered to hibernate, to hide ourselves away. Suddenly introverts around the world began to understand that their entire lives had been leading to this one moment. This was what they had been born to do!

Hide!

Suddenly, and quite without warning, introverts and recluses had been given a hall pass. We've all seen that hilarious movie when some guy is given a hall pass by his partner to go out and shag whomever he wants. This was a bit the same but without the get-to-shag-free-card.

All my life I have been in hide-mode. I've literally gone to parties and hidden in cupboards. I've gone to family gatherings and hidden in outhouses. I've worn clothes that deliberately make me look like a potted plant standing in the corner. I've made ten trillion excuses to arrive late and to leave early or not arrive at all, having become 'lost' on the way. At one of my book launches I was, for some astonishing reason, asked by the publisher to remain as one of the crowd and not to stand out. I should point out that this was not my present publisher. I actually thought that this was both bizarre and, at the same time, totally acceptable. I watched as the publisher literally launched the book while I simply sat as a member of the audience. It was strange, wonderful, liberating and at the same time totally freaky. I have never in my life felt more like an alien.

Yet a long life of making excuses and pretending not to be in a room is tiring. Finding just the right excuse to leave early or, better still, not to come at all, is either repetitive or draining on the soul. I don't know what it is, but for some unfathomable reason noisy people like having quiet people in the room with them. Perhaps it gives them an opportunity to demonstrate how colourfully full of life they are compared to that skinny little twit standing in the corner pretending to be a rubber tree. I was the grey-green foil to their ultra-violet, luminous, splutteringly bright incandescence.

It was bloody exhausting!

Then along came Covid and we were ordered not to socialise or mix. We were to 'socially distance' (pardon the government-issued split infinitive) and, better still, to remain at home and ignore the entire world as it went about destroying itself.

The time had come. For introverts, this was the greatest hall pass in the history of the world!

Let's start at the beginning. Everyone everywhere was ordered to hide. It was like a massive game of hide and seek involving billions of people. In the U.K. it began with the elderly and the term used was 'shielded', rather than isolated, which was, at least, psychologically more acceptable. Naturally not everyone was capable of it. In fact almost everyone apart from the introverts and hermits of the world had considerable trouble dealing with the entire concept of shutting themselves away even if it did mean that by doing so their lives might be saved.

In Indonesia, for example, people in some areas had so much trouble coming to terms with shutting themselves off for the duration of the pandemic that volunteers were asked to dress up as ghosts by wrapping themselves in white sheets and sitting on public benches *pretending* to be the spirits of the dearly departed. The concept, apparently, was that if people saw a bunch of ghosts occupying these public spaces then they would be scared enough to stay indoors, presumably hidden beneath their own sheets, but it never really worked that way. Local Indonesians found the idea so intriguing that they were leaving the protection of their homes to look for fake ghosts which actually defeated the whole object of the exercise. In Indonesian folklore images such as these ghostly figures are known as *Pocong* and reputedly represent the trapped souls of the dearly departed. In other areas of Indonesia people who were found to be out in public while not wearing a mask were sometimes jailed in abandoned houses that were said to have been haunted. But it didn't stop there. In other regions people were made to do push-ups in the street for not wearing a mask, sometimes while also reciting the nation's national anthem. It was like a nationalistic fitness workout with whips. In East Java some bureaucrat who evidently had been drinking gallons of Javanese coffee ordered that anyone not wearing a mask should be punished by being made to dig the graves of those who had died of the virus. There were no further reports of how many conscripted grave-diggers might have died as a result of this policy. Bamboo canons were also fired at the entrance to villages in an attempt to keep non-residents away. It's probably unlikely that any of the villagers managed to get any sleep with the Battle of Trafalgar roaring just beyond their *atap* huts.

Indian authorities also attempted to scare people indoors by issuing some of their police officers with helmets crazily coloured and shaped like the microscopic Covid cell — only bigger, naturally because they had to fit onto a size-seven cop's head. That particular innovation almost certainly frightened nobody but it did result in about ten trillion selfies, the police officers themselves looking a little stunned and embarrassed with massive Covid balls and coloured suckers stuck to their heads like alien fashion attire.

If people were not scared off the streets by this incredible sight then there was another terrifying weapon in the Indian arsenal. Tourists caught on the street during lock-down were being forced to write: 'I did not follow the rules of lock-down. I'm very sorry,' five hundred times. It was a bit like going back to 10th grade after being caught snogging Wendy Turnbull behind the teachers' bogs!

Crikey — did I really write that!

One Indian priest went too far, however, when he hacked off a man's head with an axe as a kind of ritualistic sacrifice, firmly believing that by doing so he would appease his rather unpleasant gods and thus end the world pandemic entirely. I have news for him. It didn't work. The priest claimed that he had received the sacrificial order from his gods while having a dream, although the fact that he was a bit pissed at the time probably had something to do with it too.

For most people the lock-down was difficult. Being shut off from the rest of humanity went against the grain of the normal human condition. Almost everyone, apart from introverts, of course, are born to be with others, to socialise, to gain comfort and support, to play a part in each other's lives.

There are limits to this, naturally, and not even the most extroverted of extroverts are capable of handling unlimited human contact. They gather energy and charge batteries while glowing in the dark, even their joggers wink with those little coloured lights every time they take a step, but extroversion is limited by brain capacity and emotional bandwidth.

You didn't know that did you!

This was all very cleverly diagnosed by a quite brilliant chap named Robin Dunbar who demonstrated that, on average, even the most social of people can deal with only about 150 friends and acquaintances. Anyone above that number, roughly, is consigned to the friendship pit which is a dark place where no one actually wants to go apart from introverts who happily live there all the time.

Robin Dunbar is a British anthropologist who came up with this important number after studying primates compared to an observable group of humans. He became completely convinced that brain size directly influences the sizes of social groups. This basically means that if you are storming the Capitol Building you have the brain the size of a lentil and three friends, whereas if you are a professor at Oxford University you have 150 friends and acquaintances all of whom think that you are ridiculously brilliant. I've simplified it here in satirical terms, of course, but the concept is actually quite clever. It even has a name, it's known as Dunbar's Number. Isn't that imaginative?

More somberly, Dunbar outlines that most people of reasonable intelligence have similar numbers of friends and associates. Christmas card lists, phone contacts and Facebook friends appear to prove his point. The numbers also come in concentric circles, a bit like the rings of a tree. Beginning with five people who are usually the closest family or friends — those who are loved dearly, followed by fifteen good friends, then fifty friends who might be meaningful contacts such as people you like in your business organisation, followed by the remainder, out to around 150, with whom you can maintain some kind of stable relationship. The numbers actually continue to grow beyond that point to 500 more distant acquaintances and 1500 people you could recognise, but the inner core is the magical number of about 150 people.

There is no known reason why these numbers multiply in fives but Dunbar stated that this is the number that had been fundamental to the primates and humans he had studied. Extroverts, however, have even greater capacity for these social networks, but while the numbers are greater they actually spread themselves more thinly around their particular network. Introverts are quite the opposite. Those introverts who do have close friends spread themselves far more thickly.

Extroverts spread like water. Introverts spread like strawberry jam.

Now I know that most of you think I'm going crazy here but this is a fact. The Swedish Tax Office, which I'm sure is a wonderful organisation as much loved, for example, as the ATO in Australia or the IRS in America, has actually restructured its offices to accommodate the 150 person threshold, so it must all be true. Neanderthals, who, contrary to popular belief, were actually a really intelligent species, organised themselves into farming villages of around 150 people. Even the Mafia has recognised the importance of this number. It's true. Mafia families in the U.S. are roughly split into groups of around 150 although it's probably unlikely that they have ever heard of Dunbar's Number and it's far more likely that membership is defined by the precise quantity of brass knuckle-dusters available at any one time.

So for a large number of super-bored people without toilet paper, especially the extroverts, isolation was the yawning chasm of hell. Suddenly they were unable to dazzle their (at least) 150 friends with their unerring brightness and noise.

For most people the first few days or even a week or so of isolation were usually fine. (I've been in almost complete isolation now for well over two years and I'm as happy as a cherry). They had their mobile phones and could text, email or doom-scroll as much as they wanted. Doom-scrolling, by the way, is the practice of checking the mobile every half hour to see how many more cases there are of Covid contagion or to check to see if a lamented *el presidente* has at last been mortally afflicted by eating a cat-meat burger imported from Wuhan or if Putin has admitted that the invasion of Ukraine was an indication that he should be locked up in a rubber-lined cell.

Isolation internees found that they suddenly had time to do some cooking, study a new language or darn all the socks that had been lying in a drawer for the past ten years. One person tweeted that he had a load of unmatched socks that would come in handy if he ran out of toilet paper. Apart from the potential of causing very serious bog-clog in one's sewage pipes, I guess that wasn't such a bad concept. In Italy, Pornhub thoughtfully offered free membership, advising that some of its sister-site's revenue was being donated to public hospitals so I guess there was a fair bit of patriotic wanking going on during the Italian lock-down. (Don't look at me like that, it's true!)

Meanwhile other less porn-addicted Italians were gathering on their window ledges and balconies to sing arias or bang pots and pans together to keep each other amused. Actually it was quite lovely to watch these singers, talented or untalented, belting out some of Puccini's better known pieces, even if they were usually songs about death and tragedy. It didn't matter. It was Italian opera at its heartfelt best.

The clanging pots were a bit irritating though!

Alcoholics Anonymous will, however, have a bit of a problem in future years when the fallout begins from all the Zoom parties that took place during the lock-downs. Apparently it was all so simple. One had only to start a chat on the teleconferencing app and then begin drinking with everyone who turned up. In fact you could never be quite sure who you were drinking with or what they were drinking. Iranians were ingesting gallons of methanol in the unshaken belief that it would cure Covid 19. I have no idea how many people died as a result, but it was a lot. That was a bit extreme, but people from all over the world were joining in the Zoom-booze parties and you might be drinking Irish whiskey in your home while in Latin America, for example, people might be drinking *Chicha* — a corn beer in which human saliva had been dribbled in order to break down the starches into sugars.

I know, it's bloody disgusting but apparently it does make you incredibly pissed.

In Korea, Zoom-boozing was known as *on-nomi* or online drinking, but I guess it passed the time even if you couldn't remember the next day who you had been digitally sharing your booze with. One can only hope that the Koreans you had been drinking with were not actually guzzling Baby Mice Wine. Now I know you think I'm either slightly demented or having you on, but really, there are folk in Korea and also in China, unsurprisingly, who like this stuff. It's made by taking baby mice immediately after birth and dropping them alive into a jug of rice wine where, of course, they drown. The wine is then left to ferment.

After the fermentation process has been completed the wine is drunk and whatever fragments are left of the little mice are eaten.

Yep, that's why we have pandemics, folks!

In fact there was one group of Indian people who hosted a cow's urine drinking party, believing that the sacred cow somehow has magical qualities that could shield the drinker from Covid infection. It's likely that the cow-piss vendors made a fortune but the people who drank the stuff almost certainly ended up being as sick as if they had actually contracted the virus.

Alcohol actually caught on as one of the possible cures for the virus and people were soon gulping it in gallons. Even if they were not cured or protected then at least they could claim to having had a jolly good time. The reasoning behind this practice was the well publicised instruction that we should all be washing our hands in some kind of alcohol-based sanitiser as often as possible. The reasoning went from there. If alcohol can kill bugs on the hands then it should also be able to kill the little buggers in the throat and the belly and even intestines. It made perfect sense. None of that was true, of course, apart from the hand-sanitising, but at least squillions of people had great fun trying it out.

In South Africa the sale of alcohol was banned completely during the term of the lock-down. Now, everyone knows that South Africans are brilliant boozers, almost as destructively joyous as Australians in their determination to turn their livers into gooey fish-paste, so not being able to drown a few cold beers at night was a bad omen. One group of rather naughty people managed to resolve this terrible issue by breaking into a local mortician's premises and stealing four gallons of 97 proof exhumation fluid. I can't believe I just wrote that! The fluid was normally used to preserve body parts after a corpse had been dug up for examination. One can only hope, of course, that the fluid stolen by alcoholics had not been recycled otherwise it would have been be a bit too fruity in a cocktail.

In Peru, a curfew largely put an end to everyone going out to drinking parties. One man who missed his round of social boozing decided to break the curfew so that he could slam back a few tequilas and chill with his mates. No one was more surprised than he when the local police arrived to break up the party and arrest everyone in sight. The man, however, thought he might get away with it by jumping into an open coffin, (face-mask on for safety's sake, of course) and lie perfectly still so that the cops would think he was a lately deceased Covid victim. That ruse lasted for all of ten seconds and then he was arrested by a gaggle of cops who were probably pissing themselves laughing at the time. No one explained, however, why there were piles of coffins lying around the drinking hole — but then, this was South America!

Which reminds me to mention the astonishing story of the deceased man in Trinidad who, dressed beautifully in a pink blazer with matching tie, perfectly pressed, pure white trousers and white running shoes, was driven to his funeral seated upright in a chair on the back tray of a utility. He was even wearing sunglasses (Trinidad being a particularly sunny place) and there is no doubt that it was a beautiful final drive for the poor dead chappy. Parked outside the church, however, the body, still seated upright in the back of the ute, was not allowed to be brought inside for the funeral service. Apparently the rules stated categorically that all bodies had to be in coffins. Some people passing by did not realise that the late and lamented chap was actually dead and reprimanded him for not wearing a face-mask in the middle of a global pandemic. That was really quite naughty of him, they said.

The funeral directors should really have thought of that one beforehand!

Holding your breath was also touted as being a sure-fire way of discovering if you had the virus. One guru in India instructed his followers to hold their breath for a full minute if they were young and healthy and for half a minute if they were a bit decrepit. If you couldn't do that you were stuffed, he said, and already had the virus.

I guess that would mean you would not need to undergo one of those rather nasty nasal probes which just about draws your brains out through your nostrils. It was also suggested that mustard seed oil should be shoved up the nostrils which would then force the Covid bugs out of the respiratory tract and into the stomach where they would be set upon rather brutally by gallons of stomach acid which would destroy them completely. What a brilliant cure that would have been if even a microscopic fragment of it had been true! Other people were experimenting with hair-dryers believing that breathing in the hot air would kill the virus. However, all that was achieved, apparently, were a few roasted tonsils.

The Chinese, meanwhile, always the clever little buggers of the world, despite the blood-baths taking place in their wet markets, were attempting to demonstrate that they have always been the most hygienic race on earth. One bank, for example, began flooding all the banknotes they received with ultra violet light to disinfect them. That was probably at around the same time that Trump brought up the maniacal proposition that we should flood our bodies with strong light so that the virus within us would have to wear sunglasses as apparently it does not like any kind of light, especially ultra violet light which is known to cause cancer, by the way. Trump was almost inviting mockery just so he could bite off another journalist's head and feed it back to him.

Comedians in the U.S. were principally the ones highlighting the absurdity of Donald Trump's views on the virus. Let's face it, any kind of political idiocy, folly, farce or failure, especially in an atmosphere of blatant lies and wholesale disinformation is always fare game for satire and Trump seemed to be unaware that every time he opened his mouth the satirists would be ready with their ironic pens and brushes pointing out in humorous and very clever ways what it takes to be a real leader.

Meanwhile the 'Big Crazy' continued around the world. No one really knew what to do especially after reading reports that all kinds of things were being infected. In Tanzania, for example, a pawpaw came back with a positive result, although it was not revealed where the nasal probe had been placed to take *that* particular test. A quail had similarly tested positive and also a goat, but there was some concern by this time that the Chinese testing kits might not have been quite up to standard.

In India the 'Big Crazy' could not have been more clearly amplified when it was revealed that a total of eighteen men had somehow managed to cram themselves into a cement mixer, along with their luggage, so that they could travel across the country during the middle of a national lock-down. One can only assume what would have happened if the 'rotate' lever had been pulled accidentally during the journey. The men would have arrived at their destination looking like some kind of horrific human porridge.

On the Swedish island of Gotland there was almost a medieval air as a group of 'knights' all of whom were members of some local jousting club, decided that they would use the full power of their impressive suits of armour, war-horses, replica swords and pine-lances to keep people apart. In effect they formed a crusade against the virus. You might be trying to grab a few rays on one of Sweden's freezing beaches but be a smidgen too close to some other sun-lover and suddenly you would be descended upon by King Arthur, Sir Lancelot and possibly even Merlin waving his magic wand in a chivalrous attempt to keep you safe and virus free. You just have to applaud the effort though. The only problem I have with the people of Gotland is that they just adore eating the heads of sheep complete with their brains which, to a vegan is slightly more than vaguely disgusting.

Sports of all kinds were among the activities that people apparently missed the most. I can't quite understand it myself but if people could not get to their footy games or baseball tournaments there was hell to pay. In Australia the prime minister used the promise of opening up sporting venues in an effort to get people to download a virus tracing app. It almost worked but not enough people would agree to download the app because they distrusted it more than they wanted to get to the sporting grounds, which, for sports-worshipping Australia, was a phenomenon of staggering proportions.

Then the TV stations suddenly realised that when they again began broadcasting football games there would be just ten people in the stands designed to hold tens of thousands and therefore no roaring crowds to inject that vital element of raw barbarism into the game. In Germany they had already solved this diabolical conundrum by using fake crowd roars — a bit like the canned laughter you would see in Benny Hill shows when the girls showed their bums and Benny's eyes popped out on springs. The Yanks cleverly call this ruse the 'laff-box' and use it in those awful sitcoms about families hilariously tearing each other apart with the help of their psychiatrists. Australians thought that the concept of canned crowds was absolutely bloody brilliant and immediately pinched the idea. All the viewers had to do was to black out the empty seats from their consciousness when listening to a hundred thousand voices chanting 'You sheep shagger, Baaaaaaaa', whatever that means in English. I'm not kidding.

In Korea a massive fake cardboard-cutout crowd was placed onto spectators' seats when the baseball season began. The cardboard effigies actually had photographs of real fans pasted onto the heads. Real cheerleaders, people who were actually alive I mean, suitably masked to prevent them from catching the virus from the cardboard cutouts, jumped enthusiastically up and down and chanted and waved their tassels so that the cutouts could really get enthused about the game. It's a phenomenon known as self-delusion. Even TV cameramen were filming the 'crowd's' response and nobody seems to care how quiet they were. A similar but far more hilarious event took place during the resumption of football matches in Seoul when sex dolls, (would you believe?) were placed into the stands in place of real people.

Red faced organisers later stated that they had no idea that the 'dummies' were actually sex dolls, despite the fact that some of the dolls were holding placards advertising x-rated websites. I had a look at some of the photographs and really, the dolls were quite sweet in, you know, a 'Hi sailor, fifty bucks, short-time' kind of way.

And while I'm in the mood to talk about cardboard I should point out that Columbia put cardboard to unfathomably good use during the height of that country's Covid outbreak. An advertising company designed and created a hospital bed made almost entirely from cardboard that could be folded conveniently into a coffin once the patient in the bed had, well, passed on.

And innovation, of sorts, did not end there. In Singapore, for example, people walking in the Bishan-Ang Mo Kio Park were astounded to see something that looked suspiciously like some kind of monstrous cricket lurching towards them. (I'm taking about the insect cricket not the diabolical Ashes performance of the English team in Australia in 2022). This cricket was actually a robot named Spot which had been developed by Boston Dynamics and was being used to warn people who were not sufficiently 'socially distanced'. It sounds fine in theory but the video footage I saw was slightly terrifying as people jogged through the trees being maniacally chased by a massive yellow insect yelling almost intelligibly in an electronic voice that they were being very naughty indeed. The people I saw on camera were turning their heads in frightened confusion, and while it did not appear to make any difference to social distancing space, it certainly sped up the joggers as they ran like buggery from the horrifying object.

Introverts like me, banged up in their lofts and attics with the dust of generations and two white mice, looked out of their cobwebbed windows, including their digital windows, of course, with intense curiosity. Somehow, all this was merely confirming what they already believed about humanity generally. Civilization was literally as thin as a sheet of toilet paper. It could be shredded in a second. If people did not have the ability to wipe their bottoms they became really *really* angry. Then the anger and frustration began spilling out in all kinds of directions. Shops and restaurants were closed, as were parks and beaches. I think it was the closure of the beaches more than anything that caused the greatest frustration among my cousins the extroverts, but actually access to retail businesses and coffee shops was almost as problematic as people realised that there was nothing to do in a day but work. And then the work dried up too and they were left at home in lock-down, with only an old Monopoly set, which is not a good place to be for people who are used to bright colours, loud music, jumping wildly up and down and being in everyone's face simultaneously on both sides of Sydney Harbour.

The great lock-downs which took place around the world also meant something more for introverts: they were at last able to bathe in guilt-free isolation. The thing about introversion and reclusiveness is that it does not come easily in a world that expects human contact. Introversion is a basic human characteristic in people like myself, but for a major part of our lives we have felt guilt at not going out as others expect us to. We have not taken any active part in society by joining clubs, attending meetings, going to dances or taking part in any kind of activity that demands the participation of more than two people — preferably one. And we often felt guilty about that. Now, however, the world lock-down had occurred and introverts no longer had to feel guilty about staying at home. Normally I would frequently be interrupted in my work with the need to go down town for a variety of reasons. Now I was free just to stay at home. I utilised the time by proofreading a book that was soon to be published (*Tragedy at Évian*) and then writing another (*Sea Monsters*) while also drafting another chapter for this book. Additionally, I wrote another book: (*Spies, Saboteurs and Secret Missions of World War Two*). I also worked on an anthology of autobiographical narrative poetry, and sent a new novel to my publisher (*Entombed*) so my time in isolation was not only comforting, it was also hugely productive. *Sea Monsters*, for example, was written in less than two months. On the very day I completed it the manuscript was accepted by my publisher, so I was more than happy to have been banged up for a while.

My point here is that because of the lock-downs, introverts no longer had to feel that they were in any way a lesser kind of personality nor did they have to pretend to be ambiverts or extroverts. The lock-down was the new normal.

Introverts could just hang.

And we did. We sat quietly at home making notes, and through our digital prisms carefully studied the antics of everyone else because that's what introverts do. We are students of human nature and we love to turn our studies into some kind of art form, whether it be books, theatre, paintings or just telling incredulous yarns to each other via Zoom which would only happen rarely as introverts just don't do Zoom unless their hands are tied behind their backs with barbed wire. Yet the one thing that the outbreak of Covid meant for people-gazing-people like myself is that we have had an astonishing opportunity to study and comment about humankind generally and sometimes we've noticed that it's not always quite as kind as it's made out to be. And there appears to be an explanation for this.

As strange as this might sound, we are not new to social distancing. In fact we have been practising it for years and our embrace of social distancing has been slowly increasing, almost without our being aware of it. Introverts have always practised social distancing but extroverts are not newcomers to it either. Let's look at how society has been changing over the past couple of decades with the advances made in electronic communications, social media and the internet generally. I've seen kids seated in the same room, at either end of a couch, texting each other. That's social distancing. In business organisations, groups often communicate via Zoom or other electronic conference facilities; neighbours now more often text each other rather than actually popping next door for a chat, a cuppa and a custard cream. Technology is allowing us to retreat within ourselves. Children in their bedrooms are texted by their parents to let them know that their tea is on the table. Friends chat by text rather than going out to meet in the park. In busy offices people remain at their desks and text or inter-office message each other rather than getting up and physically going to another person's workspace. Drive-through fast-food outlets, self checkouts at supermarkets, ATM machines, automatic airport check-in, home delivered meals, grocery deliveries, all these are forms of social distancing and are facilities we would now have difficulty doing without.

This kind of self quarantining has been going on for years and we've become so used to it we hardly know that social distancing is taking place right under our noses. We've found, sometimes even without realising it, that we have the ability to socially distance (there's that *damned* split infinitive again!) while still retaining our connectivity. In effect we were already implementing what is now known as 'non-pharmaceutical intervention' — the kind of response that's been used for centuries to fight epidemics and pandemics around the world. Yet this kind of social distancing has come with a cost, and psychologists believe that the cost is a growing lack of empathy. In short, as we distance ourselves farther from society so we come to feel less empathetic, even more hostile, towards people generally. A clear example of this may be seen in the senseless battles for toilet paper. There have even been reports of people bashing each other stupidly over a single face-mask.

Of course, scarcity almost immediately brought about the usual tidal surge of greed and the price of toilet paper rose markedly. It became something of a joke with people asking the question as to how much one would be willing to pay to wipe one's bottom. One jeweller with a powerful sense of toilet humour satirically placed a roll of loo-paper in his window beautifully wrapped in a gold ribbon. Next to the bog-roll was a stunning diamond ring behind which was a sign which offered the single roll of toilet paper at a cost of $3999 with a one-caret diamond ring thrown in for free. I bet he sold it too!

One particularly brilliant cartoonist portrayed several people standing together wrapped completely from head toe in toilet paper. They looked like Egyptian mummies. The tongue-in-cheek caption insightfully asked if this was how people were actually attempting to protect themselves from the virus.

Actually I can never really come to terms with buying toilet paper. To me it is the quintessential form of mind-boggling embarrassment and it is impossible for me to imagine rolling up (sorry about the pun) to some checkout operator at my local supermarket with a shopping trolley loaded to the gunnels with massive packets of bog roll.

Sometimes, (at least in pre-virus history) my lovely wife would come out of the supermarket with a trolley basket filled to capacity with organic fruit and vegetables on top of which would be a massive plastic package of double-thickness, baby-soft, toilet paper, at least fourteen miles of it, all furled into recycled rolls and covered in pink plastic that, apparently, could be seen from outer space. Additionally, the packaging would absolutely scream 'Ahoy There! Toilet Paper Alert'. It told everyone that this plastic-wrapped bundle of pure-joy-to-the-bum was the softest, most environmentally friendly toilet paper in the entire world. The words on the high visibility plastic screamed out to absolutely everyone in the supermarket. Even people in the cafe at the other end of the shopping-centre could read the words. This is the *crème de la crème* of bog-roll, the advertisement on the package would say, although not quite in those words, harvested only from sustainable forests and made from the juiciest of pine trees, swamped in softening chemicals not only to make the paper gentle on the old bot-bot but also to give it that lasting perfume of fake wild pine so important when sitting in a really tiny room, two metres in length by one metre wide, which smells rather alarmingly of recently hatched poo.

Interestingly, I reflect, while pondering the toilet paper wars, after packaged loo paper had been invented in 1880 (in America, actually), it took another fifty-five years before a splinter-free variety came onto the market. Up until then one took the inordinate risk of having bum-splinters an inch long which would really have brought tears to one's eyes.

That's a true story, by the way.

Yet toilet paper wars and face-mask fracas aside, the pandemic also brought out some of the basest needs in human nature. Even for an introvert it's almost impossible to understand. The world was falling apart and fear of the unknown was beginning to kick in. Part of this, I guess, is Hollywood's fault. We have all seen post-apocalyptic movies where really nasty stuff was happening on screen. Zombies suddenly appearing on trains and eating everyone's brains; aliens parking massive spaceships overhead and destroying the world with super weapons, and the classic, in my opinion, *The Road*, starring Viggo Mortensen in one of the bleakest and probably the most accurate post-apocalyptic movies ever made. We were now beginning to relate to these depictions of horror in a very personal way. Would we be among the millions of victims or would we be among the few left standing, still clutching our much tattered bog-rolls, when it was all over? Would we also be scavenging for food while being hunted as food by gangs of starving red-necks in MAGA hats?

Hollywood has a lot to answer for.

But even for those who had never seen a post-apocalyptic movie in their lives (all three of them), fear of the unknown was very real. Covid appeared in the world at just a period in our history where things were buzzing and I don't mean in a good way.

America was trying to crush Chinese business. China was (and still is) trying to dominate the China Sea region while also expanding its influence globally. Ultra right-wing organisations and all kinds of heavily armed neo-Nazi groups were filling the air-waves and social media sites with dangerously effective hate-filled rhetoric; The Trump had just garnered sufficient right-wing backing from his Republican sycophants to have him found not guilty at his first impeachment trial and Putin had declared himself *El Presidente* for life. Brazil was in the grip of a president who said that Covid was a man's disease and that men should be *hombres* and go out there to face it like men and stop being bloody-well girly about it. Then hundreds of thousands of Brazilians died. The doctor who had revealed the existence of Covid had been condemned by his government and killed by the very disease he was trying to expose to the world. At least half of America and about the same number of people in the world believed that a biological weapon had either been released by China or had been developed by China and had now gone rogue, although there was absolutely no evidence to prove that. Racism was on the rise, George Floyd had been murdered by a Redneck's knee; statues around the world were being pulled down and there was a cultural and historical war going on to decide which national monuments should or should not be cast into the flames. Pharmaceutical companies and manufacturers were racing to change the names of some of their products or take them off the market altogether which, for example, brought about the complete demise of skin-lightening creams. Climate-deniers were refusing to admit defeat even as their feet were burning on the bitumen streets of Washington and Canberra and it was estimated that the entire global economy would very quickly collapse as a result of the viral outbreak. Absolutely nothing was looking good. Then came the news that not even people who had contracted the virus were immune from further infection, and a vaccine, if one were ever to be developed, would be at least eighteen months away during which time millions could die, most of them, apparently, either Americans or Brazilians. About half the population of America actually believed that Bill Gates was paying to develop a vaccine so that people could be injected with a serum that would be used to track them forever. Trump was demanding that he be awarded a 'Noble' Peace Prize (really!) and holding up a Bible while his gang sprayed humans with quite unpleasant chemicals. People everywhere were beginning to become really terrified, and what was terrifying them the most was the possibility that Trump might actually have received his long sought 'My Precious' award because that was how crazy the world had now become.

In America, people were rushing out to buy guns and ammunition almost as much as they were rushing out to buy, borrow or beg bog-roll. This says a lot about the human psyche generally and a great deal more about Americans. It is quite understandable, of course, that people were beginning to fear for their own safety. The opposite of truth, by the way, is not only untruth, it's also chaos. And chaos is a wonderfully malleable element, a bit like kiddies' plasticine. It can be moulded into any evil shape one wishes. In times of chaos, safety is a high priority and a delicate balance. But when that chaos is being manipulated from the highest echelons of government to create even more chaos and then to benefit from that chaos in any way, especially politically, then it quite clearly becomes of great concern for everybody, and many people, especially in America, believed that they would need a Vietnam War-sized arms horde in order to protect themselves.

Weapons dealers across America were (and still are) being rushed off their plate-sized hunting feet to keep up with demand and there were long queues outside their stores. One would think that with the 'shelter-in-place' order in effect, gun violence would actually drop, and it's true that crime was dropping dramatically but gun violence was actually rising. Why was that? It seems that when you have a lot of guns being waved about in a lot of homes, accidents just happen, especially when the guns have just been purchased and the gunsters who purchased them are not quite up to speed in methods of keeping them safe. ('Gunsters' is another word I've just invented by the way. I thought I'd just chuck that in, in case anyone missed it).

Of course there has also been something of a spike in deliberate gun violence as people at home have become bored with one another and decided that divorce settlements are just too bothersome and inconvenient. One would think that with gun violence on the increase, American authorities would have moved decisively to make attempts to lessen the carnage. They moved decisively all right but in completely the wrong direction. They not only classified gun stores as essential services but also allowed the same insane category to apply to shooting ranges and weapons manufacturers. In March 2020 almost two million weapons were legally sold in the United States, a phenomenon that almost matched the same fear-driven paranoia that had taken place following the Sandy Hook massacre in 2013, and since then sales have grown exponentially like the virus. So here were millions of people, many of them sad, depressed and angry that they were now unemployed, and also banged up in their tiny New York apartments, and all they had to pass the time was to watch Netflix and polish their new Colt .45s. It was a recipe for disaster especially at a time when the health and hospital services were swamped with Covid cases and people were being turned away.

Is any of this making sense to anyone out there?

But for me, I was most fearful for the animals. If people wanted to tear each other apart then who was I to stop them but many of these people were buying weapons because they believed that if food shortages were to occur then they would resort to feeding their families through hunting. The killing apparently began almost immediately even though the supermarket shelves were still stuffed to capacity with sides of beef, legs of pork, black-puddings and Wuhan sausages that happily had escaped the tariff duties. Apparently people just love any opportunity and excuse to kill something. I'm told it makes them feel good. It gives them a thrill. You can see examples of this online every day with people publishing photographs of themselves hunting in Africa, for example, where they pose with their bloodied 'kills'. Killing for them is fun and a sport, and therefore, to them at least, it all makes perfect sense.

American abattoirs began closing due to outbreaks of the virus so that also inspired people to dress up like Rambo on steroids and trek into the wilds after elk and Bambi. There was also the major advantage, of course, of being able to glue massive antlers to the walls of their aluminium trailer cabins so that they could practise bragging about them while playing strip-poker with themselves. There was something really macho about having an unwashed hunting knife in the kitchen sink while playing cards naked and drinking home brew, even if all your mates were also locked down in their own $50 a week trailer-park cabins buried in crushed beer cans, spent bullet cases and overflowing ashtrays.

Some people claimed that for them personally the killing of animals created a kind of mental cleansing. Killing, apparently, is spiritual. One young woman who killed her first deer described the experience as thrilling, exciting and remorseful, all, rather strangely, in the same nonsensical sentence.

In Indiana, applications to acquire turkey-shooting licences went through the roof which resulted in a turkey holocaust. Two wildlife ecologists claimed at the time that wild turkeys could only sustain so many hunters and that the population was declining steeply. The FBI was drawn into the picture too. In one month alone it processed 3.7 million background checks for new firearms permits, and a couple of months later, during the height of the Black Lives Matter demonstrations, the number of permit applications reached 3.9 million for the month. In Illinois, 706,000 background checks were made in just the month of June 2020. In Georgia, turkey hunting increased by 47 per cent. The American wildlife and especially the turkeys didn't stand a chance in hell. The American gun lobby was in the fray, boots and all, stirring up public fears of all kinds of looming disasters: fear of crime, fear of the government itself (which nonsensically supported them) and even, would you believe, a fear of a zombie apocalypse which some predicted was coming very soon.

Actually, animals in many parts of the world, and zombies too, I guess, were either enjoying a well deserved holiday from the violence and crush of humanity or were suffering because there were not enough humans around. It is a rather complex paradox. I read stories where zoo keepers were stating that there was not enough money to feed all the animals because the zoos had been closed so the keepers were on the verge of feeding the animals to each other. That story depressed me for weeks. Then I saw video footage of hundreds, possibly thousands of monkeys surging through the streets of a city in Thailand because they were starving. The tourists who once happily fed them had disappeared and now the animals were foraging quite madly for food. It was a staggering sight to see them running in their hundreds around traffic, sometimes turning on each other if one found a scrap of food while the others did not. Meanwhile, in China, dogs were being abandoned in the streets because Covid had been linked to the consumption of animals, particularly wild animals and dogs. It was quite common to see expensive pedigree dogs facing starvation. In the end they probably just got stewed.

Yet animals were happily turning up in the most unexpected of places: massive jungle lizards were taking advantage of swimming pools in tropical resorts; deer were seen on the streets of London and beneath the cherry blossom trees in Japan; dolphins were seen cavorting in the Bosporus which was normally thronged with massive tankers and other forms of shipping and passenger boats.

In Haifa wild boars began to come onto the streets in search of food, raiding residents' rubbish bins. Many people loved seeing them but there were, of course, the few who just wanted them destroyed! Pink flamingos thronged an Indian city in their tens of thousands while in Albania the same birds increased by a third in number and could be seen enjoying life on the otherwise deserted waterways and lagoons. In Kansas City, zoo officials took their penguins to the local art gallery for a cultural afternoon. It was brilliant! I watched the video footage and it was pure magic because the little guys dressed in their best tuxes were really enjoying that art. I expect there were a few fishy poo-stains on the extensive red carpets though.

At the Chao Mai National Park in Thailand the highly unusual sight of thirty or more plump dugongs were seen in a waterway that would normally be crowded with plump tourists. In fact the entire park had come alive with wildlife. In Hong Kong two pandas were able to mate successfully after ten years of trying. Apparently they had been put off by constantly being watched by tourists, but in the privacy of their Covid-induced isolation they happily got it on. At a 'rewilding' estate in England, conservationists were astonished to see a nest with white stork eggs, the first recorded wild breeding of white storks in more than six hundred years. Imagine that! The last time that white storks had a successful bag-off in the wilderness of the UK had been during the 15th century. Glazed glass and just been invented, Leonardo de Vinci had recently invented the parachute and Joan of Arc was swanning around France hoping to buy a fire extinguisher before it was too late.

Now, however, cougars were seen to be stalking the streets of Santiago in Chile and one was even discovered sleeping in an apartment complex. In my own home country of Wales, Kashmiri goats were seen in the streets, some of which were helping themselves to flowers and other culinary delights in people's gardens and window-boxes. In Germany, however, which had already advocated feeding zoo animals to each other, pigeons which, normally relied on food from tourists, were left in a parlous state as their food source had dried up along with the tourists. However, in Poland organisations were being formed to remedy a similar situation. There was even a piece of now iconic video footage of a large jellyfish making its way peacefully up a canal in Venice, a waterway that was normally thronged with gondolas, tourists and plastic boats shaped like pizzas.

The world turned. Nothing was the same any more and we began to pose questions which before Covid could never possibly have been asked. We were banned from going outside except for essential reasons such as the purchase of groceries. Was buying a new dildo during lock-down an essential item, one woman asked. She apparently had a lot of time to fill and no Monopoly set. In America the same question was asked about marijuana. In Illinois, not surprisingly, the governor decided that guns were, indeed, essential items.

Why am I not surprised?

As Covid galloped ahead in the United States, Mexico closed its borders banning Americans from crossing — an event that would have been unthinkable only a few weeks previously when Trump had been busily constructing his wall-to-end-all-walls to prevent Mexicans from coming the other way. It was a highly controversial wall anyway. Mexican nationals and others from Latin American countries were easily climbing it. It came in for some scathing criticism in the world press and its efficacy as a human barrier was severely tested. Only a few kilometres of it were ever built and guess what: while Americans forked out billions to have it constructed, Mexicans never actually paid a single peso!

Even the Mafia was suffering Covid pains. People stopped gambling, and with businesses closed everywhere the entire protection racket business fell into a massive vacuum-toilet like they used to have on aircraft before everyone stopped flying and the airline companies began recycling their aircraft to make aluminum saucepans — which is exactly the reverse of what happened during the Second World War. Strip-club dancers and hostesses really began to feel the pinch, (no pun intended) and rather than shedding their clothes in front of a hundred leering men they decided that they would instead deliver food to them in isolation. At least the revolving tassels would have brightened everyone's day.

Boredom became the major issue of the lock-downs, probably relieved somewhat by the universal groaning of bedsprings. I am expecting there to be a new generation in the future that will be called something like the CoviKids. These will be a wave of children, just like the boomers, who have been born or conceived during the Covid crisis and they too will have to face the stigma that boomers currently face: being a drain on resources and with attitudes too firmly steeped in the past — those kinds of things. In fact the virus also became known as the 'Boomer Remover' and appeared in tens of thousands of tweets and retweets, probably posted by a bunch of fifteen year olds suffering from some kind of acne-induced moronavirus. At time of writing, this hypothesis actually seems to be coming true and the Indonesians are already expecting there to be a massive baby boom as a direct result of the crisis. People are not only staying at home shagging like bunnies but they are also staying at home because they are afraid to attend crowded family planning clinics or go to supermarkets to purchase condoms or to see their doctor or pharmacist to obtain birth control pills. The Indonesians alone are expecting hundreds of thousands of additional babies to be born as a result of the pandemic — possibly upwards of close to half a million. That's an awful lot of bonking in the tropics!

But among all this mayhem, bored shagging and confusion, introverts were beginning to find a kind of psychological freedom. Up until now, introverts have been regarded as residents of the loony fringe. Susan Cain's best selling and really wonderful book, *Quiet*, did much to dispel this myth but Susan was just one voice of reason in a world of discrimination. Introverts were always regarded as peculiar, no matter how much Susan Cain's book explained and justified the issue. Yet now everyone was being forced to become a recluse and suddenly psychologists around the world were stating that it was actually okay. The principal question I have for those psychologists is this. Where in hell were you when all the introverts of the world were protesting (quietly) that it's okay to be an introvert and to stay at home tucked up with a book and tub of soy ice-cream? Introverts have been social distancing all their lives but have also been stigmatised and marginalised for it. It's not just that we are usually totally germophobic, although that's important too, but we also don't like being too close to people. Suddenly Covid gave us some kind of astonishing validity. We have been right all along. We are not nuts. We are just quiet people who don't like to mix and mash with other people.

There was even a tiny element of rejoicing our kind of quiet superiority. Extroverts were tearing their hair out, jumping up and down with cabin fever, while we introverts had been flattening the curve all our lives. We were smugly confident that nothing could kill us especially not some horrible bug that was clearly designed to target extroverts because they dressed so colourfully and inhaled vast amounts of other people's saliva while jumping up and down and shouting out to the world how brilliant they are. We, on the other hand, were shielded by our own personalities. It was a bit like having Covid antibodies in our DNA.

There was a small downside, however. Introverts are not always banged up alone. Introverts also like to go out to the beach and parks and they rather missed that. The only difference was that introverts like to go to those places alone and if they take their dogs for a walk you can always spot the introvert: they are the ones wearing dark sunglasses even on cloudy days and have super-long leads so they can keep their distance while passers-by stop and pat their dogs.

Yet there were hangups to this too. Where people would normally not visit because they knew that we preferred our own company, and so left us alone, they suddenly found an excuse to contact us using Skype or Zoom or texts and emails. Social distancing was still in place but suddenly introverts were being inundated with electronic communications asking them to 'hangout' in some weird chat-room or to take part in an online drinking party or play chess or show their bums. Anything to pass the time. It was not even possible to use the age-old excuse that we had somewhere to go or we needed to go home. We were in lock-down and we were already home. We were caught in a web of super-bored extroverts wanting to do something — anything — as long as it wasn't something quiet like sitting down with a good book or knitting a pair of grandpa-socks. It was impossible to use the simple excuse that you just didn't feel like it. Somehow the excuse to be alone failed to connect with anyone in the new normal of Covid 19. The only way out of this, of course, was to disconnect all electronic communications which was not always possible. For introverts it was a conundrum they would have to face with courage, just like going to grocery stores.

Actually most introverts loath grocery stores and the Covid thing amplified that to an unprecedented degree. Shopping aisles in busy supermarkets have always been like the Hall of Horror you see in cheap fairgrounds full of spooky images and green skeletons dangling from plastic gibbets. The crush of people with their grocery trolleys pushing and shoving and trying to squeeze around you to get at the coffee or condoms leaves introverts shrieking inside, and that was *before* the toilet-paper wars had begun. The situation was not helped at all when someone put a video animation online that demonstrated how easily the sucker-bugs fly around in shopping aisles once someone has sneezed. In the video a thick green soup of animated bug-mist began to swarm like bees. It literally flew in all directions and especially enveloped a chap standing in the next aisle who was innocently but unsuccessfully looking for toilet paper. You could see by the digital bug-swarm that he was almost certainly going to die. The poor sod didn't have a glowworm's chance in a snowstorm.

There was also the problem of introverts with families who were used to working quietly from home after the husbands or partners had gone to work and the children had gone to school. Now, suddenly, the partners were working from home and the children were not at school but taking up valuable broadband data trying to do their lessons online. For the average introvert this was exactly like trying to weave through the Chicago downtown traffic on a wet Monday morning in winter with the radio blasting a piece of hip-hop doggerel. It was a disaster. And the most difficult thing of all was when partners pressed them into taking part in lengthy Zoom communications that seemed to go on forever because the extroverts on the other end of the line knew that you were trapped with nowhere to go and took full advantage of that.

It was like one of those occasions in the past when you had met up with the kind of people I call professional conversationalists. We had one in a town where I used to live. Greenie, as I called him, was a photographer. I had made the hilarious mistake at one time of agreeing to be a model for some men's fashion photographs which were published in the press and on the local TV channel, and to get the shots I had to visit Greenie in his photographic studio. Thereafter it was impossible to pass his studio without Greenie dashing out to grab me with his tongue like a lizard. He was like one of those really big Monitors with tongues about three feet long, only chumpier, of course, with tortoiseshell glasses and really serious halitosis. Greenie literally could not stop talking. It was anathema to his DNA. He would talk for hours and no matter how I tried to get away he always found a way to manoeuvre around me, cunningly blocking my exit without seeming to do so, constantly talking, shifting the focus of his diatribe from one subject to the next without even the hint of a pause while also not allowing me to say, 'Sorry but I have to get going,' or even if I did magically manage to say those words he would say: 'Oh okay then it's been great to talk to you, and oh, by the way, before you go I should let you know that ....' And so it went on, seemingly endlessly, until his assistant would come from the studio, apparently taking pity on me, to tell Greenie that his cuppa was ready or his mum was dead, but even then he disengaged with the reluctance of a hyena unlocking jaws from its prey. That too was an introvert's kind of hell, not only because I was glued inescapably to a chumpy lizard's tongue but also because I don't like people looking at me. People would be passing me in the street and giving me pitying looks knowing full well that I had been trapped in Greenie's conversational web-of-hell and I didn't stand a snowball's chance of getting out of there any time soon.

I would need to be invisible to do that!

Slowly but unsurely, we began to see a tentative light at the end of the Covid tunnel and even recluses like myself found that we were able to breath a small sigh of relief, especially if the much cherished stock of loo paper was becoming critically low. One by one countries began opening up, some far too early and rapidly and others slowly and, for a while at least, more safely, although, in reality, as we now know, the illusion of safety was to prove only too ephemeral. In Switzerland, for example, brothels were among the first types of businesses to resume operations. What a relief that must have been, especially for the overworked Gnomes of Zurich who obviously needed a jolly good shag after all that money-counting they had been doing all day!

Actually I was astonished to discover that the Swiss had legalised brothels way back in 1942 so at that time there were probably rather a lot of nasty Nazis ducking regularly across the border to roger away their ill-gotten *reichsmarks*.

Now however, more than three-quarters of a highly erotic century later, the Swiss authorities, and particularly the health ministry, had made it very clear that while brothels were being allowed to restart bonking operations, there were certain activities that would remain strictly off the menu — if brothels have menus, that is. The first thing to be forbidden was, of course, kissing. Faces were to be kept the length of a forearm apart which would have been a peculiar position to hold while you were having sex unless you were doing it missionary, but apparently that was *verboten* too. Clients also had to give up their personal details so that they could be traced in case of an outbreak at the massage joint. That rule alone probably deflected a few married erections from walking through the door. Now, I expect you think I'm being rude here, or pulling your leg, but I'm just giving you the rules as outlined by the Swiss authorities who, after all, were probably well experienced in these important matters. Doggy style sex was permitted, and also the much favoured reverse cowgirl position. If you don't know what that is you can Google it or get a friend to draw a naughty diagram. Threesomes were completely banned, naturally because that would have meant far too many hands and appendages being in altogether far too many recipient places. The wearing of masks was recommended during the sex act which would probably just about kill the mood for any kind of hanky-panky-spanky. Any kind of sex that might cause the transmission of 'droplets' was seriously discouraged so unless you were having sex with someone in the next room or one of the shag-dolls in a Korean sports stadium it would be difficult to know how it would be possible to comply with that particular guideline. I expect all these rules certainly helped to keep people safe while they got their rocks off, but really, you have to ask if it was worth the effort?

While doing my extensive research for this story, by the way, I never once visited a Swiss brothel personally but I would have loved to have seen the actual Department of Health regulations that explained all the rules in the usual official jargon. By the time you had waded through all the guff and rushed out to buy the latex gloves without actually knowing why you needed them you would probably have forgotten why you were in the brothel in the first place and you definitely would not have been able to maintain an erection.

People were out and about but they were still bored — at least those not shagging their brains out in Swiss brothels. In Taiwan, for example, some people were missing airline travel so much that the Songshan airport put on special 'flights'. 'Passengers' could go through check-in, luggage-checks, passport-control, security, gift-shop buying, drinking coffee in the waiting lounge, saying goodbye to friends and relatives, boarding the aircraft and everything associated with a wonderful trip to exotic places such as Bali or Clapham Common but without actually going anywhere. The aircraft never left the ground. After five or six hours being served microwaved food in plastic containers and drinking double-price half-measure scotch and sodas, the passengers could disembark knowing that at least they didn't have to worry about their luggage ending up in Moscow, which was a jolly good result for everyone especially the baggage handlers because they were all at home busily creating Covikids.

Actually I think I'm getting crazier as I write this book!

Conclusion

Okay, so I'm not really invisible, although I try my best to be. I was reading a psychology article recently which stated that our personalities are not fixed. In early life we can be one person but by the time we reach adulthood we can have changed to a different person entirely. By the time we reach middle age we might have changed again and by the ripe age of pension eligibility we will possibly have taken on a whole new persona. In fact, researchers have demonstrated that it's possible to change our personalities over just sixteen weeks under an intensive training period. Well the fact is that I was an introvert as a child and wished then that I were invisible and have remained that way all my life without any desire to change. I admit, however, that I shall probably never be completely invisible until I eventually melt like a musty old lollipop in a terramation chamber.

Invisibility is a myth. That's a fact. Everyone knows it.

Or is it?

Researchers at Duke University in the U.S.A. believe that real invisibility might actually be achievable. Working with Imperial College, London, the university now speculates that the answer to achieving invisibility might be an invisibility 'cloak' made of what they call 'metamaterial' which would be able to guide light waves and electromagnetic waves around it thus creating a space that would theoretically be invisible. A bit like water flowing around a rock in the centre of a stream. It's all quite beyond my limited understanding of science, but researchers at both Duke and Imperial College are optimistic that this phenomenon might become a reality in the not too distant future.

As of time of writing a U.K. company, Invisibility Shield Co., and also a company in Canada, are developing systems based broadly upon this concept, and demonstrations of their effectiveness may be seen online. I can see introverts worldwide, after reading this book, beginning a massive crowdfunding campaign to hurry things along a bit.

As I have become older my seclusion has increased, rather than decreasing. I was once a university lecturer and although I struggled to stand and teach in front of my students, mainly because, as I have explained a few times prior to this, I just don't like being the centre of attention, I forced myself to do what I had to do because everyone needs to work. Today I wouldn't do that. If someone offered me a similar job I'd be running like Roger Bannister in the opposite direction and as we all know he could run a mile in about the same time as it takes to boil a runny egg.

Basically I have two lives. The private life where I live, and my public life as a writer. The two are so distinct that at times it would seem that I am two different people.

Today, in my private life, I rarely use the telephone, in fact I only use it when I irregularly remember to phone my dear sister. I never go into small shops because that would mean that the shop assistant would actually be looking at me. I never go into banks and I am yet to use an ATM for any reason. All I want to do is write and research. Alone. Quietly. That's it. I also like to campaign for animal rights but that too is done as anonymously and as quietly as possible while at the same time hopefully making a massive amount of electronic noise and saving animals from human-imposed suffering and death.

On the other hand there is my public life as a writer and as I have said many times to publishers, for a book to be successful it has to be a full and willing collaboration between the author and the publisher. About the only time I'm seen in public is when I do a book-launch or book-signings in shops or libraries, although at the time of writing even these activities have ceased due to

Covid or 'post-Covid' issues. Yes, I'm uncomfortable doing them but people would never know that because even though I dislike public speaking I'm very experienced at it and I work hard at appearing to be relaxed and natural. It seems to work. To date most of those events have been particularly successful, often with hundreds of guests, and signings that have gone on until the wee hours. What I'm trying to say in all this is that being an introvert does not necessarily mean that one is doomed to failure or to a dull life living in a shoebox. Even reclusive introverts like myself can succeed and can make a significant difference. I receive fan mail from people here in Australia and overseas telling me how much my books have meant to them. One person told the press quite recently that my books had literally changed his life. He had never been much of a reader, and history had held little interest for him. Then he had read one of my books and it had altered his perspective entirely. He now reads avidly, especially histories, and volunteers his time at a historical museum. That kind of feedback makes it all worthwhile.

Seclusion has been a major part of my life but I have to say that I have also been guided and influenced by my deep love for all animals. It's just who I am, and while I absolutely don't wish to turn the conclusion of this book into a lecture on ethics, I should at least attempt to explain why I love animals so much and why, therefore, I am an ethical vegan and will remain so until the day I die. Perhaps in this way readers might gain a better understanding of why this book has been written.

When I first arrived in Australia, almost by accident, in 1972, I faced a long trek right across the continent from west to east, a distance of almost three thousand miles, some of it through rough, dry, desert country including the Nullabor which had no sealed road at that time. That story is for another book but I have to say that although I have lived permanently in Australia since 1972 it has never ceased to amaze me how animals, both farm animals and wild creatures, are exploited here. Millions of kangaroos are 'culled' each year and probably an equal number are killed on the roads by cars and trucks. Sometimes I lie in bed at night and can hear the kangaroo shooters at work, just outside the city boundaries were I live: the distinctive two shots, the first to bring the animal down the second to finish it off. It is a heartrending experience and for anyone who knows these beautiful, gentle, vegan creatures it's quite obvious that this kind of behaviour is completely intolerable. When I first saw a kangaroo-shooter's vehicle during my long hitchhiking journey across Australia I had to rub my eyes in disbelief. I thought for a moment that they were the butchered and beheaded remains of human beings hanging bloodily from the hooks of the utility. The horror of it didn't just take my breath away, it scarred me forever. That, by the way, isn't something you see in the glossy tourist brochures!

This, I soon discovered, was a country that had once waged war against its own emu population. Most people will not have had any connection with emus but they are a hugely intelligent and loving animal, much like ostriches, who make great animal companions although they can be a bit naughty and peck where they shouldn't at times. My brother-in-law had an emu which he raised from a chick, just out of the egg, and when it had grown sufficiently, and was independent, it was returned to the wild. Emus are funny, mischievous and marvellously bright, but the Australian government had once ordered that they be massacred by machine-guns. It almost beggars belief. That's so stupid that John Cleese is making a movie out of it.

By the way, I should mention, just as a matter of curiosity, that it could also have happened to the hedgehogs in England until the British Government passed the Wildlife and Countryside Act specifically preventing the machine-gunning of the prickly little creatures. I'm not sure why anyone would actually want to machine-gun hedgehogs but it's true and proves that the mass slaughter of any species, large or small, can be prevented with a good bit of sound legislation, no matter how crazy it sounds. In any case, I have to ask this really important question: how many people in England actually own a machine-gun and even if they did own such a weapon why would they want to use it on hedgehogs? It all sounds a bit nutty to me.

I love all animals and insects and am delighted that ethical veganism is growing around the world, although I was somewhat disheartened to read recently that someone had invented a vending machine for dispensing edible insects including salted roasted crickets and chocolate-coated beetles, which demonstrates with cutting clarity that we still have a long way to go on the road to compassion for all living creatures.

Attitudes are changing, however, as our levels of education improve and our need for ethical reform increases. Education and the passing of new laws are playing a leading role in that. For example, in January 2020 during a landmark legal case brought by ethical vegan Jordi Casamitjana in the U.K., ethical veganism was ruled to be a 'philosophical belief under the Equality Act of 2010', because it satisfied several tests including that of being ' … worthy of respect in a democratic society', and that it was also, ' … not incompatible with human dignity and not conflicting with the fundamental rights of others'. The judge hearing the case, Robin Postle, ruled that ethical veganism was both 'worthy' and 'important' within democratic society. This vital ruling meant that employers in the U.K., at last, would have to respect ethical veganism and that they would be unable to discriminate against ethical vegans for their beliefs.

The struggle to have veganism recognised as a 'mainstream' ethical belief has taken decades and, of course, the ethos has been attacked on all fronts, principally by those who work in, or control, the meat industry. Yet even ordinary people on the streets who have no connection to the meat industry will frequently attack (sometimes physically) and 'troll' vegans, believing that vegans just want to take away their right to eat meat or use animal products such as milk, eggs, fur and body parts. However, this is not true. Vegans would love the world to become completely vegan but we are realist enough to know that this will only happen over many years — possibly centuries — and more for reasons *other* than ethics. However, vegans hope to convince meat-eaters that consuming animals is nothing more than 'eating the dead', as I often phrase it on social media, and that when one eats a corpse one is basically grave-robbing. Harsh words, I know, and emotive, but also true and effective.

Even before the advent of Covid 19 which wrought worldwide devastation on meatworks and their employees, abattoirs were closing, especially in regional centres, and although I deplore the fact that people are put out of work, if we are to move forward to a kinder, more sustainable form of food management in the world, and recent very detailed and carefully researched academic reports prove that we need to do just that, then such closures are inevitable and jobs will be lost in a variety of meat-related industries. Yet it's not all bad news and there are solutions that will provide both employment and a sustainable, less cruel, food supply for humans.

It's a way off yet but rapid progress is being made with healthier, cleaner, cheaper, cruelty-free meat substitutes and proteins. As public consciousness grows, as empathy through education towards the plight of animals increases, and as technology improves, so the meat industry will slowly fade to be replaced by more ethical and efficient proteins including 'manufactured' meats, that are now becoming known as 'clean' meats or 'cultured' meats, and real dairy products that have not come directly from farmed animals.

Winston Churchill actually predicted that this day would come when he wrote in 1931 that in the future it would no longer be necessary to kill a chicken just to eat a wing or leg and that those body parts would be able to be manufactured in a 'suitable medium'. For his time, Churchill was being acutely perspicacious because what he was predicting was a kind of agricultural revolution that is happening around the world right now. Even traditional meat production companies and owners of abattoirs like Cargills and Tyson are beginning to come on board and are investing in cultured meat technology because they can see that profits in the future will come principally from cultured meats rather than slaughtered animals.

There are now quite a number of manufacturing enterprises bringing out meat, dairy and egg products without the use of animals that are so much like the original it is difficult, if not impossible, to tell the difference. One of the national American radio networks, NPR, recently broadcast an in-depth story about some of these businesses. The story included details of a company named Perfect Day, of Berkley, California, which is currently in the process of releasing a vegan ice-cream and other 'dairy' products made with synthetic whey proteins. Apparently the end product is every bit as good as 'real' ice-cream but no animals have been farmed or harmed in the process. Co-founders of the Perfect Day company, Perumal Gandhi and Ryan Pandya, have developed gene sequences that are used by cows to produce milk proteins rather than taking DNA from an actual cow. These proteins are converted into fungi in a process known as cellular agriculture. Utilising such methods of production would mean that we would never again need to raise, utilise or slaughter animals.

Impossible Burger, and another company called Beyond Meat, are now in the process of introducing meatless meat to the world, using biochemistry to copy the taste and texture of meat. Clara Foods is using synthetic biology to create egg-whites which are proving to be every bit as good as real hen's eggs. New Culture is a California company utilising microbial fermentation to manufacture casein, the essential element that gives cheese its 'stretchy' quality. This will make vegan cheeses more closely resemble and taste like animal cheeses.

In Singapore, Turtle Tree Labs was the first company in the world to use stem cells from mammals to produce milk. Indeed, Singapore is one of the countries leading the world in such technology and it became the first country in the world to allow the sale of cultured chicken meat.

In 2022 Professor Johannes le Coutre of the University of New South Wales stated that cultivated meat was almost certainly going to be a normal grocery item in supermarket shelves by 2030, adding that as the impact of animal farming placed increasing pressures on the environment, livestock farming would become unsustainable. There are ethical issues involved too but in reality there is no comparison between the ethics of utilising cultivated meat over 'death-meat'. Death-meat is an environmental disaster for the world and also transgresses the basic human ethic that we should not kill for any reason. Stem cell production is also considered to be a grey area in the ethics of cultivated meat, however, in reality, consumer resentment towards the use of stem cells in cultured meats is invalid because stem cells are present in *every* form of food and fibre. When you eat a vegetable, you are consuming plant stem cells.

You could want no more telling indication that veganism is growing dramatically around the world than to learn that in 2019 KFC in the UK introduced a vegan version of their world-famous chicken meals. This was an astonishing development addressing the needs of those who do not wish to consume dead animals. Similar moves are now underway in America where vegan KFC is being rolled out at numerous locations. In late August 2019 online digital press sources were headlining, '*A Day in History! KFC sells out of vegan chicken in five hours flat.*' The story went on to state that when a vegan version of KFC was released in Smyrna, Georgia, a line of people went right around the parking lot and that this 'smashing success' proved that people were turning to cruelty-free foods in an unprecedented way. In mid 2020 after extensive and successful trials at Altanta, Nashville and Charlotte, KFC began rolling out vegan 'chicken' in South California with more than fifty KFC restaurants beginning to sell the Beyond Meats alternative to dead birds in the Los Angeles, Orange County and San Diego areas. For a country that has a massive amount of continuous chicken-guzzlers, where chickens, sadly, are virtually guaranteed to end their lives being sacrificed to the great poo-gods, that is an astonishing achievement.

KFC is only doing it, of course, because they've realised that there is a demand for cruelty-free foods and that they can make money by attracting new buyers to their food chains. However, many vegans will probably not be taking up the offer on purely ethical grounds because dead chickens still form the principal part of the company's business. Even so, it is a step in the right direction, albeit a tiny toddler's step, and we have to thank PETA (People for the Ethical Treatment of Animals), plus many other organisations such as Animals Australia, Sentient Media and hundreds of thousands of their supporters for working to convince businesses around the world, including KFC, that it is time to begin an evolution revolution to introduce a kinder and less animal-cruel ethos to the planet.

Studies have been done on what would happen to the world if everyone suddenly became vegetarian and the outlook is actually quite promising. To begin with, the impact on climate change would be staggering. Not that the world generally is likely to adopt a vegetarian or vegan diet any time soon, and even when it does occur it will only happen over time, despite the clear correlation between Covid 19 and the destruction of habitat and animals for food.

The climate change question is important for it stands out as one of the key issues surrounding the need to cut back on meat and dairy consumption and to replace them with other more world-friendly and animal-friendly proteins. A study at Colombia's International Centre for Tropical Agriculture has revealed that up to one third of all anthropogenic greenhouse gas emissions is generated by the world's livestock industry. It has been calculated that a family of four people eating meat as a regular part of their diet is responsible for creating as much greenhouse gasses as would be emitted from running two cars.

The same study has revealed that there would also be a global death rate reduction of around ten per cent brought about by reductions in the numbers of people suffering from heart diseases, diabetes, stroke and cancers. The death rate could be reduced by up to eight million each year.

It should also be emphasised that 'cultured meat', is not a meat substitute but real meat grown from a single animal cell. It is not yet available widely on the open market but it is coming and when it becomes readily available it appears likely that it will quickly become a very real and compassionate alternative to traditional meat. As cultured meat producers grow in size (and Israel is leading the charge) this new form of meat will challenge traditional meat on pricing, availability, ethical production and also on other vitally important issues. Unlike traditional meat, cultured meat will be free of pesticides, hormones, antibiotics and diseases. It will free up billions of acres of land for crops for human consumption and will, eventually, be environmentally non-destructive.

Of course, it's going to take time. Trillions more animals will be killed before cultured meat becomes a major force in world food consumption but when it does arrive it's likely that it will come as something of a tsunami. People are now ready to take on the challenge of embracing a new protein source that does not selfishly take innocent and harmless animal lives. People want to do something to help solve the problem of climate change and this is one of the really important methods that we can utilise to do that. Additionally, for cultured meat to catch on globally, it will also be necessary to have the major supermarkets and retailers on board and it would appear from their past history that they will embrace cultured meat as they have embraced organic foods, fair dairy pricing and cage-free eggs. It all comes down to just a few important issues. To provide a product that people want at a fair price; to ensure that the product is clean, healthy and uncontaminated, and that it makes a profit for everyone involved from manufacturing through to retail sales. In these respects cultured meat ticks all the boxes.

One thing in all this is that when cultured meat becomes commercially available there will be dissent from the traditional meat industry. Human nature being what it is, that almost goes without saying. In fact, in some areas the meat industry opposition to cultured meat is already starting. Meat producers, abattoir workers and owners, butchers and many members of the public who just like eating dead animals will be vociferous in their condemnation of cultured meat, but I predict that what happens next will mirror almost exactly what we have already seen in fairly modern history. The dramatic change from butter consumption to margarine, for example, and the consequent closure of countless butter factories, is a clear example of that.

~~~~~~

Now, I know you are going to think I'm completely nutty (if you haven't already come to that conclusion), but I also believe that we are on the very cusp of creating something quite unique. Vegan Space! Mankind is yet to begin colonising space although we are making slow progress towards that eventual goal. As technology improves, and certainly if it improves at the rapid rate achieved throughout the latter half of the 20th century, and through this century, then realistically the colonisation of space may be closer than we think. We are, apparently, going to begin with Mars and this is our golden opportunity *not* to take dead animals into space for food.

There, you see, I told you you'd think I'm crazy!
~~~~~~

Now I know that vegans all over the world will applaud this concept. In fact some already have after I tweeted it on several occasions in 2022, but there are loads of people out there who believe that the colonisation of space could not be achieved without animal nutrition and proteins. The fact is, however, that plant proteins will not only be needed, they will be essential.

One of the problems associated with very long space journeys will be the provision of fresh, nutritious food. Mars-bound astronauts, for example, will require lots of fresh food for the eighteen months it will take to travel there from Earth and, of course, the same amount of food for the return journey. That's three years of fresh food. However, there is a major problem. Astronauts lose about one per cent of their bone mass for every month they are in space. To counter that, the men and women manning the space station have had to undertake rigorous exercise regimes. Astronauts to Mars would also have to inject themselves with hormones every day. Additionally, as has been proven on the space station, astronauts quickly begin suffering from what is termed 'menu fatigue' and have been known to lose a significant amount of weight in space because the food, mainly reconstituted rations, is monotonous and uninteresting. Imagine the havoc that 'menu fatigue' would cause on the bodies of those men and women travelling to Mars and back for three long years!

The answer, apparently is lettuce and other plants such as barley and radish which NASA has been experimenting with for some years. Vitamins often last only about twelve months in perishable items so it will be essential to find ways to grow fresh food in space. Additionally, plant-based foods can be the source for the production of edible natural drugs and even a range of home-grown 'plastics'. At present this work is still in the experimental stages, and while there are important ethical issues involved, including that of GMO modification, it appears that plants are going to be essential to the success of future space travel.

However, beyond the science of this, we also have to examine the ethics and practicability of animal consumption in space. We can't fill a spaceship with crates of live pigs and chickens, as the early explorers filled the ships that once carried them around the world. Frozen, canned and dehydrated foods lose their nutrition rapidly, most vitamins disappear almost completely once the food has been cooked and processed. We don't need the corpses of animals to conquer space. We will not need to eat the dead. Fresh plant-based food, grown aboard the spaceships, space stations and colonies in specially designed gardens is the only realistic, healthy and ethical way for mankind to reach for the stars and begin our amazing journey into a vegan universe.

~~~~~~

Well that brings me to the end of this little story. Time to shoot this manuscript off to my publisher, keep my fingers crossed that they don't think I'm a complete Mr Magoo, and hope for the best. I should admit that this entire book has been written at night in my 'spare time' when it is totally quiet and I am completely alone and no one can see that I'm in my pyjamas. I write all day, usually history books or novels, and when I finish work for the night and after a nice vegan sandwich I pop my laptop onto my lap where it belongs and write some more, usually something idiotically different like this. I call it the 'wobbly-knobbly' method of writing, which entails being seated in my wobbly chair with the laptop perched on my knobbly knees! That's a writer's life, I guess. We just can't stop ourselves scribbling. I swear that if I had only an old soy ice-cream wrapper and the stub of a pencil to lick, I'd be scratching out some dialogue for my next tome.

Yet hopefully this book will do something, even if it's just something small, to assist with the plight of animals worldwide and also create a better understanding among the public that
~~~~~~

introverts are, in reality, neither weird nor alien. They are just the quiet version of everyone else. So the next time you see a reclusive vegan introvert, just say hello and pat them on the head like a good little muppet — oh, I almost forgot — you'll never *actually* see one because, like me, they are all invisible!

So that's it. I'm going back down my burrow now!

About the Author

Tony Matthews is a Welsh-Australian author who has dedicated almost his entire adult life to writing and researching Australian and world history. Tony is the author of more than thirty books. He is also a novelist and deeply committed vegan advocate with a significant social media presence which he uses to promote a vegan lifestyle highlighting the many ethical issues involved in the deliberate destruction of billions of animals annually to provide food, clothing and other products. He advocates continually for the transformation of humanity to create a cruelty-free world where all species are able to live in harmony.

Tony worked in the television industry for many years, writing, producing and directing, and during that time wrote a number of highly acclaimed historical documentaries which were broadcast on the Seven Network and ABC Television. He has also written and narrated more than five hundred historical programmes for ABC Radio. Tony Matthews' books and articles have been published in Australia, England, New Zealand, the United States and Europe and his television documentaries have been widely distributed to schools, universities, colleges and libraries across Australia.

For further details of Tony's published and broadcast works, please see the author's website:

https://drtonymatthews.weebly.com
Twitter: @tonytheauthor

Other Books

By Tony Matthews

PUBLISHED BY BIG SKY PUBLISHING

Tragedy at Évian

How the World Allowed Hitler to Proceed with the Holocaust

In July 1938 the United States, Great Britain and thirty other countries participated in a vital conference at Évian-les-Bains, France, to discuss the persecution and possible emigration of the European Jews, specifically those caught under the anvil of Nazi atrocities. However, most of those nations rejected the pleas then being made by the Jewish communities, thus condemning them to the Holocaust.

There is no doubt that the Évian conference was a critical turning point in world history. The disastrous outcome of the conference set the stage for the murder of six million people. Today we live in a world defined by turmoil with a disturbing rise of authoritarian governments and ultra right-wing nationalism. Now is the time to reflect on the past to ensure we never again make the same mistakes.

QUIET COURAGE

Forgotten Heroes of World War Two

What could induce a young pilot to walk out onto the wing of his burning aircraft at 13,000 feet?

Why would a plucky young woman descend into the bowels of a sinking ship knowing that she would almost certainly die there?

Why did a family remain on their farm, tending crops while suffering four long years of deadly artillery shelling?

How did a former fishing trawler sink one of Hitler's deadliest U-boats, and who were the two Australian nurses who protected wounded patients with their own bodies while experiencing a savage machine-gun attack?

Why did a young naval apprentice keep rowing when his hands had been so badly burned they were literally glued to his oar? And who were the two selfless 'Dad's Army' soldiers who miraculously saved the lives of hundreds of their comrades even when it meant sacrificing their own?

These and many other fascinating questions are answered in one of the most remarkable books of gallantry, fortitude and self-sacrifice you will ever read. *Quiet Courage — Forgotten Heroes of World War Two* is a book about thoughtful, intelligent actions and above all, an enviable capacity for bravery.

Sea Monsters

Savage Submarine Commanders of World War II

The true story of a deeply murderous intent that lurked menacingly beneath the waves during World War Two.

The torpedoes strike explosively and nine thousand people die — five thousand of them are just defenceless children.

Another ship founders after being attacked by a brutal submarine commander and the ship's crew and passengers are used in a murderous kind of blood-sport.

Merchant seamen are savagely machine-gunned in the water, callously slaughtered with hand-grenades or simply left to the circling sharks.

And hundreds of doctors, nurses, ship's crew, ambulance drivers and hospital orderlies are viciously killed without compassion, despite being protected by the Geneva Convention.

From the heart-rending account of the sinking of the German liner *Wilhelm Gustloff* in 1945 — the worst maritime disaster in world history — through to a variety of other brutal actions carried out by numerous submarine commanders, including the sinking of the hospital ship *Centaur* in 1943, this book comes from the deep shadows of a tragic past. It reveals the terrible truth of a secretive war that was responsible for an unimaginable number of deaths.

Sea Monsters includes powerful and poignant interviews with survivors — never before published.

INSPIRED BY A TRUE STORY

ENTOMBED

Six Men Buried Alive for Six Years

The year is 1945. Six German soldiers led by Captain Hans von Roth, have been accidentally buried alive deep underground in a military stores bunker at the port of Gydnia, Poland. At first they believe they will be rescued, but as the hours drag into days, months and finally years, it is appallingly clear that the men will almost certainly face a terrifying death in the grim darkness that surrounds them. They struggle to find a way out of their personal hell, but each fierce attempt leads only to failure and despair. Unaware that they will be trapped for six terrible years, the men face debilitating disease, violent death, and even madness as they attempt to understand the horror of what lies ahead.

This is a story of immense struggle against immeasurable odds but it is also a story of great love and anguish — the anguish of Erika von Roth who, unaware that her husband, Hans, is still trapped underground in Poland, and believing him to be dead, is fighting to survive in a brutal post-war Germany. Erika must find her own way through the love she retains for her husband and the growing, unexpected and self-betraying love she is experiencing for a man who was once one of her sworn enemies.

Inspired by actual events, *Entombed* is an agonising struggle for survival and one of the most important untold stories to emerge from the era of the Second World War.

SPIES, SABOTEURS AND SECRET MISSIONS OF WORLD WAR II

What kind of courage does it take for an ordinary married couple to confront the Nazi regime of Hitler's vicious Third Reich?

And why did two men betray their fellow secret agents after landing on American shores with the intention of carrying out sabotage attacks on a massive scale?

Why did the Germans murder more than two hundred and sixty innocent men in retaliation for a botched Resistance attempt to steal a simple truckload of meat?

From technical wizardry that goes disastrously wrong, to underwater warfare with a sting in its tail, this new book by Tony Matthews delves into a wide range of top-secret stories, including black propaganda missions, calamitous Resistance operations and accounts of espionage activities at the very highest level.

Spies, Saboteurs and Secret Missions of World War II is a fascinating insight into some of the most astonishing clandestine activities of the Second World War.